MUSIC OF THE AMERICAS

Contributors' Initials

L.B. Laura Boulton · P.C. Paul Collaer · W.N.F. William N. Fenton
R.K. Rolf Krusche · E.L. Eva Lips · S.M. Samuel Marti
V.T.M. Vicente T. Mendoza · W.R. Willard Rhodes

PAUL COLLAER

MUSIC OF THE AMERICAS

An Illustrated Music Ethnology of the
Eskimo and American Indian Peoples

With contributions by
Willard Rhodes, Samuel Marti, Vicente T. Mendoza,
Eva Lips and Rolf Krusche

PRAEGER PUBLISHERS
NEW YORK · WASHINGTON

BOOKS THAT MATTER

Published in the United States of America in 1973
by Praeger Publishers, Inc., 111 Fourth Avenue,
New York, N. Y. 10003
First published in Leipzig, Germany (East), in 1968
by VEB Deutscher Verlag für Musik under the title
AMERIKA in the series *Musikgeschichte in Bildern*
Edited by Heinrich Besseler and Max Schneider
Translated from the German by Irene R. Gibbons
English translation © 1970, in London, England,
by Curzon Press Ltd.
Library of Congress Catalog Card Number: 70-112028
Printed in Germany (East)

INTRODUCTION

When the New World was opened up to Europeans in the 16th century, information about Indian music and musical instruments started to come trickling in. But these early descriptions were based almost entirely on European standards. They failed to take into account the magical and ritualistic function of Indian music and the special way in which it was bound up with their religion and their whole way of looking at the universe. As a result of sheer prejudice, the *Conquistadores*, with only a few exceptions, seemed unable to realise or were unwilling to admit that they had come across highly advanced cultures in the central and southwestern portions of the double continent that were entirely different from the form of civilisation they knew at home. For example, Hernando Cortés, who vanquished the Aztec Empire with his mercenary horde about 1520, referred to the music of the native inhabitants as "monotonous and wearisome". The Indians, no doubt, felt much the same about the equally alien music of the invaders. This emerges quite clearly from an account given by Fray Toribio de Benavente Motolinia (829, Chp. XII) in 1540 of his endeavours to teach music to the American natives: "In the third year we gave them instruction in singing and some of them laughed and scoffed at it . . . because it seemed discordant to them." But various chroniclers confirm, between the lines, that the Indians were extraordinarily musical and they refer to the amazing speed and ease with which they picked up and mastered the European melodic structure and polyphonic part-singing. A report by Juan de Torquemada (901), one of the first missionaries sent to America, is most interesting and illuminating in that respect: "The first man who taught them singing in conjunction with Pater Pedro de Gante was a venerable old priest called Pater Caro, who was very gentle and circumspect in his dealings with them. As he did not know a single word of their language and they had no conception of Spanish, he spent the entire day teaching them the rules for singing short, simple pieces merely by talking and conversing with them. He did this with great patience and enthusiasm, just as if they were Spaniards too. The boys stood there in open-mouthed amazement and listened to him very attentively, trying to grasp his meaning . . . . so in a short time and without having any other means of communication the boys contrived to understand him so well that they did not only learn and master the Gregorian chant, but were also able to engage in part-singing. They then taught the others and so there are many competent singers and *maestros de capilla* among them. . . . In short, there is no form of church music that the Indians have not managed to master and perform . . . . One thing I can positively assert, and that is that in no part of the Christian world is there such an abundance of flutes, shawms, trombones, trumpets, horns and drums as are to be found in this New Spanish Empire . . . . Having once learnt to sing, they began to compose pieces of their own – folk songs in the organ song manner, four-part songs and some Masses, also other works. When shown them, competent Spanish singers said that these compositions could, in their opinion, have been produced by superb experts, not Indians." This account not only reveals the advanced stage of musical development reached by the American natives, but at the same time gives us some idea of the priceless treasures that were irretrievably destroyed by the constant influence brought to bear by the immigrants. But the streams of ancient tradition have not dried up completely even now, and so we can see what a vital part music must have played in the lives of the Indians. In America the musical ethnologist is faced with a vast field that has not been fully explored by any means, and his special task is to separate the native from the alien, and the old from the new and uncover what has lain concealed for so long. Such material as is valuable for purposes of comparison has been found in certain tribes and groups that were only discovered in the last few decades and had been living in remote, inaccessible areas apparently free from any previous contact with the incomers. The most amazing example is probably the discovery of the Yanoama tribes in the frontier area between Brazil and Venezuela. Fresh light has been thrown on the musical culture of the Indian population by the archaeologists, who have unearthed a large number of musical instruments and illustrations of musical scenes. They give us a vivid picture of musical life in the highly advanced Andean cultures, also among the Maya and Aztecs and the older civilisations. When America was discovered, a great number of important Mayan settlements had already fallen into decay and become submerged by the jungle. Even in those days Teotihuacan, the old cultural centre that had flourished in the valley of Mexico in the classical period, was no more than a vast expanse of ruins. But the Conquerors did come across some inhabited cities, e.g., Tenochtitlan, now known as Mexico City. With her population of about 300,000 she could easily stand comparison with our own great cities of today.

The absolutely amazing architecture of these gigantic buildings, the artistic perfection of the statues, the brightly coloured frescoes, the richly decorated ceramics and the magnificent pieces worked in gold all bear witness to the high level of artistic development reached by these old American cultures. These peoples even had some knowledge of the sciences and studied astronomy. They also had a special system for reckoning time and a few of them had devised a kind of picture writing.

According to 16th-century Spanish chroniclers, Mexico possessed something in the nature of an "Academy of the Fine Arts", where the singers, dancers and musicians of the country gathered together to perform various songs, dances and pieces of music or created new ones at the command of their ruler. All this points to rich artistic traditions and definite creative talents, also to the active practice of music and strict organisation of the musicans. The chroniclers all draw a distinction between private festivals of minor importance held in the palace yards and solemn religious ceremonies, for example, the "Mitote" of the Aztecs, which must have made a very deep impression on the Spaniards. All the historians referred to that festival, basing themselves mainly on the description by Motolinia (829). His very clear account gives us valuable information about the musical customs carried on in the Aztec Empire, which was destroyed in the 16th century: "One of the most conspicuous features of that whole country was the use of songs and dances by the natives in the festivals dedicated to their daemons, whom they worshipped as gods and from whom they hoped to receive great favours, and also as a source of pleasure and enjoyment for themselves. For that reason, and because all this was considered so important, a band with the necessary singers and composers of songs and dances was maintained by each of these peoples and in the house of every ruler, and they tried to find inspiration and compose songs in keeping with their own special tonal form and rhythm. They were highly esteemed for their beautiful deep basses. In fact, the rulers instructed songs to be sung in their palaces on many different days in a deep voice. Singing and dancing took place, as a rule, at the main festivals, which were held every twenty days. For the less important festivals . . . . the singers arranged what they were to sing a few days before the event. The great peoples had many singers and, if new songs or dances had been created, others joined them so that there would be no deficiencies on the day of the festival." The writer then goes on to describe the musical instruments, but the many excavation finds give us a far better and more detailed picture of the types used. Even today some of them are still in vogue among the Indians in a virtually unchanged form. This demonstrates the striking degree of continuity in their pattern of musical evolution.

In addition to recent field studies, for example, the exciting discovery of large fresco cycles, archaeology has also supplied us with valuable information about the pre-history and early history of America. This has been greatly enriched by the radiocarbon (C-14) dating method, as far as the early phases of development are concerned. Extensive anthropological studies have also been made in an attempt to find out about certain aspects of the Indian settlements and their biological structure. The unanimous conclusion reached was that the earliest inhabitants of America must have come in from Asia. Before Europeans found their way into the country, America was occupied by people who were quite different from any type previously known. The earliest travellers and chroniclers were impressed by the relative similarity of the tribes from a somatic and also a cultural point of view. And yet the individual groups reveal quite perceptible disparities, when we compare them with one another, which could be accounted for by the succeeding waves of immigrants from Asia and the isolated existence of the various groups among the forests and mountains and in the river areas (cf. 827, p. 246). America was settled in comparatively recent times, as can be seen from the oldest data obtained by radiocarbon analysis of the various excavation finds compiled by Arthur G. Jelinek (823, p. 451 ff.),

Most areas on the American continent were presumably settled between 9000 and 3000 B.C. The majority of immigrants arrived via the Bering Strait, which was at that time crossed by a land bridge, or by way of the

Aleutian Islands. They reached South America by land and advanced into the accessible valleys in the cordilleras along the Pacific coast. We are still so poorly provided with information about the Amazon area that it is impossible to reach any definite conclusions on the subject. We have proof that the Eskimo were the most recent immigrants in the period before the discovery of America. Material from other regions is often considerably older. Ancient traces of man, in the form of carved stone arrowheads and burnt remains of bones, have been found in the Sandia Cave near Albuquerque in New Mexico.

Of more recent date are the stone arrowheads of the Folsom and the Yuman type discovered in fairly extensive areas of North America. As regards their physical appearance, the Indians of the north-west resemble the oldest inhabitants of eastern Siberia, the Palaeo-Asiatics (822, p.21). Polynesian and Melanesian influences can also be detected in Indians from certain regions, although this has not altered their general ethnic and cultural type. For example, some skulls found in Brazil bear strong Melanesian characteristics. When the migrations stopped and all contacts with their original homelands were severed, the American Indians began to reveal progressive (and quite considerable) differences, and their culture has taken on certain specific forms. In pre-Columbian America the only known domestic animal was really the dog. There were no wheels or sails or clay vessels turned on a potter's lathe. But some artistic handicrafts were carried on in certain areas, e.g., weaving, featherwork, stone carving, ceramics and working in metals. The various phases of their migrations were not conscious or organised movements carried out on a large scale. We find rather a spontaneous spreading process similar to that in the plant and animal world. Groups of Asiatic hunters, no doubt, advanced into the uninhabited continent for the first time in pursuit of the herds of animals fleeing before them.

Successive or sometimes simultaneous phases in this prehistoric period have made a deep mark on the American cultures in the various areas. Before we can give our full attention to the music of the Americas, we must present a brief picture of the peoples living in this continent.

According to Canals-Frau (818, p. 64 ff.), at least four main currents of pre-Spanish settlement can be detected. The first stream was composed chiefly of dolichocephalic types of low cultural stature. In the New World, as in Asia, the long-headed type presumably came chronologically before the short-headed type. From the point of view of anthropology these long-headed people bear a striking similarity to the Australians and have therefore been termed Australoids. In the opinion of some investigators they correspond to the Aurignac man in Europe. Their economy was based on hunting and fishing and the gathering of wild fruit. A second stream probably came in along the Aleutian Islands towards America. These people also belonged to the long-headed race, but were short in stature. As they were accustomed to a marine life, their food consisted of molluscs and sea mammals. The third stream brought in forms that were probably of the Neolithic type. They were small and thickset and short-headed and displayed Mongoloid characteristics. Apparently we cannot rule out the possibility that some of them came from south-east Asia, perhaps via Indonesia, and went straight by sea to Central America, from where they spread out towards the north and south. There (according to Canals-Frau) they introduced sun worship, stone polishing and also the bow and arrow. The fourth and last of these so-called currents brought in more new features. It is supposed to have come from Polynesia and reached the coast of Chile. These people founded states and hierarchical social structures. As they arrived just two thousand years before the Spaniards, they were only able to extend the principles of their highly advanced culture as far as Colombia and Mexico. According to Canals-Frau (818, p. 67), the anthropological and cultural features of these four currents or streams formed the basic initial material from which racial types and specific cultures finally evolved in America.

When studying the earliest inhabitants of America and their material civilisation, we find that archaeological investigation has to be confined within comparatively narrow limits. Canals-Frau (818, p.118) warns that from the few stones and remains of bones found in the various layers we would only be able to get a very poor idea of their civilisation. Fortunately, we can turn to ethnography or the science of ethnology and complete our picture by making a study of the peoples living there to-day. At the present time there are, in fact, a great many groups who are directly descended from the primitive long-heads and have changed their cultural level very little since those remote times when their forefathers were alive. It is certainly possible to explain past events by examining what we can see today, a procedure not only confined to geology. When the various waves of settlers swept over America, a number of different anthropological groups evolved in the individual regions. These groups split up, in turn, into linguistic and ethnic families, which became subdivided still further into peoples or tribes. The word "tribe" should be used with caution. Here we are interpreting it as an "ethnic unit" marked by a fairly homogeneous cultural structure and occupying a common habitat. To make it easier for the reader to pinpoint these ethnic units we have included two maps showing the living areas of the most important tribes at the time when they came into contact with the Europeans.

The cultural status of each of these Indian "tribes" presents special problems owing to the influences exerted by neighbouring peoples and movement of the individual population groups from one place to another. Bearing in mind the cultural complexity of the Indians, we shall give some details about the leading tribes and their basic way of life and economy before discussing their music.

There are about fifteen million Indians alive to-day, only about one million or so in North America and mainly (in the U.S.A.) in reservations. Hundreds of different Indian languages are known to us at the present time, but none of them is related to any linguistic family belonging to the other continents, apart from some features slightly reminiscent of Asia.   P.C.

The type of economy prevailing among the *sub-Arctic hunters*, evident among the first immigrants to reach the continent, still exists in a great number of widely distributed groups who go hunting for caribou and elk and beavers and other fur-bearing animals over a broad stretch of woodland and taiga and tundra country between Alaska and the Atlantic. The rivers and sea coasts also provide them with food in the form of fish, and the berries of the sub-Arctic region are their main vitamin sources. None of these tribes had a knowledge of agriculture. Their tribal organisation is loosely knit together. The economic unit is the male hunting group in the family. The organisation of the tribe has only to be tightened up, temporarily at least, for communal hunting expeditions in the more northerly regions. According to Wissler, the cultural links uniting the entire area are the caribou, the use of spruce wood and birch bark for canoes and receptacles, also sledges without runners, frame-style snow-shoes and tents with a covering of skins or bark. In north-western Canada, i.e., the Mackenzie district, we can detect a few cultural differences compared with the east, but there is a current of unity, both material and spiritual, running through the entire sub-Arctic region. The factors responsible for this are hunting and the ritual worship of game animals which is bound up with it, also the climate, reflected in the forms assumed by sub-Artic shamanism, with a priestly magician dancing, drumming and invoking the spirits of things animate and inanimate. The main representatives of the sub-Arctic hunting type are the Algonkin tribes in the east and the members of the Na-Déné linguistic family, who are also referred to as Athabascans and call themselves "persons" (Déné or Dineh), in the northwest. Long, long ago they were the people who came along on snow-shoes and drove the slower races belonging to the areas round the Great Bear Lake and Great Slave Lake right up to the frozen margins of the north or into the barren wastes to the west of Hudson Bay. A distinguishing feature of the Athabascans is their extraordinary ability to adapt themselves to other cultural forms. So the Hare, named after the Arctic snow hare, tend to bear a strong resemblance to their Eskimo neighbours. The Beaver Indians, whose whole way of life was destroyed by the white men appearing in their midst in the 17th century, later carried on a flourishing trade in furs with the Hudson's Bay Company. The Tanaina and Kutchin took over marked features from the culture of the north-west coast, whilst the southern Sarsi adopted almost completely the Prairie Indian existence of their neighbours. Other groups wandered along the Rocky Mountains into the south-west of North America and we find them recurring as Navaho and Apache among the maize-growing Pueblo Indians. The numerically largest group of northern Athabascans, the warlike Chipewyan, made peace with their neighbours (and enemies) the Cree in 1760 and thereby established contacts with the Algonkin of the east, who had a different language, but a similar economy. The portions of the Ojibwa people who still go in for hunting follow on to the south of the Cree, whilst the entire sub-Arctic area of the Labrador peninsula is inhabited mainly by the Montagnais and Nascapi, those magnificent trappers who follow an annual economic cycle and are on the hunting ground in winter and in their assembly place in summer, where they carry on a commercial (fur) and cultural exchange with other groups of Indians and with white traders.

The so-called Eskimo living in *the Arctic region* on the northern fringe of North America, who refer to themselves as *innuit* ("human beings"), were the most recent immigrants to reach the continent. This is evident, amongst other things, from the identical language they use, which only shows marked dialect differences in the far west — in Alaska and on the Aleutian Islands. These western areas betray clear Asiatic influences extending down as far as the Indians of the north-west coast, whilst the eastern Eskimo likewise make up a uniform cultural group stretching as far as Greenland. Very probably the first Eskimo immigrants were land hunters, like the tribes from the interior of Alaska who hardly fish at all and the so-called Caribou Eskimo on the western margin of Hudson Bay. The oldest Eskimo in the central region and the east are descended from the representatives of an ancient culture named after Cape Dorset on the north-west tip of Baffin Land. They were pushed back to the edge of the icelands by the far more mobile "Thule" people with their dog-sledges and specialised form of hunting until they became adapted to the Arctic milieu. There they devoted themselves in particular to the pursuit of marine mammals and actually reached the stage of hunting whales. In the Central Eskimo area hundreds of abandoned homes have been examined and the material found there revealed the existence of the very advanced Thule culture, the tools being fashioned mainly from stone, bone and fishbones. On the edge of the icy region a typical method of hunting seals is to wait beside a hole with a spear or a hook (or, in more modern times, a gun) until the animal comes up for breath. Men also go off singly in kayaks, or hunting boats, in pursuit of marine mammals, each man being securely tied into his boat. There is a larger travelling boat too, called an *umiak*, which is rowed by women. For travelling overland they use sledges on runners pulled by dogs which can cover up to 150 km per day. In all probability their original winter home was an earth house built partly underground, and from it the igloo, built in the form of a dome from blocks of snow, subsequently evolved. It provides snug accommodation with its entrance sheltered from the wind, the flat cooking lamp carved out of steatite burning inside and the platforms of snow covered with pelts. Their summer home is a tent, generally covered with caribou skins. Treatment of skins for making clothes has reached a high standard. The double bow and harpoon were introduced from Asia. At government expense reindeer were brought into Alaska from Lapland for the Eskimo and they learned to domesticate them. As a result of their environment they have a loosely knit social structure (their leading figures are the "great hunters") and also a special conception of the universe dominated by magic and shamanism and demanding blood revenge, whilst the main feature of their legal system is a willingness to negotiate and achieve reconciliation. Disputes are settled by means of singing contests and drumming dances or wrestling bouts. The austerity of their whole way of life has made them turn inwards and they are noted for their great wealth of myths and their special talents for carving and making human and animal figures out of walrus ivory. They engrave hunting scenes and create masks of supernatural beings and have for some years been making small plastic objects out of steatite — works of art that are greatly sought after by museums.

On the Pacific, to the south of the western Eskimo, we find the amazing Indian fishing cultures of the *North-west Coast*. They have a secure economy and so have managed to achieve a remarkable standard of craftsmanship and develop a highly artistic culture, absorbing the various influences brought in from Asia, the South Sea Islands and America and by European seamen. As a result of all these hybrid influences, a kind of trading "Esperanto" has sprung up along their coast in the form of the Chinook jargon, which is a mixture of tribal languages and fragments from the vocabularies of Europe and Asia. They adopted everything they could — Asian daggers, bows and protective armour, the magic medicine obtained from the ginseng root, bear worship and also the benefits of modern social progress. The amazing originality of their works of art can stand comparison only with the Chinese masterpieces of the early days. When referring to the North-west Coast Indians we mean the inhabitants of the coastal stretch and the islands lying off it from Mount Elias in the north to Puget Sound within the territory of the state of Washington to the south. They belong to various, and in some cases debatable, linguistic families, mainly the Wakash, Salish and Na-Déné. There are considerable differences between the northern group, of whom the Haida, Tsimshian and Tlingit are typical representatives, and the tribes of the south, e.g., the Kwakiutl and the Nootka. For instance, only the southern tribes knew how to kill whales and this set a special stamp on their entire culture. The shoals of fish which appeared seasonally and gave them the idea of finding some means of preserving them provided these tribes with a solid economic foundation. So food was also available in winter and they supplemented it with berries and roots. They were thus able to settle in villages in large houses built from planks of wood from the ubiquitous conifers. These fishing peoples were not great hunters and had no need to be. Ocasionally they used a bow and arrow to bring down any game that was easily available. But bears are feared and respected because of their great strength and also on religious grounds and so they have come

9

to play a leading part in the art and mythology of the North-west Coast Indians. Their main item of equipment was a magnificently painted canoe chiselled from a mighty cedar which was burnt out and carved into shape. These were efficient coastal boats, but, technically speaking, they cannot be compared with the boats of the South Sea Islanders, although they were artistically superior to them. Totem poles stood outside the houses of the Indians of the northern group. They bear paintings and carvings of fantastic animals, human beings and spirits and were at one time supposed to be very old, although that is not the case. They came into existence towards the end of the 19th century and were really a new Indian version of the coats of arms used by Europeans. Towering up one above the other, these poles display the human and animal clan connections of a particular person or family. The erection of a pole was always marked by great celebrations in which crowds of people took part. Like the songs and spells heard on those occasions, they were the personal property of individuals or groups. This marks the beginning of class distinctions. The whole concept of property is very important on the North-west Coast. It consisted chiefly of slaves, who had a definite exchange value. They were acquired during raids into neighbouring areas and the owner had the right to let them live or die. Slaves were killed on certain occasions to demonstrate that right. In other cases they were granted almost equal status in the families. Further indications of wealth, in addition to shell money, were the so-called "coppers", large tokens of a particular shape that were beaten out of the cold metal and were passed on from generation to generation. Valuable blankets made from bark material or woven from vegetable fibres and the hair of mountain goats (called Chilkat blankets) were also regarded as a kind of fixed assets, just like canoes, fish oil, preserved berries and fish and all other desirable objects. On the North-west Coast accumulation of wealth of this type culminated in the holding of give-away or *potlatch* festivals. Mighty chieftains used to distribute or destroy most of their accumulated wealth as a peculiar mark of generosity. Those *potlatch* festivals, which usually had to be prepared for over a period of years, were held on special occasions, to mark the installation or death of a chief, the building of a house, etc., and the host often ended up as a beggar. The *potlatch* has been viewed as a kind of control operating within the social system on the North-west Coast, wiping out the distinctions between rich and poor. The characteristic features of the northern tribes are their totem system and their belief in a mystical relationship with animals. So all Haida feel that they are members of the eagle or the raven clan and the raven is also regarded as the bringer of culture and their finest earthly possessions. There are distinctly marked social differences in the central and southern group. We find hardly any evidence of totem poles, i.e., of a coat-of-arms system. The clans have forfeited some of their social importance and fit into a highly developed system of secret societies, the culmination of which is to be seen among the Kwakiutl. All the ceremonies on the North-west Coast include elaborate artistic devices, carved masks, colourful costumes and magnificent accessories. Even today the carving done by the Haida is superior to anything existing elsewhere in North America. This was the centre of a flourishing culture with specialised artists. Material goods are stored up and a unique form of art is carried on and at the same time we encounter a grand gesture of voluntary renunciation denoting a spiritual mood akin to the Asian's profound contempt for all things visible.

The wide strip of land stretching down between the Fraser and Columbia River systems in the north as far as the deserts of Nevada is referred to as the *Plateau* in the northern portion and the *Great Basin* in the south. Here too there is an absence of agriculture and of fixed resident communities. At one time the influences of the Prairie culture were evident in the east. In the north and the centre we mainly come across river fishermen catching salmon and gatherers of the wild camas lily root, e.g., the Nez Percé tribe, but they later turned to bison hunting as well and adopted certain features of the Prairie civilisation. In the dry, sandy southern region the Shoshone, Ute and Paiute groups, probably the economically poorest of North American Indians, were living long before America was discovered. They include the Paviotso, members of the proud Uto-Aztec linguistic family, who were, however, without maize and all the human and cultural contacts of the great civilisations. And yet, as far as we can gather, they form the northernmost portion of the Chichimecs and were noted hunters who migrated to Mexico under their legendary leader Xolotl and brought about the downfall of the Toltec Empire. So in the Plateau and the Great Basin we find a compact population in the north with a sound economic basis and in the south a sparsely distributed population whose yearly economic cycle is based on the amounts of wild seeds available and the supplies of meagre supplementary foods. They live in miserable wind shelters and their low cultural level is only compensated to some extent by their great talent for plaiting vegetable fibres. The bleakness of the landscape and the meagreness of their food led to the creation of myths built up round a cultural hero, the Coyote. Visions were of high importance. Thus an Indian prophet known as Wovoka, bringing Messianic ideas, arose from the midst of the Paiute and originated the "Ghost Dance", with its exciting blend of Indian and Christian elements, which swept in great waves over the Indian territories as far up as the Great Lakes region.

The western neighbours of the Great Basin Indians are the Indians of *California*, which has been referred to as the "Caucasus of North America" because of its many different linguistic ties. Northern and southern California show particularly strong influences from neighbouring areas, but the typically Californian culture is most pronounced in central California. This is also demonstrated by the numerous prehistoric finds in the area. Before the coming of the whites, central California consisted of vast stretches of grassland with large oak-woods. There was no agriculture. Acorns were the main item of Indian food. After they were gathered, the bitter flavour was removed by ingenious methods and they were dried and stored, cracked with stone pestles, powdered down, sifted, blanched and cooked in tightly sealed baskets by using hot stones. Pottery was unknown here, as was also the canoe. Instead they used baskets to store food and rush rafts for crossing water. There was great variety in the type of dwellings, which ranged from simple wind shelters to solid structures built with posts. They had a completely uncomplicated social system — in fact, there was hardly any sense of political unity or cohesion. Here we find the friendly contacts with neighbours that are such a usual feature of gathering communities (peoples who obtain their basic food supply from some plant species growing in great abundance). As representatives of these central Californian tribes we might mention the Pomo, belonging to the Hokan linguistic family, the second largest tribal group in California, living round the Russian River. Their diet was based on acorns and this was supplemented by small game throughout the year and by fish in winter and also some species of wild grass seeds and roots. Here too we find a typical "harvesting population" as defined in the works of Julius Lips, with the characteristic relaxation of the territorial principle, friendly groups being invited to share in the acorn harvest in years of plenty as a kind of "economic insurance" to guarantee against the lean years, when the invitation was returned. They had storehouses to keep the harvested acorns and venerated them in dances and by using sacred acorn meal. In northern California, which is represented by the Yurok, who belong to the Algonkin linguistic family, the Karok (Hokan) and the Hupa (Na-Déné), there is strong evidence of influences coming through from the North-west Coast. This is confirmed by the prehistoric finds around Humboldt Bay. Here we come across houses built from planks, boats made out of a single tree trunk, wooden boxes, plaited hats and beautiful carvings — all signs of a secure economic foundation and a fairly stable social system with more ambitious cultural needs. Southern California comprises the desert area between the coastal mountains and the Colorado River and also includes the strip running along the sea from Los Angeles into lower California. There is evidence here of a strongly marked ritualistic life including the use of narcotic plants, whereas dream songs are a customary feature of the desert region. The Yuma of the Hokan linguistic family and the Mohave belong to the desert tribes. The latter are the only Californian tribe who, under the influence of their south-eastern neighbours, became farmers before the advent of the white man. They manage to make use of the river silt that accumulates every year when the Colorado floods, just as the ancient Egyptians turned the Nile mud to good account, and they sow wild seeds as well as maize.

The *south-west*, which is the area adjoining California and the Great Basin, is the classic agricultural region of North America. The main implement used in the cultivation of maize was a simple digging or grubbing stick with a sharp point, with which the ground could be broken up and holes drilled for the seed. There was sometimes a forkshaped side-branch on the stick which served as a foot-rest, but a number of these digging sticks had a spade-shaped end. The oldest known representatives of the ancient agricultural civilisation of the south-west, which dates back to the 7th millenium B.C., are the Basket-makers, of whose existence there was evidence long before the beginning of the Christian era. Associated with these were the Pueblo cultures, which are still flourishing even to-day. Pueblo is not the name of a tribe, but is the Spanish word for a "village" or "people" and so refers to the peculiar form taken by these Indian settlements. Their houses are placed on top of and alongside one another in a honeycomb formation and are constructed from slabs of stone joined together with clay or adobe (unfired brick). They built cliff dwellings, i.e., whole villages inside clefts in the rock. They have ceremonial chambers, or *kivas*, situated partly underground, and that is where

11

they begin their famed maize fertility rites. They have a typical agriculturists mentality. They venerate the dead as helpers living on in the other world and try to ensure the safe gathering in of the harvest with their assistance. In this arid land the magic associated with their ancestors and with rain has assumed grand proportions through the practice of the so-called Katčina cult. The Katčinas are masked ancestral spirits and a great many of them, all wearing individual masks, enter the village once a year as rain demons in order to bestow their blessing on their descendants and on the maize. The Pueblo are highly skilled weavers, basket-makers and workers in ceramics, and they are noted for their peaceable and conservative nature. These mild-tempered farming folk were subjected to attacks from wild Indian hunters long before the white invaders appeared on the scene. These hunters descended the steep slopes of the Rocky Mountains and brought their alien Athabascan language with them, also their Asiatic double bows and their belief in the sanctity of game animals. About 1300 according to our reckoning the first Navaho ("Enemies of Tilled Fields", as they were referred to by the terrified farmers) must have appeared in the south-west together with the Apache, with whom they originally formed a single tribe. When the Pueblo came into possession of sheep and goats about 1540, after the Coronado expedition, the Navaho began to take such an interest in these animals that they proceeded to settle down in the south-west. During the great uprising of the Pueblo against the Spaniards in 1680 many Navaho harboured Pueblo fugitives and married maize-grinding Pueblo women. In this way a cultural exchange took place in which they were the recipients rather than the main beneficiaries. They became increasingly settled and gained deep insight into the ceremonial life of the Pueblo. They introduced maize and also adopted the famous Pueblo art of weaving that had been practised since 600 and became converted from savage robbers into skilled arable farmers and tenders of sheep and goats, as well as dyers of wool and weavers and great ritualists who recited splendidly poetic songs to bless the earth and the maize. The only thing they did not adopt was the Pueblo style of house. Instead they retained their northern earth house, the semi-subterranean *hogan*. In spite of centuries of Christian influence, the Pueblo still adhere largely to their age-old beliefs. To the south of the Pueblo we still find Desert Indians, such as the Pima and Papago, whose ancestors represented the ancient Hohokam civilisation. Their traditions go away back to the wild-seed peoples of Cochise. They were highly skilled in canal-building and are receptive to modern ideas. In fact, they are well on the way to winning full rights for themselves in the south-west.

The horse reached the North American continent from the south-west — from New Mexico and Texas. Shortly after this, around 1750, i.e., in historical times, the very famous, but short-lived Indian culture of the Plains came into being. Another reason for its development apart from the horse, was the presence of millions of bison, which provided the main item of their diet. Viewed as an Indian cultural area, the Plains are a stretch of rather treeless country covering four million square kilometres and stretching from the Canadian provinces of Alberta, Saskatchewan and Manitoba as far as the Gulf of Mexico. Its width is limited on the west by the Rocky Mountains and on the east by the Mississippi and the flat lakeland country. There are two types of landscape here. There is the western part of the true "Plains", the classic bison-hunting territory (now the land of cowboys and herds of cattle). It lies at a high altitude, beginning with the rugged slopes of the Rockies, and is covered with long buffalo grass. The eastern area of short grass offers natural "Prairie" scenery and is now a fruitful region devoted to maize and pigs. Thousands of years ago the Folsom hunters killed here their moose and caribou and some bison. They were followed by a wave of very early farmers, especially in the river valleys. It has been shown that the Plains presented ideal growing conditions for buffalo grass in the 16th century and mighty herds of wild bison were concentrated in the heart of the continent, so many maize-growers of this region were obliged to leave their villages about 1700. That is how the typical nomadic bison hunters of the higher western Plains came into existence, whereas the eastern farmers from the low-lying Prairie settled down and contrived to combine agriculture with bison-hunting. According to Kroeber a kind of cultural high-pressure centre developed in the main bison areas. Groups of people uprooted by the whites streamed into the Prairie, especially from the east, in order to share in the general abundance and they came into conflict with the hunters who had arrived there first. So war became a part of the way of life of these Indians.

When we visualise the Prairie Indians, we think of bison-hunting, of the great authority of the chiefs during the hunting season, of painted tipis arranged to form a "camp circle", of leather clothing, feathered head-dresses, trials of strength and valour, and also of scalping. The most important ritual among these tribes is the "Sun Dance", a kind of fertility magic involving the bison and the sun, combined with the torture of youths about to be admitted to manhood. Typical Plains Indians, who were pure bison hunters, joined in the tribal confederation of the Blackfeet of the north-western Prairie, whose bison-hunting traditions went back to the days when there were no horses. Linguistically speaking, they are Algonkin, like other famous representatives of that group, the Arapaho and the Cheyenne, whose northern group joined together to provide three thousand warriors and wiped out General Custer and his troops at the famous Battle of Little Bighorn in 1876. The main heroes on that occasion were the Siouan Dakota. The sedentary portion of the Prairie peoples is to be found in its purest form in the Mandan, who are members of the Siouan language family and are the oldest known village Indians belonging to the Prairie. They were still living in semi-subterranean earth houses like their prehistoric forerunners. They grew maize, beans and gourds and spent the bison-hunting season in *tipis*. They have become immortal, thanks to their heroic chieftain Matotope. But the smallpox epidemic of the 19th century wiped them out as a tribe and the small surviving remnant became assimilated by other groups. Other prominent bison hunters and village Indians were the tribal confederations of the Caddo and the Pawnee. Just as the culture of the Prairie Indians came into existence in the first place as a result of the appearance of bison on a large scale, they disappeared again when these animals died out. The end came when white hunters in search of leather arrived with their quick-firing guns and tracked down the bison. The Prairie Indians who did not starve reverted in part to maize-growing or turned to handicrafts.

In the area of the *Great Lakes* the abundance of a single wild plant was responsible for creating a special cultural form among the people who gathered it. Vast crowds of different origins had swarmed together in the "wild rice district" from very early times. This nourishing plant is not the cultivated proper rice (Oryza sativa) but a wild grass, Zizania aquatica. A pattern of material and spiritual interchange evolved in the places where this "rice" was most plentiful, e.g., Green Bay on Lake Superior and Michillimackinac (now Mackinaw) on the peninsula separating Lake Michigan from Lake Huron. Here a great variety of groups came together and became united in spite of all their linguistic barriers and helped to swell the density of the population in the wild rice district. At one time the Dakota were established here, but they were driven out of the rice area in the course of protracted wars with the Ojibwa who had received firearms from the French and so they migrated into the Prairie. The Menominee (Algonkin like the Ojibwa) stayed on as neighbours — their name means "Rice People" — and the Siouan Winnebago remained beside them too. They are all united by their comprehensive economic system, which guarantees that they are supplied with food throughout the year. So work is not divided up according to sex. All members of the community share in the harvesting, drying, roasting, threshing and preserving of the "wild rice". The supplementary food of animal origin, in the shape of aquatic birds, deer and small rodents also attracted by the grain, can be obtained virtually without any effort and can easily be killed on the paddy fields even by the women. As the whole of their life is bound up with the rice, a special feature of their spiritual culture is the sanctification of that universally desired plant. Myths recount how their hero Manibosho brought wild rice to man and founded the all-powerful secret medicine society of the Midéwiwin, who extol the forces of life in their rites and songs and therefore also the *manito* powers, which enable the rice to grow. Intertribal relations are relaxed by mutual sharing in the rice harvest, which serves as a kind of economic "insurance" in the good years. This mutual economic basis has created a uniform type of culture that persists here even to-day.

The mighty *forests of the east* extended to the south and east of the Great Lakes area. At one time they stretched from the Mississippi to the Atlantic, but their continuity is now broken by the large cities. A great number of Algonkin tribes of the sub-Arctic hunting type resided in the northern areas. Farther south we are aware of increasingly powerful agrarian influences. The history of these Atlantic Algonkin, who were exposed to invasions by white men earlier than any of the other Indians, goes right back to the Micmac — originally in Nova Scotia — the first Indian tribe since Viking times to come into contact with Europeans. They were peace-loving fishermen and hunters and they also moved over to western Newfoundland and settled down as good neighbours beside the Beothuk, until the French equipped them with guns and, for the sake of the fur trade, induced them to exterminate the Beothuk, who were finally wiped out at the end of the 18th century. On the east coast we see a tendency for different tribes to form mighty leagues. They lived in the oval wigwams of the Forest, or Woodland Indians, but they had a more rigid tribal system than their relatives in

13

the sub-Arctic region, with peace and war chiefs, a tribal council and a "general council". The Micmac also belonged to the tribal confederation of the Abnaki, with the Mohegan (Mohican) adjoining them on the south — a tribe that has become famous throughout the world, thanks to the novel by Fenimore Cooper. Not far from them was the home of the Wampanoag in the present-day state of Rhode Island. In Metacom they provided these Algonkin with a hero and liberator who united all the New England tribes in a mighty campaign against the white men, but he was finally destroyed by treachery. Another tribal alliance was formed by the Delaware in the region of what is now New York City. They called themselves the *lenape* ("True Men") and left behind a tribal chronicle in the form of picture writing carved on wood, the *Walam Olum*, which starts at the Flood. The most important tribal group of eastern Algonkin was controlled by Chief Powhatan in Virginia and was the only one to come into existence as a result of conquest. Their economy was based on the cultivation of maize, beans, gourds and tobacco, which was carried on by the women, while the men, who only cleared the ground and broke it up, devoted their attention to hunting and fishing. The domain of Powhatan, with its temples, country houses, priests and holy fire, came into the full glare of world history in 1607, when, after destroying the Spanish Armada, the English founded the settlement of Jamestown in Virginia. The Shawnee in the south-east, who were maize-growers as long as they remained in their village settlements and became hunters when they moved about, were members of another Algonkin tribe. They produced the greatest Indian hero of them all, Tecumseh, at whose side stood his twin brother, the "Shawnee Prophet" Tenskwatawa. They were spiritual descendants of the great Pontiac (1729—1769), chief of the Ottawa, who at one time set himself the task of exterminating all white men. Tecumseh united all the tribes from the Blackfeet in the north to the Creek in the south in a revolt against the whites, which came to a tragic end on 7th November 1811 in the Battle of Tippecanoe. The Sauk, coming from the central Algonkin, also had a tragic hero — Black Hawk. They have often been grouped together as a tribe with the Fox, who are making a name for themselves to-day with their various modern schemes and the way they are putting them into effect. To the south of the St.Lawrence the members of the Iroquois confederacy were like a fiery wedge driven into the Algonkins' side. Around 1570 the Iroquois had been joined by the Mohawk, Oneida, Onondaga, Cayuga, Seneca and later by the Tuscarora. At the end of the 17th century they controlled the whole of the north-east from Ontario to Tennessee, from the Mississippi to the Atlantic. They were great maize-growers, but they also planted beans and gourds and continued fishing and hunting. Warlike by nature, they lived in longhouses in villages with palisades. Their famous social system was based on the *ohwachira*, or big family, led by a woman with a male adjutant. Women were also dominant in the clan, which was made up of *ohwachiras*. The clan chiefs and the warriors' representatives formed the next highest class and were presided over by the Council of the Elders. Although the Iroquois have contrived to adapt themselves very largely to the demands of present-day life, they are still deeply rooted in their old ritual existence, exemplified by their masked society of False Faces, which sets out to heal diseases. Their old enemies, the Hurons, who also spoke Iroquois, have now died out almost completely, except for about seven hundred who live in a reservation near Quebec.

The *south-east*, corresponding roughly to the present "Southern states" of the U.S.A., was mainly occupied by sedentary maize-growers, the majority of whom belonged to the linguistic family of the Muskogee. The Spaniards invaded the area as early as the 16th century and some of the Creek Indians, the Seminole or "Seceders", escaped to the swamps of southern Florida and joined forces with fugitive Negro slaves from the south, just as had happened on the east coast. The hero of the Seminole was Chief Osceola, against whom seven generals waged war for eight years from 1835 onwards, until he was finally betrayed. Other tribes from that area, which is strongly permeated by Mexican influences and is inhabited by highly organised maize-growers, made desperate attempts to adapt themselves to the Europeans, but found themselves miserably transplanted to Oklahoma, where the remnants of the "five civilised tribes" (Creek, Chickasaw, Choctaw, Cherokee and Seminole) still live to-day. But the south-east was the site of the most highly organised social systems in any part of North America and states were actually formed there. The most amazing example was the Natchez community on the lower Mississippi. At the end of the 17th century about 3500 Natchez lived in four hundred houses, ruled over by a chief bearing the name of "Big Sun". There were different social classes — the nobles and the commoners — with definitely prescribed regulations about marriage. There were temples with mummified bodies of former chiefs, also a priestly hierarchy, prophets, dances and dramatic ceremonies. On the death of a "Big Sun" chief, women and servants were sacrificed by strangulation so that they could accompany the deceased ruler on his journey into the other world. Their economy was based throughout on maize, supplemented by non-domestic animals and wild plants. The French exterminated them and since 1732 the Natchez have disappeared from the pages of history.   E. L.

The areas of *northern and central Mexico* between Rio Grande del Norte and the Isthmus of Tehuantepec display a great variety of scenic and climatic conditions, brought about both by difference in altitude and extent of that territory, running from north to south. The heart of the pre-Hispanic culture in Mexico is the *Mesa Central*, the central plateau, now dominated by Mexico City with her six million inhabitants. Even in early historical times the area round the valley of Mexico was very densely populated. It was here that the great metropolises of the Teotihuacan people, the Toltecs and the Aztecs, were built. The Indians of the *Mesa Central* have been familiar with intensive agriculture and horticulture for centuries and have invented efficient methods for irrigating their fields, improving the soil and enlarging the area suitable for cultivation. Their diet was and still is based on maize, which was cultivated 5000 years ago on the high plateau of Mexico. In contrast to the agrarian civilisation on the cool central plateau with its low rainfall, the ancient culture region on the Gulf coast comes within the *tierra caliente* region, the lowland area of eastern Veracruz and Tabasco with its abundant rain and humid heat. In this alluvial territory, covered with tropical bushland and rain forests, the population lived in more widely scattered settlements whose livelihood was based on slash-and-burn cultivation. The Indians of the Mesa Central thought highly of the Gulf coast because it was the source of certain highly desirable tropical products and luxury goods, such as cocoa, tobacco, cotton, rubber, jade, turquoise, jaguar skins and the feathers of gaily coloured tropical birds. Olman ("The Land of Rubber") was the name given by the Aztecs to the rich coastal land of the south-east, which formed the goal of their trading and military expeditions. The arid northern part of Mexico is quite different. It largely consists of desert and steppe areas, where the characteristic plants are cacti, thorn bushes, agaves and yuccas. In the eyes of city-dwellers it was the home of barbaric peoples on the fringe of the civilised world, of the roving, warlike Chichimecs. The "Gran Chichimeca" was influenced only superficially by the cultural development of the south. Rather, the hunting tribes from the northern steppes kept on advancing into the area occupied by the agrarian peoples. They represented the most dynamic element in the general interplay of the three cultural zones in Ancient Mexico. The earliest cultural remains in the form of bones or stone show that human beings lived as big game hunters in northern and central Mexico from at least 10,000 B.C. onwards (and were big game hunters). Excavations in north-eastern Mexico reveal a long tradition of gathering food plants and gradually cultivating them. Even in the oldest stratum investigated (7000—5000 B.C.) not only remains of agaves, Opuntia and wild beans were discovered, but also remnants of what was probably a cultivated type of gourd. Subsequent strata contained more and more residues of cultivated plants and illustrated a gradual transition to agriculture. From our present extent of archaeological and botanical knowledge it would appear that agriculture (i.e., the production of maize and different varieties of beans and gourds) in Central America arose out of local traditions and the practice of tending and cultivating indigenous food plants. It is, in fact, rooted in the old desert tradition of Mexico, whose material and economic foundation was a combination of gathering and hunting. The general lay-out of the villages appearing about 1500 A.D. in the central plateau and in the Gulf coast area, (e.g., El Arbolillo or Tlatilco) indicates that the transition to a more developed system of food production was by then complete.

Careful excavation work at the exploration sites of La Venta, Tres Zapotes and Cerro de las Mesas has shown that the Gulf coast population must have made a vital contribution to the ancient civilisation of Central America. Small pieces of jade, superbly fashioned, and monumental basalt carvings weighing up to forty tons can be regarded as products of the civilisation of La Venta (800—400 B.C.). The representatives of that civilisation must have invented an ancient system of writing and making calendars. Indeed, certain objects from that culture bear carefully incised glyphs and numerals that are almost identical to those of the Maya, but are certainly older than any of the calendar material from the latter culture. The widely occurring La Venta style has been attributed to an ancient people on the tropical coast of the Atlantic, who were known to the Nahua tribes of the *Mesa Central* as the Olmeca ("Dwellers in the Rubber Land"). The chroniclers of the 16th century regarded the Olmecs as the oldest civilized people in Mexico and which had even contrived to retain their individuality in Aztec times. However, the term probably did not refer to a specific ethnic or

15

linguistic group, but — more or less — to all the civilized populations of the Gulf region and — more generally — to in fact, the heirs of the pre-Toltec civilisation. The influence of the La Venta culture on neighbouring peoples can be assessed from the fact that strands of the "Olmec" culture can be seen running through all the great classical art styles of Mexico and Guatemala. It is these mature artistic achievements, above all, that justify our use of the term "classical" when referring to the Indian civilisations emerging (or developing) during the first 1000 years of the Christian era. Here we are thinking in particular of the achievements of the Maya of Chiapas and Peten. The dates given for the classical period (300—900) refer properly, only to the beginning and the end of the corresponding period in the Mayan area. In the opinion of W. Krickeberg, the Totonacs were the builders of the temple pyramid of El Tajin and the creators of those somewhat mysterious stone objects regarded as characteristic "fossils" derived from the classical Veracruz civilisation, although their original function still remains highly problematical. Along the Gulf coast and among the Maya of the lowlands no true urban centres had been formed even in the classic period, but the type of settlement was quite different in the highland regions of Mexico and Guatemala.

Excavations in the valley of Tehuacan provide evidence that some techniques of artificial irrigation had actually been developed in the pre-classic period. The dam of Tehuacan, at least 500 m long, and its canals made it possible for a great number of settlements to exist for many hundreds of years in what is now semi-desert territory and it must have represented one of the largest irrigation systems in pre-Columbian America. The most important city in the classic period was Teotihuacan on the central plateau of Mexico. Even the Aztecs saw the "holy city" lying in ruins and attributed it to an earlier era. The so-called "Pyramid of the Sun" of Teotihuacan is a monumental structure of adobes with a volume of one million cubic metres. This — and the mighty pyramid of Cholula, which has been built over on several occasions — can be regarded as the largest building in ancient America. In the mountainous country of southern Mexico the classical civilisation is represented by a large temple city on Monte Alban, a high ridge in the south-west of Oaxaca. The vast lay-out of this city, revealing traces of a settlement dating back 2000 years, has been ascribed to the Zapotecs. A characteristic feature of all the city-states of the classic period is that they were ruled over by a priestly hierarchy. The ceremonial centres were their residences and at the same time the religious focal points. The temple areas with their palaces, ball-game courts and yards were also artistic and spiritual centres. Craftsmen and artists worked for the priests and calendar calculations and a knowledge of the rituals were purely a matter for literate "specialists". The period from the late 7th to the early 8th century marked the beginnings of the earliest mythical and historical traditions, as seen in the leather codices of the Mixtecs and the old chronicles of the Nahua tribes. The Mixtecs inhabited chiefly the south and west of the valley of Oaxaca, in the area known as the *Mixteca Alta*. In the 14th century they drove the Zapotecs, who were linguistically related to them, away from Monte Alban. The Mixtecs appear as the masters of the fine arts in Mexico. They were unsurpassed as gold- and silversmiths and also made a name for themselves with their magnificently painted pottery and their beautiful picture writing painted on deerskin leather. The art of that people had such a decisive influence on the culture of the post-classical period (900—1521) in central and southern Mexico that the term "Mixteca-Puebla Culture" has been applied to that entire era. The incursions of warlike and barbaric peoples from the north in the 9th century marked the beginning of a period of large-scale social changes in the course of which the power of the priests became reduced. Their place was taken by the warriors and merchants who were gaining power and taking over control to an ever-increasing extent. The victorious invaders were, no doubt, largely made up of Nahua peoples. Tollan, corresponding to present-day Tula in the federal state of Hidalgo, became the residence of their kings and the capital of the Toltec Kingdom founded by them. After the Toltecs had taken over the civilisation of highland Mexico and made it their own, their name became used to denote the contrast between the mode of life of the cultivated city-dwellers and the habits of their wandering relatives, the warlike Chichimec. Sahagún has given us a brief ethnographical account of these Chichimec tribes. He describes how they roamed through the grasslands and steppes in fairly small bands, dressed themselves in skins and gathered roots, fruit, seeds and honey or hunted for their food with bow and arrow. He also refers to the Peyote ritual of the northern tribes. The Chichimec were, in fact, aware of the intoxicating effects of the *peyotl* cactus and used that drug in their nocturnal dance celebrations in the steppes. Around the end of the 12th century and the beginning of the 13th Chichimec tribes advanced into the Mexico valley under their leader Xolotl and brought about the

16

downfall of Tollan. After the destruction of their kingdom, the Toltecs settled in Colhuacan and other places on the plateau. But the Chichimec kingdom soon collapsed too and a number of small rival principalities remained. One Chichimec tribe that had reached the plateau in the 13th century was the Mexica or Aztecs. They did not become town builders until the second half of the 14th century. Then, in 1370, they laid out the island city of Tenochtitlan on Lake Texcoco.

In the 15th century Tenochtitlan, Texcoco and Tlacopan joined to form a triple urban federation, in which the Aztec metropolis in course of time began to play an ever more important role. When the army of Cortés moved into Mexico, Tenochtitlan was a really large city with a population approaching or even exceeding the numbers living in European cities of those days. To the north, west and south it was connected with the lake shore by means of broad highways. Two walled-in conduits provided its supply of drinking water. On Lake Texcoco rafts covered with lake mud formed small islands on which maize, flowers, pepper, tomatoes and gourds grew, so making up for the scarcity of natural horticultural potential. In addition to this system, known as *chinampa*, the Aztecs tended the ground that had been cleared with stone axes and by fire by providing it with irrigation and fertilising it with vegetable ash. Additional food was supplied by the fruit of the prickly pear and the numerous fish and game birds inhabiting the lakes on the plateau. The single-storeyed houses of sun-dried bricks that belonged to the ordinary people were overshadowed by the residences and palaces of the dignitaries and the temples. The temple area was situated in the centre of Tenochtitlan with the great pyramid bearing on its topmost platform the two temples dedicated to the rain god Tláloc and the war god Uitzilopochtli. Within the temple precincts were the priests' schools, in which future high-ranking officers and functionaries were trained, the large arsenals that were referred to as spear houses and the ball-game house. Like the other Mexican peoples, the Aztecs were familiar with playing with rubber balls. This was not a profane sporting activity, but a solemn ritual symbolising a cosmic event — the course followed by the sun.

Aztec society in the 15th and 16th century revealed a clearly developed pattern of social distinctions. Apart from the king and his relatives, who usually filled important offices of state, the persons belonging to the ruling class of *tecuhtli* (dignitaries) included deserving warriors who were granted estates in the subjugated provinces of the kingdom and represented a kind of aristocracy based on merit. Soldiers played an important part in the Aztec state and the societies of warriors known as "Eagles" and "Jaguars" probably occupied a position similar to that of the knightly orders of mediaeval Europe. The military expeditions of the Aztecs brought in spoils and tribute from the defeated provinces and also prisoners of war for their sacrifices, which in the end assumed quite terrifying proportions. Under the last king, Montezuma II, thirty-eight provinces came under the control of the Aztecs. These areas were obliged to pay tribute, but did not form a rigidly centralised state such as existed in Peru at that time — indeed, they did not even make up one continuous territory. After the conquest of Tenochtitlan (1519—1521) by the army of Hernando Cortés, the Spaniards, just like the Aztecs before them, did not initially destroy the social, political and economic institutions of the Indians after they themselves had taken over the positions formerly occupied by the Aztec ruling class. For two centuries the system of *encomiendas* and *corregimientos* was preserved in the colonies, and the Indian communities, which were still owners of the ground, remained subject to their Spanish liege lords (*encomenderos*). The Indians were at their service as *repartimientos* and were compelled to pay tribute and undertake forced labour. If any of the communities could not fulfil these demands, they had to make a number of slaves available. The mixing of the original Indian population with the Spanish colonists or their descendants led to the process of *mestizaje*, i.e., the formation of half-caste *mestizo* stock, and this union also brought about cultural changes. In most Latin American countries the term "Indian" is not used to describe a particular anthropological type — in Mexico 75 % of the entire population display quite definite Indian features — but merely indicates the fact of belonging to a community with special cultural and social characteristics. In 80 % of Mexican communities the inhabitants come into contact with people speaking Indian languages. In 1960, for example, 795,000 Indians used only the language of their tribe, whilst the number of bilingual individuals was over twice as large. We also find in Mexican Spanish a marked influx of words borrowed from the Aztecs. Such terms as tomato, cocoa, or cacao, and chocolate are well-known loanwords from the Aztec (Nahua) language. It has been estimated that at the present time about three million people living within the territory of the Republic of Mexico speak Indian languages. The majority of these are from the central area (Nahua, Aztecs above all, also Otomi, Tarasca, etc.), the Gulf zone (chiefly Maya, also Nahua, Totonac, Popoloca, Huaxtec, etc.) and the south-east, where nearly a million Indians live in the states of Oaxaca, Guerrero and Chiapas (Zapotec, Mixtec, Nahua, Mix, Zoque and Maya).

The *area of the Maya* peoples begins in the east of the isthmus of Tehuantepec, and their ancient civilisation marked the culmination of Indian art and learning. The region of rain forests in eastern Mexico and northern Guatemala can be regarded as the centre of the old Mayan civilisation. The dry, chalky land on the peninsula of Yucatan lay on the fringe of this area of cultural development in the classic era of the Maya, just like the mountainous territory of Guatemala and western Salvador, where the bulk of the Mayan population live to-day. The classical age of the Maya in the plains extended from the 4th to the 10th century. The number of ruined sites so far discovered bear ample witness to their outstanding technical achievements. This is all the more remarkable when we remember that their highly developed civilisation was based on a comparatively simple and archaic agricultural system, the ground being cleared by burning, and that the inhabitants of the rain forests possessed no intensive agrarian technique equal to that of the peoples from the *Mesa Central*. Everything would seem to indicate that the scattered type of settlement surrounded by areas cleared for cultivation was characteristic of the rural population and that there was no great Maya Empire here, but a series of smallish city-states ruled by lords of the priestly order. In all the centres of the Mayan area the priests were familiar with astronomy and arithmetic and there was a widespread knowledge of reading and writing. A calendar was also used, which enables us to date most of the Mayan "cities" and — beyond it — to correlate various cultures north and south of the Mayan territory with such Maya states. Among the Maya the numbers of the years were for the most part chiselled on large stelae, but they also appear on the walls of tombs and on clay vessels and jade ornaments. Their method of reckoning time was based on a mythical origin, corresponding to 3113 B.C. Although we are basically familiar with the features of the calendar, we can only read about a third of the hieroglyphs in spite of the ingenious work done by the various students of the Maya. Even a preliminary attempt at deciphering them with the aid of cybernetic machines has not, so far, brought the desired results. The task of deciphering has, of course, been rendered more difficult by the fact that we are not absolutely certain about the way in which their script is built up. It is probably a system containing phonetic elements, perhaps syllables, as well as word signs. The ancient Maya have left a great number of dates behind them, but we know very little about the political and social history of their city-states. There is a good deal of evidence to support the theory that the classic Maya period was mainly a time of peaceful relationships. But pictures of victorious warriors, with persons whom they had vanquished or taken prisoner paying homage to them, show that the situation changed after the middle of the 7th century. A great deal of information is contained in the brilliantly coloured fresco paintings dating from the 8th century and coming from the temples of Bonampak, discovered in 1946. In these we see not only the lords of the priestly class surrounded by numerous servants, elegant ladies and a festive procession of musicians, but enemy armies facing each other and a horde of conquered people submissively awaiting judgement. There would clearly appear to be some foundation for the view of P. Armillas that the warlike activities depicted at Bonampak are connected with the collapse of the priests' rule in the 9th century. The decline of cultural centres in the middle region actually occurred at a time when Mexican peoples might have invaded the area, and the signs of ravage and destruction evident in Piedras Negras and Palenque could readily be explained by the forcible seizure of these temple cities. At the time of the post-Classic Mayan culture of Yucatan —there is nothing corresponding to this at the classical sites — there was a new flowering of learning and the arts. The continuity of the priestly tradition is demonstrated by the famous Maya codex dating from the post-classical period and housed in the Saxon Provincial Library in Dresden, but it is really a revised "new edition" of much older hieroglyph books from the central province. A very powerful influence was exerted by the Toltecs from the end of the 11th century. The Itza, who moved in from Campeche and were either Toltecs themselves or were under Toltec leadership, were chiefly responsible for passing on the cultural heritage of Central Mexico and the Quetzalcoatl cult. The most important political entity in Yucatan was the "Liga de Mayapán", founded in 1007. The confederacy broke up when the Lord of Mayapan, with the assistance of Mexican "captains", gave the leading power to the Cocom dynasty and conquered Chichen-Itza in 1204. After the downfall of the Cocoms of Mayapan in 1441, the land soon disintegrated into a series of small rival city-states. In 1524/25 Pedro de Alvarado conquered the small states of the Mayan tribes in the highlands of Guatemala, but the conquest of the peninsula up in the north was not successfully accomplished until 1546/47. Indeed, until 1697 the small Itza state of Tayasal retained its independence in the forest area of Peten. In Yucatan the Indians repeatedly revolted against their foreign rulers, but they lost their own traditional culture in that area more rapidly than the plateau or upland peoples. Here the Indians were concentrated together in villages after they were conquered to make the task of supervision and control easier, but they often managed to avoid the new system by escaping into inaccessible mountain areas. The Indian way of life was preserved more effectively in these *sitios* than in the large Indian villages. The main maize-growing areas often coincide with those having a relatively high Indian population. Nowadays the Indians are usually forced to leave the upland regions from time to time and improve their economic position by hiring themselves out as hands on the plantations and ranches. The Catholicism of the Indians is linked to a marked degree with remnants of old religious ideas and usages. This popular and superstitious belief in *brujería*, or witchcraft, plays a vital part in the lives of the Indians and also the *ladinos* (*mestizos*). The most important Maya languages from a numerical point of view — Quiche, Cakchiquel and Mam — are spoken in the highlands of Guatemala. Out of a total Maya population of more than 2 million, 1.5 million live in the mountainous part of Guatemala. The Lacandon in the forests of eastern Chiapas, i.e., the classical culture area, form a remnant numbering hardly more than two hundred people.

As regards the *Central American land bridge*, the territory now occupied by the states of Honduras, Nicaragua, Costa Rica and Panama, our knowledge of the Indian peoples and their history is still sparse and incomplete, although detailed archaeological and ethnographical studies of the southern portion of Central America promise to yield important results with a bearing on the cultural history of both the Americas. In Costa Rica and Panama the tombs of Indian princes still provide fruitful exploration sites for modern gold-diggers, who in most cases have managed to forestall the archaeologists. Most of the finds of precious metals stem from the activities of these *huaqueros*, who generally sell their spoils to rich private collectors, giving false information about their origin and the conditions in which they were discovered. Only in a few small individual areas can we sketch out the course of history in broad outline and the connection between the archaeological finds and specific ethnic groups very often remains problematical. The Central American land bridge consists of a narrow fringe of lowland along the Pacific coast, a mountainous interior and a hot, humid zone facing the Atlantic and occupying a considerable part of Nicaragua. Apart from occasional stone arrowheads found in north-western Costa Rica and the Canal Zone, which point to a period of hunting activity, the piles of shells on the shores of the Gulf of Parita (Panama) are the oldest signs of human settlement in the area. They are the rubbish dumps of partially sedentary people living mainly from hunting, fishing and collecting shell-fish and not yet at the stage of producing ceramics. Radiocarbon testing established that these residues dated back to 4850 ± 100 years B.C. After the gradual and comparatively late introduction of agriculture, we could expect fixed settlements to spring up and cover quite large areas. In more recent strata we find more indications suggesting artisan division of labour and the existence of social classes and emphasis on the ceremonial aspects of life. The ancient inhabitants of Central America reached a high standard in the working of gold and copper. Peoples belonging to the Chibcha linguistic family, whose descendants can be found living even to-day in Colombia and adjoining areas of Central America, were masters of that artistic craft. Colombia, Costa Rica and Panama were the true Indian gold lands and we are reminded of their great wealth by the names dating from the times of the *Conquistadores*, e.g, "Costa Rica" ("Rich Coast") and "Castilla de Oro" ("Gold Castile", now Panama). As ownership of any objects made from precious metals was a prerogative of the élite, most items worked in gold have come from the tombs of the nobility. Even in their tombs these distinguished persons were accompanied by male and female escorts, so the existence of dependency and polygyny must have been a marked feature of the ruling class. In historical times the Indian population shows both cultural and linguistic connections with the peoples in the northern part of Central America and also with South American groups. Of northern origin are the Nicarao, who, like the Pipil in El Salvador, speak (or at one time spoke) an ancient Nahua language. In both tribes we see descendants of Toltec immigrants who abandoned Tula in the 12th century and moved to the south-east. The easternmost Nahua enclave, which took its origins from a troop of mercenaries or trading expedition sent out from Mexico in 1539, was, however, represented by the Sigua on the Chiriqui Lagoon (northern Panama). The Chorotega, the former carriers of the ancient culture in Nicaragua, also appear to be related to certain Mexican peoples (Otomi). The tribes from the South American lowlands advanced along the Caribbean coast into the Central American area. Apart from isolated groups, like the Choco in eastern Panama and western Colombia, or the Jicaque in Honduras, most of the representatives of this cultural type speak Chibcha languages: Cuna, Guaymi, Talamanca, Guatuso, Rama, etc. The main foods of the Forest Indians consist of tuberous plants, the fruit of the *pejibaye* palm, indigenous to the Orinoco basin, and the products of hunting and fishing. Some Indian groups live in clans even to-day. Public affairs are settled by the heads of the clans or a council of elders and the medicine man still sometimes plays an important part in social life too. In most Central American countries, however, there is a marked *mestizo* element in the Indian population, while the indigenous inhabitants in some areas have totally disappeared.

Three mountain chains, or cordilleras, form the characteristic feature of the *northern Andes area*, in the mountainous part of Colombia. Between them lie warm, humid lowlands, through which flow the large rivers of Colombia. Only the mountain range in the east widens to form a plateau, the *Meseta de Bogotá*, which in the pre-Spanish era was one of the most densely populated areas in America. The plains with their rivers and also the coast were probably settled in fairly early times, although it is not possible to give a definite date for the stone tools found on the former living sites of the nomadic hunting and gathering groups. The mysterious stone sculptures of San Agustin on the upper Magdalena date back to an agrarian type of population. They were erected in subterranean chambers used for worship or burial and on tombs. No-one can say which people fashioned these megalithic images of animal demons or gods. The rock tombs of Tierradentro, whose interiors are covered with a veritable tapestry of colourful paintings, may be rather more recent. In historical times (and owing to the absence of any written historical tradition this can only mean just a few generations before the arrival of the Spaniards) the north-west of South America was dominated by the Chibcha-speaking peoples. The spread of the Chibcha has been linked in the minds of the various investigators with the movements of peoples occurring in the north of South America, which were brought about by the expansion movements of the Carib-speaking tribes. In nearly every area maize was the most important crop, apart from tubers, such as the sweet potato, the yam and sweet manioc. The inhabitants of the plateaus grew several varieties of potato and also quinoa, oca and other plants native to the Andean countries. Fruit-trees were also cultivated. The land was made arable by means of fire, stone axes and planting sticks. A class structure and the existence of small states on the basis of village confederacies were typical of the political organisation of the Chibcha tribes inhabiting the Cauca valley and on the *Meseta de Bogotá*. At the head of a chief's area stood the *cacique*, who ruled it like a despot. Only the Muisca of the Bogota *Meseta* had reached the stage of forming relatively large states and they had nine independent principalities. The authority of the Chibcha rulers received religious sanction. Unfortunately, we are only able to form a confused and incoherent picture of the spiritual world of the Muisca from the records made by Spanish observers. It would appear that their religion, based mainly on the two stellar gods, the creator god Chiminigagua, the earth god Chibchachum and their culture hero Bochica, had not departed to any very great extent from the ancient view of the universe held by the Forest Indians. The destruction of the Chibcha states (1536—1541) was made easy for the Spaniards by the rivalry among the *caciques*. In the 16th and the early 17th century militant religious movements came into existence once again in the subject areas. They were led by Indian prophets and were aimed at the expulsion of the Spaniards and their religion. As the Indian population became increasingly more hybrid, the Muisca language finally died out in the 18th century. The numerically most powerful Indian peoples in Colombia are to-day the Aruak-speaking Goajiro of the Goajira peninsula and the Paez in the Tierradentro region. The Goajiro Indians successfully turned to the rearing of livestock and have become the owners of large herds of cattle and horses as well as flocks of sheep. About half of the indigenous population of the country live in Indian reservations and are mainly employed in agriculture.

"High Peru" was the name formerly given by the Spaniards to the *central Andes area*, the country between the two mighty cordilleras which extends far beyond the territory of present-day Peru and also includes the mountainous portions of Ecuador and Bolivia, the north of Chile and the north-west of Argentina. The chilly steppe-like plateau, 3000 to 5000 m high, is overshadowed by the towering, snow-covered peaks of the Andes ranges and carved up by deep ravines with rivers from the cordilleras flooding the fertile land. Owing to these differences in altitude, a great number of cultivated plants have become indigenous in the central Andes area. Of these, potatoes and quinoa, a seed-bearing type of Chenopodium, were adapted to the Puna region, whereas maize was grown predominantly in lower-lying areas. The extraordinary productivity attained by the Indian economy on the plateau was based on the use of intensive methods of agriculture (terraced beds, irrigation channels, systematic fertilisation), which demand cooperative effort on the part of quite large communities. The Indians of the plateau succeeded in domesticating such large animals as the llama and the alpaca and had various advanced techniques for working in metals — Indian bronze-founding, for instance — which can be traced back to these inventive people of the Andes. The coastal strip to the west of the high mountainous area is made up of arid desert country that only receives a shower of rain once in the course of several years. Permanent settlements were only possible in that unprepossessing region because of the number of small river courses running down from the slopes of the western cordilleras. Human settlements and above all their fields were mainly to be found in the narrow river valleys, which were intensively utilised. A system of oasis cultivation led to a considerable population density and the formation of urban centres. To the north of the Gulf of Guayaquil the picture changes, as the coast of Ecuador has an abundance of rain and forests. Just as happened in the eastern rain forest areas of the Montaña, the natural environment halted the advance of the upland Indians. Isolated finds in the Pampa de los Fósiles on the north coast, the Bolivian plateau and from Ecuador would appear to show the presence of early hunters in the central Andes area. Cultural remains from the sites of settlements belonging to an ancient civilisation on the coast based on a combined economy of fishing, gathering and agriculture are more recent. The introduction of the maize plant can definitely be ascribed to northern influences, but its cultivation in the central Andes area cannot, according to D. Collier, be put before 1400 B.C. An early artistic style in widespread use was probably developed in the 8th century B.C. and has been called the Chavin style after Chavin de Huantar, the old religious centre or place of pilgrimage. The quality of the metal technique is evident from certain ornamental pieces made out of copper and alloys of copper and gold. Centres of Classic civilizations were Moche or Mochica (north coast), Nazca (south coast), Recuay (northern highlands) and Tiahuanaco (southern highlands). Of these, the Moche civilisation, above all, has become famous for its tremendous output of ceramic work in the form of painted vessels with curved handles and figurative ornaments. These paintings and also the completely plastic pottery pieces provide a great amount of ethnographical information about those ancient coastal peoples, as nearly every aspect of profane and religious life was portrayed. The well-known religious centre of Tiahuanaco in the Bolivian plateau has given its name to a civilisation which must have spread over large stretches of the coast and the upland regions in the post-Classic period (from 800 A.D. onwards) and has influenced the cultural development of that entire territory to a very considerable extent. The period between 1200 and the extension of the Inca sphere of influence is known as the "period of small kingdoms". The leading principalities in the coastal lands were the Chimu Kingdom in the region of the ancient Moche civilisation and the state of Chincha in the south.

Within that same post-classical period when various states were formed we see a small dynasty of the Quechua people emerging in the Cuzco area — i.e., the Inca. Initially that small state only enjoyed local importance and its political role was confined at that time to conflicts and alliances with neighbouring groups of tribes. It was not until the second half of the 15th century that the Inca State developed into a great political and military power, the internal structure of which was, however, convulsed in the 16th century by internal quarrels and struggles among members of the Inca family. The intervention of the Spaniards under Francisco Pizarro (1532) put an end to the fateful dissensions and led at the same time to the collapse of Inca power. At the head of the well-organised Inca state stood the "Son of the Sun", an absolute ruler bearing the title of "Sapay Inca". The bulk of the population lived on the land. The structure of the agrarian communities (*ayllus*), the regulations for the distribution of water and the division of labour according to age and sex were, like the terraced cultivation beds and the irrigation channels, traditional elements of the agrarian way of life and were not created by the Inca, but were taken over by them and developed. Working parties from the resident communities undertook the building of the terraces and channels and during the time that they were working they were fed from the stocks in the state storehouses. The area of land belonging to a community that was not required for the immediate maintenance of the families was owned by the Inca and the sun god, i.e., the priestly class. The craftsmen did not form a special class, but were farmers commissioned to produce woven goods, pottery and work in feathers and metal. They received the raw materials from the state stores, where the finished products were subsequently kept. Special services included the supervision of the large suspension bridges and the relay messenger system. The administrators of the Inca state used a team of

21

runners to convey important communications. An admirable system of roads linked the various provinces in the empire together. The imperial language was Quechua. Although, as far as we know, the Indians of the Andes never reached the stage of devising a proper script, they largely made up for that deficiency when running their mighty empire by using knotted cord records (quipus) as an aid to memory for statistical information. At the time of the *Conquista*, according to J. H. Steward, approximately half of all the South American Indians lived in the high plateau areas of Peru and Bolivia and their average density of population was only equalled or exceeded in a very few specially favoured regions. In contrast to the northern part of the Andes, where the number of Indians to-day represents barely one-tenth of their original strength, we can estimate a population growth of one million since the days of the Conquest among the upland Indians of Ecuador, Peru and Bolivia. The Quechua language is actually in more widespread use to-day than at the time of the Inca Empire. It very soon became a written language and it was taught as early as 1756 at the University of San Marcos in Lima. Quechua and Aymara are parliamentary languages in Bolivia and the 1940 census in Peru showed that at that time over half of the schoolchildren used Indian languages and over a third knew no Spanish. At the present time 850,000 Bolivians are Aymaran, whilst in Peru 300,000 people use the Aymaran language. Quechua is spoken by 3.2 million in Peru, 1.5 million in Bolivia and 1 million in Ecuador. Moreover, about ten thousand Quechua and Aymaran live in the Argentinian Andes and in the northern provinces of Chile. On the other hand, the number of Uru, who are to be found on the shores of Lake Titicaca and in northern Chile, and represent the last remnants of the old fishing population in the west of South America, is very small indeed. Their language has now died out almost completely. The great majority of the Indians — as in pre-Spanish times — are farmers tilling their own small pieces of ground and still living and working together to some extent in the old Indian *ayllu* association. An example of the stability of this system is to be found in the extremely inaccessible Indian village of Collana, situated no more than 50 km away from the Bolivian capital of La Paz and yet persistently clinging (until 1946) to its judicial independence. There the village common and even the square where the inhabitants meet for their village assembly is divided up according to the *ayllu* groups, with the boundaries marked by llama bones. The mountain slopes are still laid out in terraces for cultivation — in fact, some of these date back to the time of the Inca. The Indian usually has only a small piece of unirrigated land at his disposal, whereas the fertile stretches are let out by the very powerful *hacienderos*. The Indian territory is owned by the village community who utilise the pasture and forest on a communal basis and distribute the arable area to the various members in turn. Thousands of Indian farmers obtain their livelihood from pieces of land that could not be used agriculturally if they were not worked by people adapted to the high altitude. Even mining can only be carried on by Indians at an altitude of 5000 m because of the tremendous physical exertion demanded. Stock-rearing and cottage industries play an important part in the Indian economy. Attempts have recently been made to settle upland Indians who have no ground and no work in lower and rather inaccessible districts and acclimatise them gradually to conditions in the Montaña.   R. K.

The people living in the southernmost part of the earth are the Yahgan of *Tierra del Fuego*, which has taken its name from the fires flaring up on sand and turf bases in the natives' boats. These attracted the attention of mariners in the cold island territory around Cape Horn. There were still about three thousand Yahgan eighty years ago, but they have been almost entirely wiped out by disease and brutal persecution. Of the other "Canoe Indians", living, like these, from the sea, the Chono, who dwelt to the north, have also disappeared, but groups of Alacaluf are still in existence to-day. After Ferano de Magalhàes, who reached the southern archipelago in 1519, Darwin was one of those who saw the Indians of Tierra del Fuego. In spite of the almost Antarctic climate they wore hardly any clothes. A thick coating of fat and colouring matter protected their skin and they merely tossed a seal pelt over the shoulder that was turned towards the wind, a garment reaching only halfway down. Their home was a shelter made from trees bent together and covered with leaves, ferns, seaweed and bark. Like all gathering communities, they possessed firmly plaited carrying bags and baskets. They used knives fashioned from shells and stones, bone hide-scrapers and stone hammers for breaking animal bones. Their canoes were sewn together from bark. They were familiar with five types of spear for hunting, also clubs, snares and bows. Their food consisted of marine mammals, shellfish, crustaceans, sea birds and their eggs, also mushrooms and berries. The harsh austerity of their environment greatly developed a strong inclination toward magic and religious conceptions. They had a rich store of myths.

Medicine men (also medicine women) constituted the most important members of the community, in which the family formed the basic unit. The complicated rites used when the young became initiated to adulthood may perhaps point to some earlier and higher form of civilisation. These Indians may have fallen back in that respect when they were pushed down to the southern tip of the continent. Associated with those Indians who gained their livelihood from the sea and probably reached Tierra del Fuego about 2000 years ago are the Foot or Land Indians, whose southernmost representatives, the Ona, have also died out almost entirely. The chief game sought by these hunters, who had no canoes, was the guanaco. Their skins were stitched together with sinews to form capes, with red dye and fat rubbed into the leather side. The women also wore a fur skirt. The Ona had no houses, but merely lived behind wind-breaks made from guanaco skins and set up in a semi-circle. During their wanderings all the objects that were in use were wrapped in the wind-break cover and carried on the women's backs, whilst the men pursued the game with their birchwood bows, which were almost two metres long and extremely delicately fashioned, and their feathered arrows. They also knew how to kindle fires with inflammable material obtained from fungi and pyrites, and they used leather water-pails and containers and all kinds of plaited baskets, as well as combs made from wood or whalebone, skinscrapers made from shells, clubs for processing the leather and for hunting and (the very important) awls for boring the holes through which the sinew thread was pulled. In spite of the preponderance of land game all around them, the Ona were also able to hunt aquatic animals and they went after seals, crustaceans, eels, ducks and cormorants. Their economic group consisted of the family, which formed part of a larger local community with an exactly defined hunting ground. Larger assemblies gathered only on special occasions, for example, if a whale went aground or initiation celebrations were being held. Every young Ona had to submit to an arduous two-year training period ending with the initiation ceremony, which bears a marked resemblance to the initiation practices in the Amazon area because of the masks used and the physical torture that was inflicted. From a spiritual and cultural point of view the Ona firmly believed in a world beyond and had like the "canoe Indians", a rich store of myths and a highly developed form of shamanism. Adjoining the "broken tableland" of Patagonia, the plain of the Argentine Pampas extends as far as the La Plata estuary. There is still a great deal of uncertainty about Patagonia and the Pampas in prehistoric times. Among the most interesting prehistoric finds are quantities of wedgeshaped implements which the expert Grasso feels like attributing to the Early Stone Age, but this would mean that the immigration date of the first Americans, so far accepted as correct, would have to be shifted 50,000 years further back. Quite a number of other historical mysteries have come to light. The northern neighbours of the Ona living in the Pampas were the "classic" hunters of the south, the Tehuelche, the Puelche and the Querandi, who, when out hunting, used to hurl their famous *bola*, or stoneball, attached to guanaco sinews or leather thongs. From the early 18th century onwards, under pressure from the white man, Araucanians streamed over the Andes into the Pampas, where, for a century or so, hundreds of thousands of wild horses had formed themselves into huge herds and where the white man's cattle came to be regarded as highly desirable game animals by the Indians, representing as they did a kind of artificially introduced bison. Those who left the Andes area and moved away eastwards were the Pehuenche, whose name means "Pine People". They were indeed "harvesting peoples" depending upon the wild-growing piñon-seed of the Andes pine, Araucaria. Every Pehuenche had an exclusive and hereditary right to harvest *piñons* in a particular place. Their mountainous homeland contained many open passes leading into the Pampas that were used by the Araucanian "enemies of the white man" (called Aucas or Serranos) who stole horses and cattle on their way to the Great Plains — a land of plenty like the North American Prairie later on. The great gathering of the Indian Pampas hunters was brought to an end in 1879, when General Roca set off on his terrible expedition into the Great Plains.

Farther to the north, in the heart of the South American continent, lies the *Gran Chaco*, surrounded by mountains and only open to the south, with its plains dotted with salt-pans. Its name is derived from the Quechua word *chacú* ("Great Hunt"). Here we find peoples from seven linguistic families: Guaycuru, Mascoi, Lule-Vilela, Matacan, Zamuco and splinter groups of the Aruak and Tupi-Guarani. In spite of all their variety, they do possess certain uniform traits. For example, strange to relate, pottery, which is elsewhere an art only known to farming communities, is familiar to them all, and the custom of scalping, which is rare, on the whole, in South America and is connected with agrarian head worship, is evident among Chaco tribes. Since being driven into the Chaco, all the Chaco Indians became gatherers, hunters and harvesting peoples, but farmers only to a limited extent. The chief equipment they used to obtain their food was a long and heavy digging stick, large carrying bags and a wooden hook attached to a tall pole for bending down the branches on the Algarroba tree when harvesting its beans. Those living along the rivers, like the Pilaga of the Pilcomayo, used nets of different shapes for fishing. The homes of the Chaco tribes were wind-breaks roughly built up and sometimes combined in a row to form one large community house. Their clothing consisted originally of skin cloaks, then woollen blankets and sometimes also of ponchos from the Andes, and they wore sandals on their feet. The tribes of the Chaco attracted world interest when the Jesuits began their missionary and research work among them. In 1588 the first Jesuit college was founded in Paraguay and the famous creation that has gone down in history as the "Jesuit state" came into being. The general settlement, education and advancement of the Indians proceeded there on such a large scale that the originators of all these schemes were banished from South America for a variety of reasons in 1767—68. The other great factor entering into the lives of these Indians was the coming of the horse in the early 17th century. As a result, the population became divided up into two groups: the mounted tribes, like the Abipone, Mocovi, Mbaya-Cadiueo and Payagua, with the formation of sharply defined social classes, complete with chiefs, big chiefs and an elaborate ceremony when they broke camp. The second group were the "Foot Indians", e.g., the Mataca, Chorote, Ashluslay, Lule, Chamacoco and others, who met during the large Algarroba bean harvests. Shamanism played an important role and chiefs were often qualified for their high position by their "Supernatural powers". Wild plants were used as the chief source of food by the Algarroba harvesters. To-day, most of the Chaco tribes have at least some knowledge of farming. The mounted tribes showed no inclination in that direction and obtained their cultivated fruits by theft or, like the Mbaya, by demanding tribute. There was hardly any tradition of cultivating plants there. Farmers like the Zamuco lived alongside gatherers and hunters like the Chamacoco. On the northern edge of the Chaco two members of large and famous linguistic families came to share the destiny of the Chaco dwellers: the Chiriguano of the Tupi-Guarani group and the southernmost Aruak, the Chané. As far back as the very early 16th century waves of Guarani wandered right across the Chaco from Paraguay to raid the Inca Empire and carry off gold and other treasures as booty. They hid from their enemies in the remote wilderness, where they laid out fields, then waited for the harvest and moved on. In the north they came across the Chané, whose way of life showed many Andean influences. They exterminated the men and married the women and created a hybrid culture made up of Andean, Aruak and Guarani elements. Although greatly inferior to them in number, they managed to keep the Chané, who were excellent farmers, as slaves. So, just as happened among the Navaho and the Pueblo in North America, robbers appeared on the scene and assimilated the civilisation of the farmers they had conquered.

In amongst the Tupi-Guarani peoples of eastern Brazil, we find living in the *mountainous country of Brazil* and in the areas leading to the tropical forest zone the tribes that were classified linguistically as Gês by the botanist Martius in 1867. They are at a comparatively low level and are surrounded by culturally similar members of other linguistic families. Their north-western group is composed chiefly of Timbira, Cayapa and Suya. Among the best known of the central Gês are the Chavante, the Cherente and the Acroa, whilst the southern group is formed by the Caingang — a collective term for the non-Tupians in the area. Originally the tribes of the Gês group, whose settlement area reveals traces of ancient occupation, were gatherers and hunters. However, because of the Tupi who surrounded them — and by whom they were hunted as enemies — and also because of the white settlers they came to learn about farming and they adopted it to some extent, in so far as it could be combined with their nomadic way of life. The climate in the Gês area is drier than along the Amazon and the year is divided up into a dry and a rainy season. There are three types of vegetation — the tropical rain forest, a "gallery" forest along the rivers which can be cleared annually so that the ground can be tilled with a planting stick, and also the Catinga forest and the Campos with their grassy steppes and scattered groups of trees. During the dry season the Gês peoples are busy gathering food. Even today their favourite hunting weapons are the bow and arrow, because they are noiseless. Snares are effectively used in particular by the Apinayé. Where the land is tilled at all, this is done during the rainy season. The nomadic way of life starts up again immediately after the harvest. For this they wear hardly any clothing and use a "beehive hut" rapidly built up from two wind breaks as their living quarters. Initiation ceremonies exist in a more or less marked form among all the tribes. The *couvade*, or men's childbed which is supposed to grant magical protection to the newborn child and its mother, is also customary among the Gês. They believe too in "loss of soul", the idea that disease, madness or death is caused by lost and straying souls wandering in sleep or being swept off by evil magicians. After death a second burial often takes place, the cleaned bones being painted with red *urucú* and reinterred. As regards musical instruments, there are no drums, but flutes, bamboo trumpets and whistles play an important part for giving signals during dancing. A typical cultural element used by the Gês is the anchor axe, a stone hatchet with a characteristic shape and a short shaft. It is the official attribute of high-ranking elders and chiefs and probably spread from the Apinayé over the whole area. A chieftain class holds sway everywhere, but their power is restricted by a council. We often find age classes, with special adoption rites for admission to the next stage. A typical feature of the Gês is the "ceremonial friendship" existing between members of different parts of a tribe, for which the reciprocal duties are rigidly laid down. There is also lifelong membership of confederacies with mythological ties, in which the sun and the moon, the king vulture and a legendary deer play vital roles. Another peculiarity of these tribes is the "tear greeting" given to persons returning after a long absence in order to appease the supernatural powers. Another curious practice is also a race that takes place especially among the north-western and central Gês, during which they carry on their shoulders a portion of tree trunk about one metre long and weighing up to 100 kg. This sport, which is carried on by organised teams from the tribes, serves to enhance prestige within the community and it has a parallel among the North American Jicarilla Apache, who run relay races with smaller pieces of wood for the purpose of improving plant fertility. Rubber balls are also made and are used in particular for ritual ballgames during initiation ceremonies. The Botocudo or Aymoré, who speak quite a distinct language without any South American connections and moved into the coastal area from the interior of the country, were formerly known as the eastern Gês and are now allocated with the "Macro-Gês". Culturally speaking, they come close to the Gês; they are not a single tribe, but a group of tribes, of which only some stray remnants are in existence to-day. They are nomadic hunters with mighty bows and do not go in for agriculture, pottery or weaving, nor do they use water transport. Their name is derived from the Portuguese word *botoque* ("Barrel Bung"), which is a reminder of the small wooden blocks they wear in the lobes of their ears and their lower lip. They lived in local groups numbering up to two hundred individuals, with a "strong man" noted for his supernatural powers as their leader. His main functions were the prevention of disputes, the distribution of hunting spoils and leadership in war. Protective spirits were ceremonially summoned up by shamans. The master of the spirits was "Father Whitehead", the owner of songs and lord of the rain and the storm. In the south-west of the Gês complex in the central Matto Grosso and coming between the Xingu and the Araguaya we find the Bororo, who represent a linguistic group on their own. On hunting trips, whose time and location were determined by the medicine men, the capture of peccaries and tapirs played a predominant part. The women went out with digging sticks in search of roots, seeds and palm nuts. The men of the Bororo lived in a large rectangular house encircled by the simpler family huts. The tribe was divided up into clans and moieties. There was worship of the spirits of the dead who were thought to live on in flute-like wind instruments. Their mythology is dominated by the twins Bakororo and Itubori, the sons of a jaguar and an Indian woman, to whom the dead depart. The sun and the moon are also venerated. In spite of certain cultural differences, the Guato can also be regarded as coming within this group of peoples because of their simple form of civilisation. They live immediately to the south of the Bororo and are neighbours of the Gês. They too own mighty bows about two metres long with six different types of arrows belonging to them. With their spears they could kill alligators and the gigantic anaconda snakes, which are up to eleven metres long. In the swamps they built artificial earth mounds on which they grew useful wild plants to protect them from flooding — an interesting reason for passing over from mere food-gathering to agriculture. Characteristic cultural features of the Guato are their mosquito nets and a kind of spherical clay bow about whose origin interesting theories have been put forward. The tear greeting of the Gês peoples is also usual among them. To the south of the Gês complex the Guayaki live in groups of up to twenty individuals in the woods of eastern Paraguay purely as gatherers and hunters. They kill mainly fish with their bows and arrows. Jaguars and tapirs are caught in snares. The main foods of these people are wild honey and beetle larvae. They do not even have proper homes, but just creep into the undergrowth, so access to their camps is difficult. Their cultural poverty is practically unequalled anywhere in America.

On the *east coast of Brazil*, in the Pernambuco area, we find a number of tribes in whom the basic Indian element is now hardly recognisable owing to the admixture of negro and *mestizo* stock. They include, for example, the Fulnio, who have retained some of their old animal and plant rituals. To the west of them live the Pancaruru, amongst whom even to-day we come across animal dances and what might be described as communion with a wild plant. A few isolated tribes are still to be found to the south of these, shut up inside the Tupian area, e.g., the Cariri, who form a linguistic family of their own and came culturally higher up the scale than the Gês and their neighbours. If we move further south along the coastal fringe, we come to members of the large Tupi-Guarani linguistic family, whose representatives, if they have not culturally declined, work as farmers. Tupinamba is the collective name for the groups situated on the coast. We use the name Guarani to-day for the members of the same linguistic group located in Paraguay and southern Brazil. Because of their religious beliefs, those groups migrated eastwards after the coming of the Portuguese or shortly before in order to reach the much-vaunted land of their mythological "grandfather", the god of thunder, just like the North American tribes, who are obsessed by the idea of the "Ghost Dance". They spread out along the Atlantic coast over an area of two thousand miles. The prosperity of the Tupinamba can be ascribed to their combination of agriculture and coastal fishing. They lived in large villages surrounded by palisades with about eight big houses, in each of which up to two hundred persons bound by family ties lived together. These cannibals found their victims in the course of their warlike expeditions and fed on them in accordance with the prescribed rituals. They cultivated numerous varieties of maize and manioc. For fishing they used boats made from a single tree trunk, also bark canoes and rafts. To the south of São Paulo, in Cananea, comes the boundary of the Tupinikin who adjoin the Tupinamba on the south side. That marks the beginning of the territory of the Guarani, the "metal people" who showed Juan Diaz de Solis, the discoverer of La Plata, in 1513 the gold and silver that gave the river its name. These metals came, however, from plundering forays into the Inca Empire on the part of Guarani crossing the Chaco. The Spanish *encomienda* system ruined the Guarani, but the large population of *mestizos* that came into being saved their race and also their language from complete extinction. To-day these *mestizos* form the bulk of the population of Paraguay, and the Guarani language is still spoken by a million people. The present-day Guarani are thus remnants of the Tupinamba groups who moved into the interior of the country. Their culture and whole mode of life are comparable to those of the Tupinamba. Every village had a chief whose power was, however, restricted by the might of the shaman. Modern research has revealed that the "Guarani culture" referred to in such sentimental terms in present-day Paraguay does not exist at all and hardly any survivals from the old period can be detected. Of course, the officially dominant Catholic religion has taken on definite exotic traits in those areas, but the plants and animals seen in the villages are of European origin.

In the tropical *rain forests of the Amazon*, which extend roughly 2000 km in a north-south direction and about 3500 km from east to west, we find, in contrast to the maize-growers of Mexico and the Andes, the classic cultivators of the poisonous manioc tuber, who have devised an effective means of removing the high prussic acid content present in that plant. We know very little about the area in prehistoric times, as the perishable nature of the materials used by these Indians in the moist, hot climate has practically eliminated the possibility of any finds being made, so ceramic products are virtually the only fruits of their labours that have survived. These Indians lived along the great rivers and travelled on them to reach the south, and it was by river that the various cultural influences were introduced from the north. The whites also came by river as enemies and destroyers. Most of the tribal groups that had settled at one time along the rivers have since disappeared, i.e., they have not endured as sizable cultural units. If they survived at all, they withdrew into the interior in scattered groups, but, in spite of everything, they remained so numerous that even today we are still unable to pinpoint the "hundreds of tribes" said to be living in isolation, because we do not have enough exact information. The chief representatives of the culture of the tropical forest area are the Aruak and Carib in the north and, to the south of the Amazon, the Tupi. They have picked up and assimilated a great deal, especially on the technical side, not from the Andes, but from the areas round the Pacific — knowledge and features that could be adopted within their own environment, e.g., the weaver's loom, the hammock, the art of producing bark fabric, the *maloca*, built from thin posts and covered with grass or leaves and often used as a community house, also pottery and boats fashioned from a single tree trunk. So the destiny of the Indians in the tropical forest has, above all, been a wandering life, the directions of their journeys being determined by the rivers which provided them with a route and also with food. There they found not only fish, but the game animals who came down to drink. The rivers therefore play an extremely important part in their lives, equivalent to that played by plants, although these links with the water were severed in some groups when they were pushed back into trackless areas. We can therefore regard the basic foods of these Indians as tubers, grown on land cleared by slash-burning, river fish and game. In addition they make extensive use of wild plants, obtaining fruit and artisan materials from the palms in particular. Animal food, if it comes from the rivers, is killed by means of poisons, snares, weir-baskets, spears, bows and arrows. The movements of shoals of fish often have a profound effect on the Indians' pattern of life. For example, in the Rio Negro area of north-western Brazil the smaller tributaries become dried up from December to March and the fish withdraw to the large river arms. This compels the Indians who have become sedentary there as manioc-growers to lead a nomadic life for three months and for this they equip themselves with baskets filled with their staple food — flat cakes made of dried manioc. Along the rivers hunting is less important than fishing, but in the interior all conceivable methods are used to catch game, e.g., imitating animal calls, kindling steppe fires, shooting from some ambush spot, digging out armadillos and capturing ducks, as in China, by using a calabash to conceal the hunter's head. The main weapons employed are spears, snares, bows and arrows. But the typical weapon of the tropical forest tribes is the blow-gun, which kills noiselessly and is extensively used in the north-west of the Amazon area. It is utilised exclusively for hunting and not in war and is only effective if the small wooden arrows have been smeared with poison. Its pattern of distribution is linked with that of curare poison and can be accurately traced from the north and north-west of the continent. Curare is a mixture of at least thirty-five nerve poisons with a predominance of strychnos varieties. Its active principle is curarine, an alkaloid which impedes the transference of stimuli from the motor nerves to the skeletal muscles and so, by paralysing the respiratory muscles, leads to death. Curare is harmless to the stomach, so the hunter can eat any game animal killed in this way without danger. Older than the bow or the arrow or the blow-gun is the spear thrower, once used in the tropical forest region; the Mexican term for it is *atl-atl*. The typical forms of watercraft are dugout canoes, fashioned from a single trunk and also two lighter forms — rafts made from balsa wood and bark canoes. The hammock can be described as the classic sleeping device found in the tropical forest area. Gourd bottles, wooden troughs, clay vessels and baskets are the most important types of receptacle. Decoration with feathers and painting of the body are widespread and often serve as a substitute for clothing. Plaiting, weaving and pottery are carried on everywhere. In the community house, or *maloca*, separate compartments are usually erected for the different families and only two vital objects are shared by all — the fireplace where beer is prepared and a large container for the occasional maize-pounding process. In some tribes there is a separate men's house, set apart from the family dwellings. The village community is also the most important economic unit. In the clan house authority is vested in the eldest of the group and in the larger communities a man with the qualities of a shaman held the rank of chief. Although these are warlike tribes, their reasons for fighting are quite different from those of the mounted tribes of the south, who are impelled by valour. Here war is waged in order to avenge any wrongs that have been suffered and also to acquire heads as trophies, as they believe that magical powers reside in human heads. Their very strong magic convictions start right from birth and are evident in the practice known as the *couvade*, which exists everywhere. It prescribes certain standards of conduct and dietary rules for the father and mother of the child. The puberty rites for both sexes are nearly always connected with physical torture of the adolescents. As for the ceremonies for the dead, we find in them a mixture of ancestor worship and fertility magic. Alcoholic beverages and narcotics occur among these farmers in a great number of different forms, often determined by magic. The sun, the moon or the thunder may be looked on as deities. More important than these are their cultural heroes, the bringers of all fine earthly possessions. They appear as a single figure or as twin brothers or even a trinity and are often linked with jaguar myths. In spite of all the features that they exhibit in common, the many tribes living in the mighty rain forest complex of the Amazon region cannot be compressed into one single stereotyped culture. A great number of separate forms have evolved as a result of many different influences and historical events, and we can only give a few examples of them here. For instance, the Mura, who can be counted among the warlike tribes of South America, gave up agriculture after the coming of the whites and have become a people purely of canoes and fishermen because they live on the Madeira River, in an area extending as far as

Rio Purus. They lived so exclusively in their bark canoes, which were up to six metres long, and were only replaced at a later date by single trunks hollowed out with fire, that they even made provision for babies to be born on board, so that their water trips did not have to be interrupted. They fish with bows and arrows and kill large aquatic animals with skilfully manipulated harpoons. Farther to the north of the Amazon the fierce Waica and Shiriana live on the upper Orinoco. These old enemies both managed to make a number of smaller splinter groups, e.g., the Pakidai and the Surara, the remnants of an ancient population driven out by the invading Aruak, pay tribute to them. The Omagua of Rio Napo, belonging to the Tupian family, have probably died out by now. At one time they owned numerous villages and cultivated various food plants. Among the best-known tribes of the tropical forest area are the Caraya of the Island of Bananal, who form a linguistic family on their own and have always been enemies of the Gês and the Tupi. Of equal importance among them are agriculture and fishing, carried on as a communal venture with vegetable poisons. As hunters they pursue peccaries for their meat, but specialise in hunting for birds, in search of the magnificent feather ornaments of which they are so fond. Their special distinguishing features are the beautiful stools carved out of wood, their rules of etiquette and the tonsures that they wear for ritualistic reasons. Their spiritual culture is dominated by their cult of the dead and mask cult. Prominent representatives of the Tupians of the southern Amazon are the Mundrucu. They were well organised in the growing of manioc and in their warlike campaigns under a big chief, conducted for the purpose of acquiring heads as trophies. In their religion there are certain dominant rites devoted to increasing the fertility of fish, game and manioc. Today the Mundrucu have become involved in the cultural transformation brought about by the rubber trade in the Amazon area. They left their villages and now live beside rivers, collecting latex, and have entered into well organised barter dealings with the whites.

The *Montaña* is the name applied to the eastern parts of Ecuador and Peru, and the Yunga of Bolivia is associated with it too. In the old Spanish source documents the word *Montaña* is used to describe the primeval forest and this is contrasted with the mountainous region, or *Sierra*. So there is also a predominance of tropical rain forest territory in the Montaña, but the area is very mountainous, reaching up to 2000 metres in altitude. Here we find the source waters of the Amazon, whose valleys are carved deep into the Andes. This is the region with the greatest linguistic diversity in the whole of South America. Characteristic features often present in the Montaña and diverging from the usual tropical forest civilisation are the absence of manioc-growing and of the vertical weaver's loom, the trumpet and masks. On the other hand, the Chuncho (for that is the name give to the eastern peoples in the Andes) are able to rear the musk-duck, which was indigenous to this area. They can also grow white potatoes and in the higher regions use the llama and the alpaca. Sleeping platforms are found instead of hammocks. The blow-gun and curare also appear to have spread here from the Montaña. Owing to the isolated lives of the Chuncho in the valleys and forests, a very great variety of cultural forms have evolved. The Uitoto can be regarded as representatives of the Montaña Indians. They live on the frontier of Brazil and Colombia with Peru and go in for hunting and fishing, as well as growing some plants, and they have a very strongly developed ceremonial life including cannibalistic traits. They had flutes made from human and animal bones and "male" and "female" signalling drums that could "talk" over a distance of up to twelve kilometres. Skull trophies were obtained from prisoners caught on their war missions. Even more famous are the head trophies of another Montaña tribe, the Jivaro, who hoped to gain magical powers from the *tsantsas* or shrunken heads that they produced. The skin was pulled off the skull and it was filled with hot sand and prepared in such a way that they obtained a human head resembling a portrait, but about the size of an orange, with the long hair which had once reached to the shoulders still hanging from it. Among the Jivaro a large amount of vegetable intoxicants are smoked or drunk. To sum up, the Montaña tribes occupy a rather indeterminate intermediate position between the Indians of the tropical forest area and those of the Andes. Their conception of the universe is strongly magical and they have a knowledge of secret beverages and remedies. Having originated from many different sources they speak a multiplicity of languages. For all these reasons they have been greatly sought after down the years as magicians, but also as traders.

Ethnologically speaking, the highlands of *Guyana* extend as far south as the Amazon lowlands, westwards to the Orinoco plains and north-east to the Atlantic. They also form part of the tropical forest area, but here a very special ingredient has been added, i.e., the African element in the population, which has given this area quite a different cultural flavour. For a long time three European powers. Britain, Holland and France, were able to retain in Guiana part of their once considerable American colonial possessions. Remarkable ethnical developments have taken place there, where members of nine Indian linguistic families can be found. As regards what was once known as British Guiana, with her 332,000 square kilometres, only small parts have so far been investigated. According to Pahlen, the rest is primeval forest and, together with the adjacent forests of the other Guianas and those of Venezuela and Brazil, can be reckoned among the least known areas anywhere in the world. At the present time 9300 Indians live there. Surinam, or former Dutch Guiana, which actually numbers less than 200,000 inhabitants, still contains as many as 4500 Indians. It was here that the so-called Bush Negro culture came into existence about the first half of the eighteenth century. This owed its existence to fugitive West African slaves and it proceeded to establish very interesting trading relations both with the Indians and the whites. The smallest of the three, formerly known as French Guiana, was notorious for its cruel penal colony, the "dry guillotine" of Cayenne. The Indians of Guiana were and still are farmers and, as a general rule, follow the practices of the Indians living in the tropical forests. At one time they led a decidedly warlike existence with a view to acquiring slaves and subsequently devouring them. This was a specifically Carib custom. In the post-Columbian period the prisoners who were captured were sold to the whites as working slaves. Shamanism was a very pronounced feature of their religion. The magician possessed a beautifully carved seat and a rattle filled with crystals. Magic also played a leading role in their everyday lives. Thus the *couvade* is extremely important in Guyana and all the prescribed standards of behaviour were strictly adhered to. The same applies to the puberty ceremonies, the rules of marriage — "service marriage" was the usual form here — and also the burial rituals, during which the participants were soundly whipped in order to drive out the evil spirits.

The Indians departed from the *Antilles* and the Africans arrived. But the old traditions of the Ciboney, the Aruak and the Carib still remain alive when the drum rhythms of Africa sound forth beneath the "Caribbean moon" and the dark-skinned island poets of our own days sing of the destinies of the Indians and the Negroes of long ago.   E.L.

MUSIC OF THE ESKIMO AND INDIANS

There are so many cultural aspects to be considered and there have been so many migrations within the American continent and such an interchange of trends and influences that it is difficult to draw any firm lines of demarcation and pinpoint the musical styles used by the different ethnic groups of Eskimo and Indians, Nearly everywhere, for example, among the Eskimo, the Indians of northern California, the scattered groups of peoples living in the heart of the Amazon forests and among the inhabitants of Tierra del Fuego, archaic types of music appear side by side with more highly developed or more modern forms. This can be observed, not only in the case of two tribes coming in contact with each other, but within the same community, which often retains musical ideas and structures, as well as functions and modes of expression belonging to quite different epochs. This type of stratification or superimposing of varying levels of musical awareness can also be found in other continents, often as the exception rather than the rule. But in America this is a universal phenomenon. In some Indian tribes there are scales containing definitely fixed intervals, whereas others have no clearly established scales and no precise intervals. Of course, it is impossible to give a complete and exhaustive picture of Indian music within the restricted compass of this book. An attempt is merely being made to give some idea of the most marked stylistic differences and indicate the significance of music in the life of the Indians, by quoting a few typical examples. In view of the centuries of direct contact existing between the various Indians and the proportion of the American population that has come in from Europe and Africa, original Indian music and its special features have only survived unchanged in a few regions. These are, in fact, the regions that have been given prime consideration here in our choice of examples.

The music of the Eskimo, of which Zygmunt Estreicher in particular has made detailed studies (496—502), is almost entirely vocal. Their only musical instrument is the round frame drum with which the Eskimo accompany their songs by banging a stick against the underside of the frame. But they were also familiar with the bullroarer and the clapper. Why did they give up these instruments? Certainly not because they had found others to replace them. Possibly they were trying to reduce their movable property to the bare minimum. This very necessary limitation was brought about by their living conditions and the difficulties they experienced when migrating across the endless frozen wastes. But in some places having connections with the more southerly Indians we do find a kind of Eskimo violin, copied from European or northern Asiatic models. The drum rhythm is very often independent of the metre of the song. There are various kinds of Eskimo song — entreaties to animals to let themselves be killed, thanksgiving songs for successful hunting, magic chants for the healing of sickness, cradle songs, narrative songs and, last but not least, songs of scorn. As a rule, conflicts here are not settled by fighting, but in a drumming contest by the persuasive power of the songs with which the opponents mock each other and reveal their mutual weaknesses and shortcomings. There is plenty of singing, often lasting for hours on end, at the frequent dancing festivals and the evening entertainments. One of the people present sings a song composed by himself, beating a drum as he does so, and the others join in the refrain. Any pentatonic songs we hear among the Eskimo to-day appear to have been introduced in more recent times. The oldest songs noted down (up to 1902) actually consist of only two or three notes. These songs with two or three notes are still the general rule in Greenland according to quite recent observations by Poul Rovsing Olsen (719). This author points out the relative indifference of Eskimo to the size of the interval. For example, the combination sol-la-re has the same significance for them as sol-la-do or sol-si-mi. The following musical transcription should illustrate our point — i.e., the sequence of intervals, one small and the other larger. This can be shown graphically as follows:

East Greenland (P. R. Olsen)

The melodic structure of Eskimo music has a kind of "fixed centre of gravity" functioning as the fundamental note. According to Zygmunt Estreicher (500, p. 663), the purest form of musical style is to be found, as far as the Eskimo are concerned, among the Padleirmiut, a tribe of Reindeer (Caribou) Eskimo living to the west of Hudson Bay. The following two examples reveal the two basic types of melody with a centre of gravity (g'—f'—g' or f'—g'—f') and a centre of movement as their most important features:

Padleirmiut Eskimo (Z. Estreicher), ca. ♩ = 92

Padleirmiut Eskimo (Z. Estreicher), ca. ♩ = 92

In the musical culture of the Eskimo we can detect a kind of stratification pattern, the phases of which are in keeping with those evident in their general cultural development, as indicated by Birket-Smith. Estreicher (500, p. 685) agrees with Poul Rovsing Olsen about the close relationships existing between the inhabitants of East Greenland and the Reindeer Eskimo (Caribou), who have both obviously sprung from a common origin and have preserved the oldest style of Eskimo music. Estreicher felt that the musical style of the Eskimo should not be regarded as a degenerate form of Indian music, but that both were fairly closely connected together. He was struck by the stylistic similarities, e.g., the interconnections between the drum and song rhythms, certain structural types, melodic profiles, tectonic forms and so on.   P. C.
The music of the Indians of North America is essentially vocal and intended for a solo voice. There are, of course, examples of heterophony, a bourdon or drone effect and singing in parallels but these are extremely rare

and are not an essential feature of the general musical style. As for the instruments, we find a great multiplicity of idiophones, membranophones, aerophones and some chordophones, but those used to accompany singing and dancing are the idiophones and membranophones and occasionally a one-tone whistle. Although there is a certain degree of homogeneity which differentiates the music of that continent from that found in other regions of the world, Bruno Nettl (686, p. 105 ff.) has picked out and described six variants of the general style in North America. The form of musical expression ranges from the simple melodies of the Eskimo and the inhabitants of the desert areas of the Great Basin in Nevada and Utah to the more extended and ambitious forms that are favoured by the coastal tribes in the north-west and the Pueblo Indians of the south-west. But there appears to be a direct connection between the complexity of the musical style and the social and economic status of the area in question, also its population density and general cultural level.

Analysis of the various melodies reveals a multiplicity of scale formations, with a predominance of pentatonic structures. Tunes devised to go with words and used for singing the myths of creation are, as a rule, confined to a scale of two or three notes only falling within the range of a fifth. In contrast to this, the melodies used for the healing of diseases have interval gaps of fourths and thirds and cover an octave or a tenth. A specially characteristic type shows a falling melodic line moving from the highest note through a series of ascending phrases to the lowest note, the final or fundamental. Other melodies are marked by a wave-like or oscillating movement. Some rise to begin with and then decline, giving the form of an arc.

The rhythm of the music is generally heterometric, with phrases of differing length obtained by repeating rhythmical motifs in melodic sequence. Isorhythmic structures only occur in a few tribes. We find a multiplicity of forms, ranging from the litany type with constant repetition of short phrases to strophic songs and complete compositions. The drum rhythm rarely departs from a regular sequence of beats, but it is by no means unusual for the song and the drum rhythm to proceed in different tempi.

The most prominent distinguishing feature of Indian music — and something which has not yet been fully examined — is the vocal technique that gives the melodies their peculiar and quite characteristic quality. There are several singing styles, but what we most frequently encounter among the Indians is a hard and vibrant type of voice production, produced by extreme tension of the vocal cords, and the use of grace-notes or embellishments to lend "colour" to the song. Falsetto singing can also be heard occasionally. The whole style and technique of singing adapted to suit the character and function of the songs differ between the individual areas, but also within a single tribe.

For the Indian, music is not an art, but an expression or manifestation of life. Generally speaking, he would hardly describe it as "beautiful", but rather as "powerful" or "effective". The functions it performs in his life are just as natural and varied as all his other activities taken as a whole. Music for the individual represents a source of power and for the tribal association a means of reaching an understanding with the supernatural beings from whom they ask for all good things. Although modern civilisation has made an impact on the Indian way of life, his psyche has remained unchanged and still finds its most perfect expression in music.   W. R.

The music of the Indians is essentially religious and is functionally bound up with worship. The native does not sing or dance in order to demonstrate his skill or express the way he is feeling. And he does not set out to entertain or flatter his audience. He sings and dances in order to honour his ancient deities and appease them. His music is an expression of his beliefs and hopes and his fear of the gods. It is not inspired by any subjective need for exhibitionism or a display of virtuosity, but by a kind of impersonal fervour, roughly comparable to the religious music of Europe in the early Middle Ages, and by the highly evocative and expressive and in many cases almost terrifying qualities that can be present in art and music.   S. M.

The Indians of North America have no sense of harmony or polyphony. The dominant element is the rhythm and the melody is secondary to it. It must be stressed that Indians are not familiar with compasses, scales or modes in the European sense. There is a perpetual gliding from one note to another, and this, together with their throbbing voices and sustained vibratos, gives the impression that their singing technique with its many modulations does not include any absolutely fixed notes. The melodic line generally falls after a rapid rise, but this depends on the energy intensity and the length of the phrase sung without taking another breath. As the singer runs out of breath, the line falls for physiological reasons. The individual tribes show preferences for different interval patterns. Sometimes we find thirds and fourths, or a complete tone and the

31

minor third or even other intervals not contained in the European tonic system. The Iroquois, for example, have a definite melodic type with three or four notes and frequent repetition of the same note in an irregular time.

Seneca, Harvest Song (T. Baker)

Ka yon a hi a de ni ta - a ha wi-non he he han han son guai hua yo ni

he he ahan han ka yon hi ya de he he ahan han

Frances Densmore has analysed six hundred melodies from the Chippewa (Ojibwa) and Sioux. She points out that about a third of them have no semi-tones and are pentatonic and that numerous melodies range over one octave. Other types, like the following example, are built up from a widely differing selection of intervals.

The remarks made by Frances Densmore can generally be applied also to the music of the other North American Indians, at least the Athabascans, the Algonkin and the Sioux. But it can hardly be asserted that the pentatonic pattern is predominant. It would be better to say that it is a structural element underlying Indian music. When discussing rhythm (426, p. 18), she asserts that in many songs the time unit is the beat and not the internal subdivision of the beat. The stressed notes of the starting beats follow an extremely slow tempo, metronomically speaking. Within these time units there are intermediate notes of irregular duration and they cannot be noted down as exact values . . . . The drum and the singing voice are usually independent of each other. The drums give out rapid, unaccentuated beats, whilst the voice follows a rhythm prescribed by the content and significance of the song. For the song we can therefore assume ♩ = 92, when the drum beats ♩ = 88, or ♩ = 88 for the song and ♩ = 120 for the drum (measurements by Gilbert Chase, 412, p. 420 ff.).

In this large northern group the Sioux obviously show a clearer tendency towards a pentatonic system than the other tribes. The Navaho, who belong to the Athabascans, rather show a preference for structures in which the fundamental note, the third and the fifth predominate, as we see from the foregoing example. The tendency towards a pentatonic system is often merely hinted at and is stressed rather by a tetratonic structure — with transposition.

Teton Dakota, "Song of the White Buffalo Maiden" (F. Densmore), ♩ = 58

Ni ya taninyan mawani ye ni ya taninyan mawani ye e e o

ya - te le i - ma - wa ni - na ho ho ho - taninyan mawani ye ye ye

ye a ye a ye ni - ya taninyan mawani...

32

Among these old songs there are many with no clear or definite words to go with them. They are often merely sung as vowels, e.g.:

Ojibwa, Visiting Song (F. R. Burton)

Hey-ah hey - ah   hey - ah hey   hey-ah-a hey - ah   hey - ah   hey - ah   hey-ah hey - ah...

This phenomenon, which is typical of the Indians, has been examined in a study on Omaha music by Alice Fletcher (513, p. 12). According to her, the Indians think that clearly enunciated words in singing break up the melody and distort the music. They accuse us of speaking too much as we sing. There are relatively few Indian songs with a text. If words are used at all, they are changed to make them more melodic. The choice of words and their connection are not in keeping with the rules for the spoken language. Most songs consist of syllables that are not parts of words and are completely made up of sounds that are suitable for singing and have no definite meaning. Once a musican has made a choice of phonemas for his song, he will not change them. They are kept with the very same care and precision as a poem that has to be preserve unaltered.

We must also say a word here about the variability of notes and intervals. The flute with three finger-holes is practically the only melodic instrument of the North American Indians. Charles Hofmann (560) stresses that the finger-holes of the flutes are arranged in different ways. These variations between instruments are found not only between one region or settlement and another, but even within quite a small group. This confirms that the melodic line is more important than the size of the intervals. The Chippewa and probably other groups too use a special instrument for each type of song. Frances Densmore (426, p. 6) comments that the hand drum is used in many tribes by a singer performing hunting songs, but the big drum is used for dances, with the singers sitting round it in a circle on the ground and each of them holding a wooden beater in his hand. The shaman, or medicine man, has a rattle made out of a calabash or in the form of a disc. Water drums and rattles form part of the ceremonies of the Midéwiwin (Grand Medicine Society). From the north-west (Puget Sound) Willard Rhodes (831, p. 5) reports that among the Makah and other tribes belonging to the Wakash linguistic family whale-hunting is of ritualistic importance. In the village, which forms the social and political unit, whale-catchers occupy a leading position. The owner of a house carves on the beams an image of his guardian spirit, who is attached to him alone. The songs used to conjure up the spirit are his own personal property. The young man goes out into the forest and looks for his spirit, who grants him protection. Then he returns with a song and a dance. If anyone happened to be oppressed by a spirit and could not reply with his protective song and dance, the power of the hostile spirit would be strong enough to kill him. So singing and dancing are a means of appeasing or exorcising demons. The guardian spirit manifests itself by animating the musical instruments. The "power boards", which two men hold securely, are animated by the spirit if the owner of the boards is able to sing the appropriate song (831, p. 20). The creation songs of the Iroquois are also quite remarkable. They are really songs of thanksgiving to the creator. According to the Iroquois view of the universe, the earth rests on a turtle's back. So the rattles and clappers for the two ritual dances, the "Dance of the Big Feather" and the "Dance of the False Faces", in which wooden masks supposedly endowed with great healing powers are worn, are made from the shell of that animal (cf. W. Fenton, 506, p. 9). The Indians think that a man receives many songs in the course of dreams or in a trance. He is then in contact with the supernatural beings who can give him their support in all he undertakes. He is able to demand this contact and assistance again and again by singing the song, the words and tune of which are known only to him. If others learned that song, it would gradually lose its potency. Like all shamans, the Chippewa medicine men use songs to heal the sick. They are members of the Grand Medicine Society (Midéwiwin). These medicine songs are very similar to one another in their melodic structure because of their small intervals of the order of a whole tone. They are often introduced by a rising fourth.

Ottawa, Medicine Song (G. Prokosch Kurath), ♩ = 108

In war songs, on the other hand, we generally find a preference for melodic leaps of larger intervals:

Iroquois, Scalping Song (G. Prokosch Kurath), ♩ = 96

The music and dancing of the Pueblo Indians show a predominant leaning towards agrarian rites. Ceremonies include dances in which they plead for rain or celebrate the ripening of the maize. The Dance of the Ko-ko, which has been described by J. Walter Fewkes (507, p. 17), acquired special importance around 1900. Every Ko-ko wore a painted mask, complete with a long horse-hair beard that covered his chest, whilst his own carefully combed hair fell down over his back. On his head he wore two or three brilliant yellow feathers. A cord with small white fluffy feathers inserted in it hung over his hair. The blue mask had two slits for his eyes and there was a third, jagged, slit to depict his mouth and teeth. Chains of small shells and carded wool were suspended round his neck . . . His shoulders and torso were naked down to the hips, but his shoulders were painted with reddish zigzag lines, to symbolise rain . . . In one hand he held a calabash rattle and in the other a cedar twig. His body was bent slightly forward and his elbows were held in such a position that the forearms could be thrust in front of him. Some Ko-ko carried a live turtle in their hand. Every one of them had a dancing cloth tied round his hips, a kind of sash with long white threads hanging down and knotted at the end. Over his back a fox fur hung head downwards, with the tail trailing on the ground. Turtle shells were fastened to the back of the belt. The Ko-ko's legs and feet were bare except for a black woollen band on the left knee. Small animal hooves were attached to the shells by means of hide thongs. The striking of these hooves against the shells produced a sound that could be heard a great distance away when the dancers stamped their feet on the ground in time with the song.
The following Ko-ko melody was written down by Fewkes himself:

Zuñi, Dance of the Ko-Ko (B. I. Gilman), ♩ = 80

In this example, as in the case of other Zuñi songs, the melodic flow is clearly ordered by points of emphasis. The intonation is clearly and precisely determined. It differs from the musical style of the Indian tribes living farther to the north because it is so precise. B. I. Gilman (525, 526) has made transcriptions of this music and according to him these melodies are musically powerful and show a defined scalar structure. But they have not been composed according to a plan. They merely follow the intervals already implanted in the singer's mind. Although no scales have as yet been formed at this archaic stage of art, these people are already on the way to producing them.

Snake dances are characteristic of the Hopi. The Hopi priests dance with a rattle-snake in their mouths to encourage rain. Afterwards the snakes are joined to form a circle divided into six (this symbolises the universe) and are sprinkled with maizemeal. Then they are chased out of the village so that they can tell the rain gods about the ceremony.

Hopi, Snake Song (B. I. Gilman)

The music of this Snake Dance shares with the Ko-ko Dance of the Zuñi (reproduced above) a meandering melodic line and a clear structure. But these two songs, intended for quite different rites, contain different intervals. The penultimate example is pentatonic and devoid of semi-tones, whereas the last one tends rather to produce a chromatic effect, in which the semi-tone has a kind of modulating function. It will also be noticed that these songs hardly contain any passages with a uniform descent or demonstrating the archaic system of "stepped-melody", which is, for example, a favourite structural feature farther to the north among the Algonkin.

In Hopi communities the *kiva*, i.e., the ceremonial house or chamber, is situated underground, but among the Indians on the Rio Grande it is above the ground. The Katčinas are ancestral spirits from the other world that rule as rain demons in the *pueblo* for six months. They are represented by dancers in disguise and wearing masks. The songs of the Katčinas are among the most complicated pieces sung by the Pueblo Indians. They use long, sustained notes, often enlivened by a tremulo effect. The singing technique favoured by these Indians is quite different from the nasal and unnaturally coloured or even distorted singing of the Indians living farther north. The singer's mouth is only slightly open, and the position of his mouth and lips changes very little while he is singing. The strong pressure of air on the larynx produces a curious sound. The whole quality of the songs is altered not merely by the choice of notes, but also by the timbre (L. Boulton, 395). In the north the texts of the songs are often without any precise meaning, but in the south-west they frequently betray great poetic beauty, are copiously adorned with allusions to maize, seeds and flowers, and contain references to the rain, clouds, thunder and lightning and the rainbow, the main points of the universe, also the colours attributed to them. The number four has a ritualistic significance and this is reflected in the songs which are often repeated four times. Among the instruments, we should make special mention of the scraping stick, a notched stick over which another stick is passed. It is used for specific ceremonial songs, for example, during the festivities in connection with the winter solstice and the dances of the Katčinas. The bullroarer represents the voice of the spirits. Because of its special form of symbolism and its melodic structure, the music of the Zuñi and the Hopi comes close to the music of the Indian population resident in Mexico.

In musical research special interest has been shown in the centres of the ancient and highly advanced civilisations of Central and South America — the area of the Teotihuacan people, the Toltecs, Aztecs and Mixtecs in the plateau of Mexico, the Maya in Chiapas, the Chibcha in the northern region of the Andes and the Inca in the central Andes. Archaeological digs in these areas have led to surprising discoveries again and again. They have brought to light superb musical instruments demonstrating the high level reached by those people in music and their knowledge of acoustics, as well as their artistic and artisan talents. This evidence regarding the instrumental side of musical life among the ancient American civilisations has been supplemented by the many art objects portraying their form of music and by old documents and, last but not least, by studies of living traditions. A special issue of the "Illustrated History of Music" (Vol. II, No. 6, Samuel Martí, Old America) has been devoted to this subject.   P. C.

We encounter typically Mexican folk music of the present time in its characteristic form among the Indian natives and *mestizos* of Mexico, especially in the centre of the country, in the states of Mexico, Morelos, Tlaxcala, Puebla and Oaxaca. But it can also be found in the outlying areas. It consists of melodies with a strong emphasis on rhythm that can be performed on aboriginal sounding devices and on others of Spanish origin and also on hybrid instruments combining both forms. They are used in two ways — in connection with religious rites and to accompany dances.

The religious type of music amazes any person hearing it for the first time. On the day of the patron saint the thrilling and persistent rhythms of the *huéhuetl* and the penetrating nasal sound of the *chirimía* start up in the early light of morning, accompanied by the crackle of fireworks and the pealing of bells. This music is performed in the forecourt of the church and never inside the actual building, as, according to tradition, it is supposed to have a heathen "taint". The instruments used here are a *huéhuetl*, the old pre-Cortesian temple drum, or a drum and two oboes of differing pitch or a *chirimía* (a simple oboe or shawm) made by the Indians, either in the ancient Aztec form of the *toco totoco* or in the Spanish form of the *tiruli tirula*, whose tone colour is rather reminiscent of bagpipes. These musical relics of Indian folk music are coupled with the sung portions of the Mass (Kyrie, Gloria, Credo, Sanctus, etc.) and are interspersed with the mysteries of the Rosary in the evening. When these have come to an end, the group of musicians also fall silent and go away.

The music used to accompany dancing is performed by other persons and in structure and rhythm is made to suit that particular function. It can be played by a village band with metal wind instruments, on the Spanish flute with a drum accompaniment or on a violin. There are children's dances, in which the sequence of steps is marked by beating the *huéhuetl* and ringing a small bell (tied to a few sticks that are struck on the ground). According to a Mexican saying, every dance has its own musicians. So it often happens that every dancer plays his own instrument himself, as, for example, in the Dance of the "Concheros" or the Dance of the "Voladores", in which the individual dancers blow a one-handed flute and beat a small drum. In this type of music we find a powerful mixture of styles, with pre-Spanish forms and phrasing and alien features originating from a great variety of countries.

The following instruments, some of them pre-Cortesian and some of European origin, are used by the Mexican population to accompany their songs and dances:

The *huéhuetl*, made from a tree trunk, is a vertical drum about 80 cm high and 40 cm in diameter, covered with a membrane on top and equipped with feet underneath. It is placed on the ground and is beaten with special drumsticks called *bolillos*, padded at the end with soft chamois-dressed cow hide, or may even be beaten with clenched fists. The use of this instrument is confined to the states of Nayarit, Mexico, Puebla and Tlaxcala, also to one particular area of Chiapas.

The *teponaztli* is a horizontal slotted wooden "drum" of varying size and so belong to the idiophone class. In Huehuetla (Hidalgo) we find instruments like this barely 20 cm long, whereas in Yucatan they are considerably larger — up to 150 cm long and 50 cm in diameter. Hard wood is used to make a *teponaztli* — e.g., rosewood, Brazil wood, oak or *tepeguaje*. It is hollowed out inside to produce a resonance chamber. By means of several incisions, one to four wooden tongues are exposed in the upper part of the cylindrical instrument. They are rather thicker at the end and have thinner walls at the base. The length and also the strength of the wood determine the particular pitch. The instrument rests on a brushwood pad or the ground or on a wooden stand and is beaten with sticks padded with rubber. The distribution area of the *teponaztli* extends from Michoacan as far as Yucatan and Chiapas. On the edge of this region it is called the *quiringua* or the *tinco*. Another name for it is the *teponahuaztli*, i.e., "hollowed-out object".

The *áyotl*, an old Mexican instrument of worship, also belongs to the idiophone class. It takes the form of a turtle shell, beaten with the branch of a deer's antler, and is still in use in the states of Oaxaca and Chiapas.

The *chicahuaztles* are sounding or rattle sticks, as seen in the Dance of the "Sonajeros" in Jalisco or in the Pascola Dance of the Yaqui (here termed *zenazo*). Incisions are made in a wooden stick and small metal discs are inserted in them. When the stick is shaken, they strike against one another and produce a rattling noise. Occasionally this instrument has notches along the side and is used as a scraping stick (*jerucia yaqui*). The end of the rod is then propped up on a gourd shell lying inverted on the ground and a thinner stick is drawn over the notches.

The *guiro antillano* is occasionally used to accompany dances from the Carib area. This is a scraping instrument consisting of an oblong gourd resonator with notches on the outside over which the player runs a stick. This instrument is encountered, above all, among the Yaqui in the state of Sonora.

The calabash rattle known as the *ayacachtli*, mostly used in pairs, is made in different sizes with a short or a longish handle and is decorated with ribbons or feathers. It can be found from Sonora as far as central Mexico, but also occurs in many regions of North and South America under another name. A beautiful example is seen in the frescoes of Bonampak in Chiapas. But, in addition to these instruments from the pre-Spanish period, there are also rattles that were brought over by the inhabitants of the Iberian peninsula.

Apart from the *teponaztli* mentioned above, both the military drums of the 16th century, the so-called "lansquenet's drum", and small drums (*redoblante* or *tarola*) and big drums (*gran caja*) are in use. The latter are usually set on the ground and beaten by several players. Mention should also be made of the typical Yaqui drum.

As a successor to the Aztec *tlapitzalli*, an internal-ducted flute usually made of clay, similar instruments (*pito*) carved from wood or a piece of cane are now played. Besides these there are modern flutes of European construction. The vertical cane flute is usually played in conjunction with the small Spanish hand drum.

The *chirimía* (shawm), a reed instrument of Arabic origin, was brought to Mexico by the Spaniards in the 16th century as a part of their military music. Nowadays we often hear it being played together with the *huéhuetl*. They can be classified into two different kinds. On the one hand, there are the oboe-type instruments imported from Europe and, on the other, the kinds manufactured by the inhabitants of the Puebla and Tlaxcala regions. The latter are short, but have an appreciably greater range than the European double-reed instruments and generally possess six finger-holes. A great deal of practice and energy are needed by the player.

The European metal trumpet has by now very largely replaced the shell horn (*tecciztli*) and the large flute made of wood or fired clay from the pre-Spanish era. It is interesting to observe how the trumpet taken across from Europe has frequently been converted by the natives and extended by about one-third. Quite often we see curious copies of older curved wind instruments in metal foil, only the mouthpiece of which is European. The small clay trumpets are still used as children's instruments. The larger trumpet-type instruments of clay, wood or even gold that have been brought to light during excavations of material from pre-Spanish times have now evidently been replaced by wind instruments made from a bored elderberry cane, with a steer's horn fastened to the end as a bell-mouth. This instrument, called a *totochaca*, is often sounded during the ceremonies of Holy Week. The serpent, the bassoon and the ophicleide disappeared from popular and church music about the middle of the 19th century. The *bajo sexto* or *bajo de espiga* has been preserved among the "Cancioneros", the *corridos* players and the Huapango accompanists in the Panuco area (Veracruz). Its loud, resonant sound is still in great favour with the public.

The typical stringed instrument for accompanying songs and dances is the mandola (*bandolón*), which is tuned in various ways.

The musical bow is used by the Cora Indians of Nayarit in connection with ancestor worship. To amplify the string sound — it is struck with a thin wooden stick — a calabash is employed. In other regions, for example, in Tlaxcala, the player holds the end of the musical bow against his open mouth and the oral cavity acts here as a resonator.

The monochord, a pathetic substitute for the violin, is played by the Seri Indians on the coast of Sonora. The resonator is shaped like an elongated prism and, as its name suggests, it is fitted with a single string that is lifted up from the resonator by means of a bridge. To play this instrument they use a simple cane bow strung with horse-hair.

The violin is one of the instruments of the Tarahumare Indians, who play it mainly for entertainment. The Huichol Indians are also familiar with the technique of violin-playing, whilst in Jalisco and Michoacan it has become a virtuoso instrument on which difficult pieces and *sones*, which differ according to the region, are played. But in Veracruz, from the Huaxtec region right down to the Jarocha area farther to the south, it serves to accompany fandangos. Since the time of the Conquest the harp has played a definite part in the musical life of the natives. It occurs over a vast area extending from Sonora to Chiapas and serves as an accompaniment for the Pascola Dances among the Chamula Indians. We find it even more frequently along the coast — from Nayarit to beyond Guerrero — where it is referred to as the *arpa grande de la costa* ("Great Coastal Harp"). Its characteristic use is as an accompaniment for *sones* and *malagueñas*.

To sum up, the musical instruments of Central America comprise both instruments from the pre-Spanish era and European types as well as copies and modifications of both kinds. The hybrid culture of this area

37

is also reflected in the music. Only in a very few ethnic groups living in rather isolated conditions do we still find remains of archaic musical forms.   V.T.M.

From the Indian population of the island of Tiburon and the coast of the Gulf of California in the Sonora area only a small group of about two hundred Seri still remain today. They live as hunters, fishermen and fruit-pickers. They dance on beams covering a pit scooped out of the earth and acting as a kind of resonator, and the singers accompany themselves on different kinds of idiophones.

Seri, Religious Music (P. Collaer), ♩ = 66

According to Ekholm and Yurchenko (495) the shamans of the Huichol and the Cora use the *huéhuetl* drum and a musical bow bearing the pre-Columbian name *mitote*. The instrument was obviously given that name because it was played during the "Mitote" festival of the Aztecs, which took place amid music and dancing and solemn ceremonial. It is really a kind of hunting bow to which a calabash is attached as resonator. It is propped up on the ground and held with the legs. In each hand the player holds a thin stick with which he strikes the string. Another musical bow that is manipulated in much the same way is short and consists of a broad, flattened piece of wood with a hole in the middle, through which an arrow is stuck. The latter is arrested by a wooden bar which beats against the wood of the bow.

Cora, Harvest Song (P. Collaer)

The Lacandon living in the forests of eastern Chiapas, i.e., in the area of the classical Mayan civilisation, are a mere remnant numbering hardly more than two hundred persons. Palacios (830) made a reasonably careful study of them in 1926. The following musical example, a magic song to the god of fire, clearly reveals its archaic style. The only prominent consonant is "r". Otherwise vowels are used. The interval playing a special part in the melody is the fourth.

Lacandon, Magic Song to the God of Fire, Kak (B. Samper), ♩ = 132

The traditional music of the Indian population of Chiapas plays a prominent part in church festivals. In the forecourt of the church the old traditional musical instruments from the pre-Cortesian period can still occasionally be heard. But they are often replaced by instruments based on imported prototypes. Music is performed on them in the same way as on the old indigenous instruments, as the following two musical examples reveal. They have been transcribed for us by Samper *et al.* (725).

38

A further example, also coming from this area, will demonstrate the local vocal style. The text accompanying it is in Quiche, one of the commonest Mayan languages. The song is accompanied on the *teponaztli*.

Tzotzil, Church Music ("*para componer al altar*"), ♩ = 120

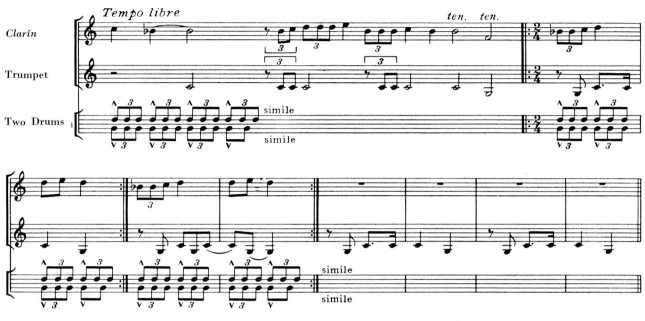

Maya-Quiché (Chiapas), Ritual Song in the Chiapa Language, Nambarimu (B. Samper), ♩ = 76

Here we are dealing with archaic forms of musical expression that have been affected relatively little by more recent influences. This music is far removed from the pentatonic system and is very much closer to what can be heard in various regions of South America, for example, in the forests of the Amazon. There is often a clear tendency to use small intervals of about the size of a semi-tone.

Repeated references have been made in the literature to features that are common to the Indian music of North and South America and also to certain differences. Comparisons in the field of musical instruments, with all their great multiplicity, are extremely interesting. In South America alone Izikowitz (579) recorded approximately seven hundred different types of instruments and described and classified them. Vicente T. Mendoza listed thirty-one kinds from the pre-Spanish period. The only stringed instrument on the list, the musical bow, which is quite common from California to Patagonia, cannot, however, be definitely traced back to the pre-Cortesian era.

The Andean civilisations offer interesting comparative research material for the musical ethnologist. The numerous musical instruments discovered at excavation sites in the central and northern Andes area, the many pictures portraying music on clay vessels coming from sites in Moche or Mochica and Nazca, also the fairly recognisable traditions present in the contemporary music of the Andes, enable us to form some sort of picture of musical life in the region of the Chibcha and the Inca. In Peru and Bolivia, which, together with Ecuador and the north of Chile, formed parts of the *tiwantansuyo*, or Inca Empire, the traditional instruments, some of which are, however, no longer played, include the *tinya*, a hand drum with two membranes, drums similar to the Aztec *huéhuetl* with only one membrane, clay kettle-drums, whistling jars or vessel flutes (ocarinas) made from shells, clay or calabashes, the notched flute called the *quena* and, above all, the pan-pipes. Our interest is also awakened by the artistic *silbadores*, the elaborate flutes and trumpets of the Nazca civilisation and whistles made from animals' skulls. In Cajamarca (Peru) and Cuenca (Ecuador) bamboo trumpets up to two metres long are still in use even to-day, the term used for them being *clarín* or *bocina*. The Frankfurt expedition to Bolivia (1927—1929) brought back interesting information regarding the use of giant pan-pipes by the Tacanan Indians. These instruments, called *bajones*, are carried in boys' processions. One of the specimens brought back consists of fifteen tubes plaited from reeds with an oblong notch at the blow-hole.

As a relic of the instrumental music performed, the pan-pipe ensembles of the Aymarans are of special significance. Up to forty players are involved in these ensembles. They blow instruments of different sizes tuned to a fifth or an octave apart. This music is based on a simple form of organum. The melody is played in parallels of fifths and octaves — usually with a slow movement. Large tubular drums beat out the rhythm.

An attempt has been made to describe the whole essence of Andean music as pentatonic, which has led to discussions between R. and M. d'Harcourt, E. M. von Hornbostel, C. Mead, S. L. Moreno and others. This and the heptatonic theory have long since lost their appeal. Nor is it right to say that all melodies with a diatonic scale show a Spanish influence. Besides the more spacious type of melody composed mainly of thirds and fourths and corresponding to a pentatonic system devoid of semi-tones, we often find here a melodic system which is closely graduated and using seconds as its means of progression.

If we make an objective examination of the songs collected in the Andes and compare them with the scales on the flutes and pan-pipes discovered at the excavation sites, we are struck by the fact that there are instruments with five notes in the octave. But the intervals between these five notes vary from one instrument to another, so we cannot speak of a fixed pentatonic "system". Some instruments have more and some less than five notes, and the intervals that can be produced on them have caused confusion among some of the investigators. They thought they had determined the "natural" intervals. The two d'Harcourts, whose work has been superseded in many respects, held the following view (539, p. 46). They tried out a very great number of vertical flutes and pan-pipes that had remained in an excellent state of preservation in tombs and became convinced that they all reproduced a scale of five notes in the octave without any semi-tones. But some instruments had other intervals that were either more "musical" or seemed "incoherent" to their European ears. We do not need to explain here that present-day research no longer upholds any such distinction between what is "musical" and what is "incoherent". The widely held view that the pentatonic system was the dominant one in Andean music was not accepted by Robert Stevenson (758, p. 3 f.). There certainly are a great number of pentatonic songs in Peru, but this does not mean *ipso facto* that they reflect the oldest cultural level. Another point to consider is that the old pan-pipes seldom have five tubes. The list given by Izikowitz (579, p. 408) contains sixteen instruments. They include nine with four and only two with five tubes. This last author does not make any detailed reference to the pitch of the instruments, but Stevenson (758, p. 3 f.) supplies the relevant information.

The tendency to use small intervals amounting to a semi-tone, already mentioned in our description of Central American music, is even more marked among the Indians of South America, above all in ethnic groups belonging to a low cultural level. In addition to pentatonic tunes, the Araucanians, for example, play melodies like the following on their flutes:

Araucanians, Lamentation, Flute (C. Lavin), ♩ = 92

Among the Alacaluf, who live on the islands lying off the Chilean coast, songs are confined essentially to two notes. The higher of the two is situated only half a tone above the lower one. These songs, or chants, are intended to imitate the cries of animals.

Alacaluf, "Huémul" (J. Emperaire)

Yé - yol - kans   yé - yol - kans   yé - nak ek - ser   yé - fé - na - won   ar - ka - ta - won   ka - ya - sa.

When referring to the songs of the Patagonians, the two d'Harcourts speak of a "state of wild and disorderly chromatics", but the question, of course, arises as to whether we can apply the term "chromatics" to a form of music completely ignorant of the European heptatonic structure. In the above-mentioned work (539, p. 222) the songs of the Aomucan Patagonians are described as follows: "The melody, which has a narrow compass and small intervals . . . . revolves around itself. Moreover, the aural impression made by the chromatics is intensified by the mode of execution which gives no more than an imprecise reproduction of the semi-tone interval. In this way they create a kind of lament, a very odd moaning effect which can be regarded as one of the most primitive forms of musical expression."

We should stress here once again that we no longer refer nowadays to deviations from a definite musical system or faulty interpretation of it. At that cultural level there is no such thing as a fixed system, but merely certain usual melodic structures or particular tendencies — e.g., a preference for small intervals which it would be superfluous to measure exactly, as they are not stable or constant. The "score" of a Yahgan song, or chant, cannot be regarded as a sequence of semi-tones. It is rather a sequence of small intervals of varying size, hovering approximately round our own semi-tone. The musical examples presented here can at any rate give us some idea of the melodic structure, but not of all the niceties involved in the dynamics of movement and the rich nuances of the actual recital.

Yahgan (R. Lehmann-Nitsche)

The tendency to favour small intervals, which we find everywhere in South America, especially among Indians at a low cultural level, and also the very widespread inclination to avoid any rather small intervals (evident in the various pentatonic forms devoid of semi-tones and with different sizes of intervals) can both be observed in the endless expanses of the Amazon forests.

Of the two contrasting tendencies, the older one appears to be the form with the small intervals. The pentatonic forms without any semi-tones may arise from a desire to produce pure and precise music, which would be typical of advanced cultures. The typical life of the individual tribes in the vast primeval forests of the Amazon and the upper Orinoco is one of complete isolation. Peoples displaying ethnical differences have sometimes lived in the same region without ever mixing or establishing any contact with one another. These tribes, some of whom were only discovered in recent years, have often preserved archaic traditions in their music without any strong influences impinging on them from outside. But, in spite of this, their musical instruments appear to be fairly homogeneous. The number of records of songs and instrumental music from the Amazon basin has increased considerably in the course of the last few years. But, owing to the vastness of the area, they are not yet sufficient to give us a properly detailed picture of the music of the people who live there. There are a very great number of pentatonic forms taking more or less the following shape:

Yaruro, Song for Healing the Sick (P. Collaer), $\downarrow = 120$

4. Mode of the pentatonic series on c   4. Mode on g

In the Amazon area we very often encounter a preference for small intervals:

Siriono (M. Key)

In the Orinoco basin (Puinave, Maquiritare) and among some Carib in Venezuela we find very stable and constant intervals roughly similar to those of the Maya-Quiché.

Puinave, Pan-Pipes (P. Collaer), $\downarrow = 104$

cents:165 119 120   138
511   120 138 511   331 260   71

We have measured these intervals and must point out their similarity to those of the Indonesian *Pelog* (417, p. 136).

We shall conclude this brief analysis of Indian music with a reference to elementary forms of part-music. Among the North American Indians there are hardly any tendencies towards polyphony, but this occurs quite frequently in South America, in the form of parallel fourths and fifths.

Aymaran, Marching Song (P. Collaer), $\downarrow = 80$

Nacurap, Leader and Choir (M. Schneider)

Pseudo-parallel imitations for three voices can also be detected repeatedly.

Craho (P. Collaer), $\downarrow = 80$

The use of three-note parallels is comparatively rare, but evidence of their distribution — for example, among the Craho — supports the view that the so-called mathematical "simplicity" of the pure fourths and fifths and their "natural" character are mere illusions that have taken shape *a posteriori* in the rationalising minds of Europeans scholars and theorists. In actual fact the parallels are usually built up on irrational intervals among peoples with a poor cultural status.

In the Amazon area we occasionally come across more advanced forms for several voices. Even examples of a definitely "contrapuntal" pattern in community music can be produced.   P.C.

Aruak, Piece for Two Finger-Hole Flutes (F. Bose)

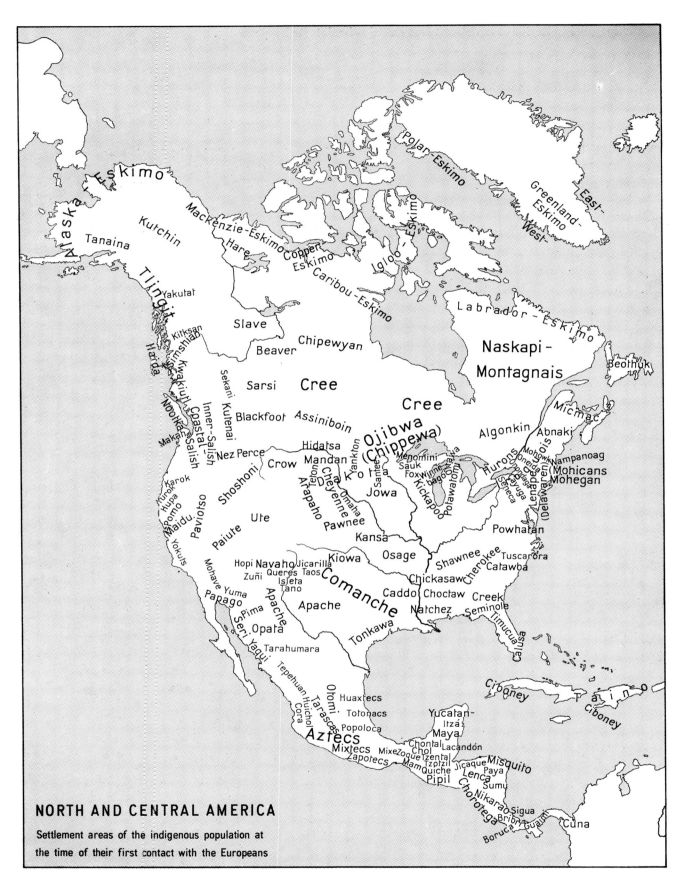

NORTH AND CENTRAL AMERICA

Settlement areas of the indigenous population at
the time of their first contact with the Europeans

44

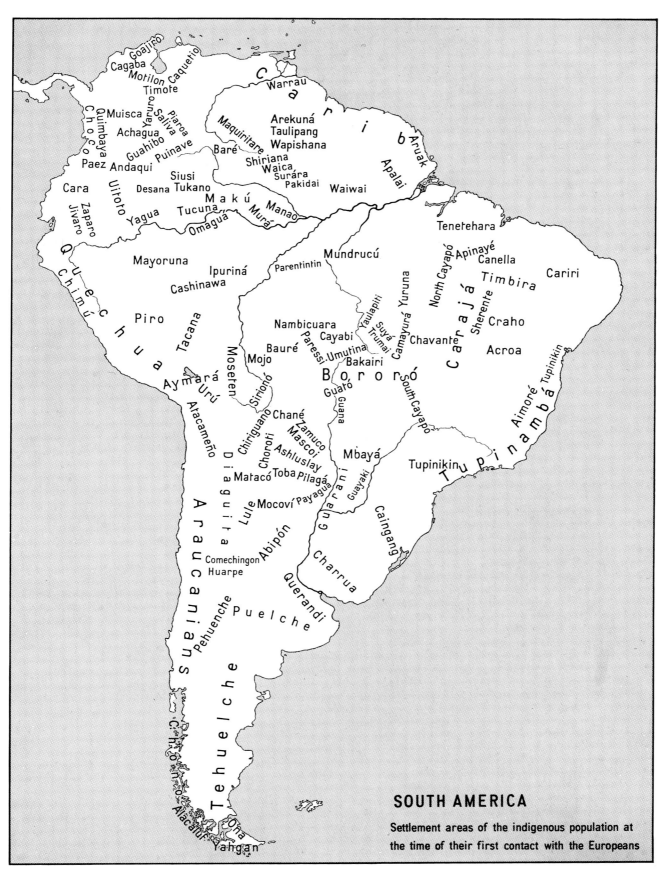

SOUTH AMERICA

Settlement areas of the indigenous population at the time of their first contact with the Europeans

45

ILLUSTRATIONS WITH DESCRIPTIONS

Illustration 1

Pan-pipes from the Hopewell Civilisation

ca. 100 A.D. Found at Helena Crossing, Arkansas

American Museum of Natural History, New York, Neg. No. 126, 285

Before we can have any idea of the high stage of development formerly attained by the Indian tribes of North America, we must refer back to prehistoric times. The prehistoric Hopewell civilisation in the Ohio and Mississippi river area covers the period roughly from 300 B.C. to 600 A.D. The Indians of that civilisation were noted for their remarkable earth mounds, so they are referred to as the "mound builders". In the state of Ohio alone there are well over 5000 of these artifical mounds, earth walls and platforms in the form of circles, squares, octagons and animal shapes, once used to enclose places of worship, festival sites and places for burying and cremating the dead. Excavation of these mounds has brought an amazing collection of extremely artistic objects to light, including several musical instruments — all testifying to the high standard reached by that civilisation.

The pan-pipes illustrated here were discovered in 1960 at Helena Crossing in the state of Arkansas by James A. Ford, Curator of North American Archaeology at the American Museum of Natural History, New York. They are regarded as a product of the Hopewell civilisation and can be dated fairly accurately by the radiocarbon method (C 14) to around 100 A.D. This instrument consists of three pieces of reed of roughly equal length enclosed in a copper jacket and with a layer of silver at the mouthpiece. That is how they are held together (cf. drawing on p. 174 left). There are wooden pegs in the two outer pipes. The bottom opening of the middle pipe, which is not stopped, was obviously closed by the finger, as it would not be suitable for use as an open pipe. After careful measurement and various tests, William S. Suggs found that the instrument was tuned to intervals of one ninth. The shortest pipe, which is on the left, produces roughly the note b''' and the next longest, on the right, the note a'', whilst the middle one, when stopped with a finger, gives g'. More instruments of the same kind and belonging to the same period have been found in the area settled by the Hopewells. Because of the importance of bird effigies in that civilisation and also the way in which the instrument is tuned, Suggs presumes that it was used for the ritual imitation of bird calls.   W.R.

Illustration 2

Painted Pottery Plate from the Hohokam Civilisation

ca. 800 A.D. Snaketown, Arizona. Diameter 26.7 cm

Arizona State Museum, University of Arizona, Tucson, Neg. No. GP-820

The word Hohokam, from the vocabulary of the Pima Indians, means "those who have gone", i.e., "ancestors". It is used to describe a civilisation from the plains in the south-west of the United States, especially the torrid desert areas of Arizona, belonging roughly to the period from 300 to 1450 A.D.

The plate illustrated here with its gay red and buff colouring was unearthed among the ruins of Snaketown, Arizona, in 1935. Its date of origin was put at about 800 A.D. Each quadrant of the plate portrays a stylised flute-player, with a dancer standing behind him and touching him with his hands. This is a very interesting picture, as similar dances are performed by the Indians even to-day. Our ceramic plate confirms the excellence of the drawings and motifs created by the Hohokam civilisation.   W.R.

1

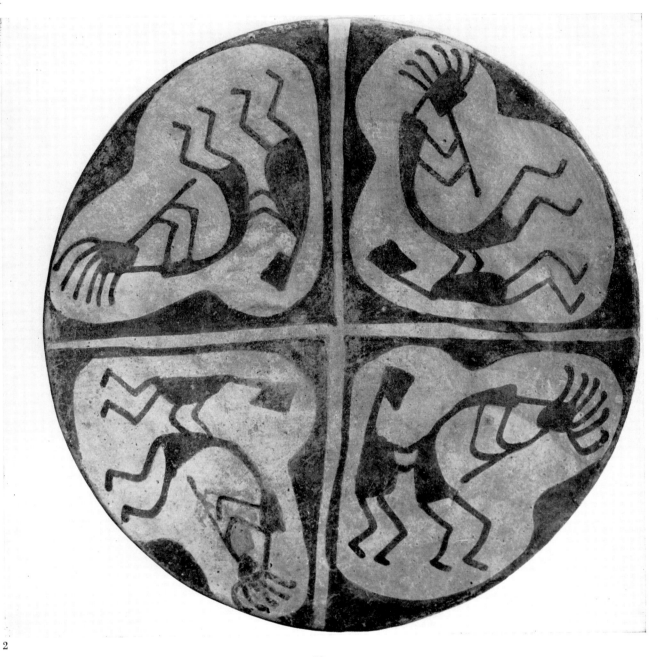

2

49

Illustration 3

Human Bone Whistle · Hopewell Civilisation

ca. 200 A.D. · Bourneville, Ohio · Length 21 cm

Ohio State Museum, Columbus, Ohio

This bone whistle made from the right forearm of a human being (radius) has been dated to about 200 A.D. by Raymond S. Baby. Such whistles were used by the Indians of the Hopewell civilisation in their prolonged burial ceremonies and were bound up with various of their customs. This instrument is quite unique and the very first one of its type to have been reported to us. It was discovered in the course of excavations at Twin (to the east of Bourneville), in the state of Ohio, in 1959. Its maximum length is 21 cm, so it can be assumed that the bone came from a woman aged between 40 and 45 years. The thicker distal portion of the bone was removed and it was bound with a thin copper band, 2 cm wide, 1.2 cm away from the cut edge. The sound hole of the whistle, a triangular opening 1.2 cm high and 0.85 cm broad, is situated immediately below the copper band. At the side of this triangular opening there are two elliptical perforations measuring 0.35 × 0.65 cm. These two small holes bored 2.7 cm above the radial protuberance were probably used for carrying the instrument. The highly developed artistic skill of these people is clearly evident from the lavish decorations on this whistle, which is an instrument with no finger-holes. W.R.

Illustration 4

Stone Flute · San Nicolas Island, California · Length 18.4 cm

Museum of the American Indian, Heye Foundation, New York, Cat. No. 20/3836, Neg. No. 22, 835

This flute fashioned from steatite is 18.4 cm long and was unearthed with other artistic objects on San Nicolas Island, California. Eight finger-holes are arranged in two parallel rows each consisting of four holes and separated from each other by five shell disc inlays. A ring of shell disc inlays encircles either end of the tube, which tapers a bare 1 cm away from these decorations at both top and bottom. The tube is hollow and we have no reason to conclude that the bottom end was closed with a stopper. As we have no information about the way in which this instrument was played, we must just form our own theories on the subject. W.R.

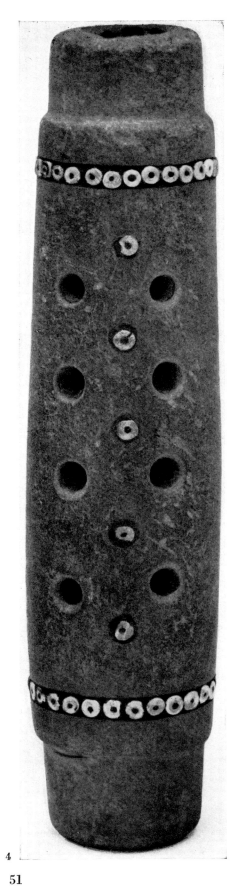

3   4

Illustration 5

Bullroarer of the Nascapi · Davis Inlet · Length 39.4 cm, Breadth 6.4 cm

National Museum of Canada, Ottawa, Inv. No. III-B-349, Neg. No. T 9138

There is an amazing variety in the shape and type of the musical instruments devised by the Eskimo and Indians of North America. Their preference for singing and their use of music for definite purposes during rites and ceremonies would seem to eliminate to a very great extent the development of any instrumental devices for producing sound. We do, nevertheless, find instruments of every kind, including primitive rattles, scraping sticks, clay drums, bullroarers, bone whistles and musical bows. But idiophones were the commonest type.

The bullroarer is an extremely simple instrument and certainly one of the oldest, judging from its worldwide distribution. It is used to imitate the voices of spirits, especially in initiation ceremonies. Curt Sachs (722, p. 42) thought that this elliptical fish-shaped object with jagged fins embodied the forces of fertility. In her work on Papago music (449, p. 141 f.) Frances Densmore described the use of bullroarers in the Viikita ceremony. The signal to assemble was given by the men with bullroarers, sixty or more of them being in action at once, when the people entered the enclosure. The noise of them being swung through the air was thought to resemble thunder and "sounds in the clouds". If a man was accidentally hit by a bullroarer that another Indian was holding, he pressed his own blade against the injured spot. If he failed to do so, that part of his body would be damaged or he would be afflicted by some general bodily disease.

The bullroarer illustrated here, with its jagged edges painted in colour, and the stick for holding it were made of wood and tied together with a leather thong. This particular specimen comes from the Nascapi living in the area of the Davis Inlet.

W.R.

Illustration 6

Bullroarers of the Central and Copper Eskimo · Length 26 cm, 21.6 cm and 22.2 cm

National Museum of Canada, Ottawa, Inv. No. IV-C-1402, IV-C-994, IV-D-162, Neg. No. T 9372

The right-hand specimen in our illustration is carved out of bone and attached to a leather cord. This bullroarer is 26 cm long and 7 cm broad and belongs to the Central Eskimo. The middle one, also acquired for the museum from the Central Eskimo, is made of wood and fitted with a sinew cord; it is 21.6 cm long and 4.8 cm broad. The left-hand bullroarer, used by the Copper Eskimo, is a wooden blade measuring 22.2 × 4.4 cm and hanging from a plaited sinew cord.

W.R.

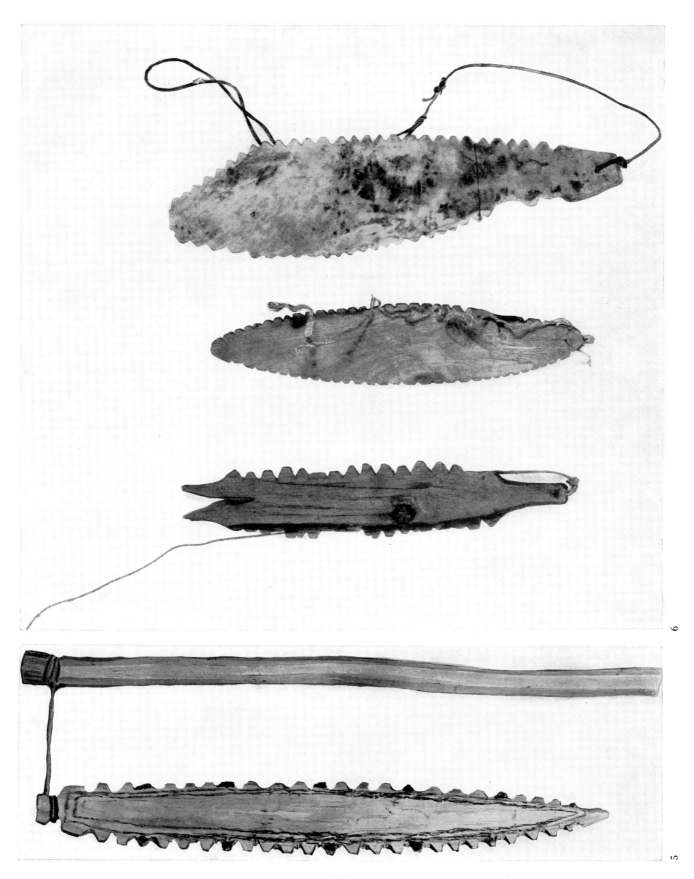

Eskimo music is essentially vocal. Only the frame drum is to be found among all the Arctic tribes of America. In some areas of Canada it is impressively large, measuring over 1 m in diameter, but is smaller elsewhere.

The flat frame drum with a handle is to be seen both among the Hudson Bay Eskimo and the Nuwungmiut of Cape Barrow on the northern tip of Alaska in the Arctic Ocean, where this group of drummers was photographed by Laura Boulton in 1946. This Eskimo drum is beaten on the frame with a thin stick. The rhythms are repeated again and again, but are punctuated with pauses from time to time to denote the different sections in the song. By singing against the membrane they manage to amplify the sound and this contributes to the distinctive timbre of their voices.

To make these drums a piece of reindeer leather is stretched over a wooden hoop about 60 cm in diameter. Pieces of whale liver or walrus stomach are occasionally used for the membrane. These instruments often have handles made from walrus tusks and these may be lavishly decorated. An Eskimo drum handle of this type (text-figure), also coming from Cape Barrow in Alaska, is now exhibited in the Museum of the American Indian, Heye Foundation, New York, Cat. No. 21/804. This specimen, 14 cm long, is an example of the Eskimo art of ivory carving. The realistic portrayals of a human and an animal head at the end of the handle reflect the magical relationship existing between man and animals. The rim of the drum was held inside the groove on the left side of the handle, whilst the three bevelled notches on the right side were fashioned for the drummer's fingers.

When writing of the customs and usages of the Caribou Eskimo, who are, of course, ancient inland hunters in the "Barren Grounds" to the west of Hudson Bay and do not hunt along the frozen margins like their northern relatives, F. Mowat (37, p. 148) mentioned that the "Ihalmiuts" produce no paintings or rock pictures or fashion effigies from clay or stone, as there is no room in the lives of these nomadic people for any large-scale or permanently placed works of art. What sense would there be in producing works of art and then having to leave them behind when they set out on their long journeys? But they do certainly have a very keen artistic sense, expressed in their songs, the gay decorations on their clothing, their ivory work, the small plastic objects they produce and the items in everyday use, and also in their various stories and legends. W. R.

Illustration 8

Eskimo Drumming Contest · Angmagssalik, East Greenland

Photograph by William Thalbitzer (1906), Photographic Collection of the Arktisk Institut Charlottenlund, Denmark,
No. 7656

Disputes and controversies among the Eskimo are usually settled either by wrestling or by drumming or singing contests. This latter form of jurisdiction is particularly common in Greenland. The two parties concerned appear with their relatives and hurl songs of contempt at each other to a drum accompaniment (501, Col. 1528). Each party tries to make the other look ridiculous and show up his weaknesses and shortcomings. This musical duel goes on until one of them is defeated by the arguments brought forward by his opponent and the persuasive power of his singing and abandons the field.

The Eskimo of West Greenland became civilised at an early date, mainly through contacts with the Danes, but the Eskimo on the inaccessible east coast remained untouched by European cultural influences until the end of the 19th century. The Eskimo of East Greenland only settled along the Ammassalik and Sermilik Fjords, close to the present township of Angmagssalik. The group of barely five hundred people living in that region were not discovered and

studied in detail till about 1885. At the beginning of this century William Thalbitzer made phonograph recordings and wrote several works on the music of East Greenland. He was also responsible for the photograph of a drumming contest (Illust. 8), shown opposite. It was taken in 1906, when such contests still served a genuine legal purpose, whereas nowadays they are often nothing more than a public show.

The illustration gives us some idea of the East Greenland scene, with its fjords and icy mountains rising to above three thousand metres. As we can see, the settling of a dispute is a matter of general interest, extending far beyond the actual members of the family. The two opponents stand facing each other with their flat frame drums and take it in turn to sing, each one ridiculing the other and publishing his shortcomings. As an example we shall quote here a literal translation of one such song noted down by Thalbitzer (771, p. 35): "You who were once afraid — you who were once a coward — have now come to take your revenge — you have now come to bite me — you miserable little wretch — just step over here — pit yourself against me with your drum — on your paltry little sledge." The song ends with a shriek of contempt. The text picture shows the bitterness of these singing duels. Note the facial expressions and postures of the two adversaries as they confront each other at close quarters. This text picture is one of the oldest photographs taken in the region. It was brought back from a Greenland expedition by F. C. P. Rüttel about 1896 and the Arktisk Institut of Denmark have kindly allowed us to use it.

Illustration 9

Dance of the Copper Eskimo

Photograph by Leo Hansen, Photographic Collection of the Nationalmuseum, Copenhagen, No. 2274

The Eskimo sing for long periods, often for hours on end, at their frequent dancing festivities and evening celebrations. One of them sings a song and beats out the rhythm to it on a frame drum. He has composed the song himself and is its "owner" and he alone is entitled to sing it. The others present frequently join in the refrain. Such songs are often difficult for outsiders to understand because of the many allusions they contain, but a great number are deeply poetic (20, p. 198). The singer dances practically on the spot with knees slightly bent and swaying hips and the top

of his body leaning forward. These dances for one person, mainly performed by men, are the only indigenous Eskimo form. The Copper Eskimo dancer illustrated here is wearing a hood made from narrow strips of skin with a diver's beak set on top.

The following is taken from a description by F. Mowat (37, p. 148) of an evening gathering of Ihalmiut Eskimo. When a number of visitors arrive in the evening, Ootek unhooks his big drum from a tent pole. He holds it over the fire so that the skin will be well stretched by the heat, then hands it over to one of the guests. These are modest folk, so the drum is passed on from one to another until one of them finally takes it — perhaps Ohoto. He rises from the circle of people sitting round and moves towards the centre of the group, quite close to the fire. For a few minutes he stays there in some embarrassment and the audience argue loudly about what he should sing. After a considerable time Ohoto says: "All right then, you people with your great bellowing voices, I will sing a song of my own that I have composed about my reputation as a hunter." He holds the drum by a handle and makes it revolve by beating the frame lightly with a stick. The song is introduced by slow, rhythmic beats and Ohoto starts dragging his legs like a circus bear. Then, leaning well forward and swaying from the hips, he suddenly begins to sing. At the end of each verse his audience take up the refrain . . . There is a quickening of the tempo and when all the verses have been sung Ohoto sinks back exhausted into his place. Then someone else seizes the drum. The songs go on for hours. In most of them the singers ridicule themselves or refer sarcastically to some notoriously

cowardly or lazy hunter. In addition to the singing contests (Illust. 8) and the dance songs (Illust. 9), there are chants with some magical or ritual significance which are sung during hunting or when they are in danger. Children's songs also have their place among the Eskimo. The Eskimo woman sings them to her child (text picture) whom she carries on her back. The photograph used for the text picture was taken by William Thalbitzer in 1905/1906 at Angmagssalik in East Greenland and has been kindly passed to us for publication by the Arktisk Institut of Denmark (File No. 7706).

Illustration 10

Singing Eskimo with his Two Wives and Daughter · Angmagssalik, East Greenland

Photograph by William Thalbitzer (1906) · Photographic Collection of the Arktisk Institut Charlottenlund, Denmark, No. 7678

The music of the Copper Eskimo of to-day is not uniform in style because of the assimilation of outside influences, but old traditions have been preserved unaltered in the songs of the indigenous population along the Ammassalik Fjord in East Greenland and in some cases have become rigidly static. According to an account by Thalbitzer (771), the local Eskimo culture has survived until quite recent times in its own peculiar form and in various respects we can regard it as the true culmination of that race. In the material civilisation of the Ammassalik Eskimo ornament occupies a prominent place and so in the more intellectual field the art of composing verse and singing has also reached a relatively advanced stage of development. In the photograph reproduced here from Thalbitzer an Eskimo with a drum can be seen singing a song to his two wives and his daughter.

9

10

59

Illustration 11

Wooden Box Drum of the Yakutat · Alaska · Height 94 cm, Breadth 83.5 cm, Depth 35.5 cm

Museum of the American Indian, Heye Foundation, New York, Cat. No. 19/9099

The rectangular box drum illustrated here belongs to the Yakutat, members of the Tlingit group living in Alaska, who form part of the Na-Déné linguistic family. It is carved out of cedar wood and must be classed among the idiophones. Two light circular patches on the narrow top show the places where the drum was beaten. The notes are roughly a major second apart. The drum is almost completely enclosed and is only open along one narrow end to allow for the emission of sound. On the front and reverse side we see artistic paintings in red, green and black in the

traditional style used by the Indians from the north-west coast of America. A totem emblem is evident in the owl, whose eyes are made of shell discs inlaid in the wood. This type of drum is played in Alaska in conjunction with lunda beak rattles on festive occasions and is quite unknown in other parts of North America.

Drums were made by the Indians in many different sizes and shapes and were often decorated with paintings. Any material readily available was used, e.g., wood, skin, pottery and iron kettles. In recent times they even put the steel rims from car wheels into service as drum frames and the rubber inner tubes of tyres as drum membranes, in place of animal skins. Small drums are played by individuals, whilst the big drums are usually beaten by a group of men standing or sitting round the instrument.

The drum is primarily a shaman instrument. The shamans play an important part, especially among the Arctic and sub-Arctic hunters. In the midst of a hostile environment they alone can offer support and protection to man against the powers of evil which are continually threatening him. The shaman scene reproduced here in the text picture was photographed in 1927 on the lower Nass River on the north-west coast. Gitiks, a Niska chief of the Eagle clan, is treating the patient set on the ground in front of him, while his assistants are singing and beating the drum (National Museum of Canada, Ottawa, Neg. No. 69,618). W.R.

11

Illustration 12

Chief's Rattle from the Haida · Skidegate, Queen Charlotte Islands, British Columbia · Length 33 cm

Museum of the American Indian, Heye Foundation, New York, Cat. No. 1/8082, Neg. No. 14,564

This artistically carved chief's rattle of the Haida from British Columbia portrays a raven with a man reclining on its back and sucking poison from a frog's tongue. It symbolises the inspiration received by the shamans when they are inventing their spells. In North America this symbol only occurs on the north-west coast and it is also connected with sun magic. Behind the frog we can see a mask with a feather ornament thought perhaps to represent a hawk's head, and the actual body of the raven is carved in such a way as to resemble a sparrow-hawk's breast. The entire instrument has been stylised with superb artistry.

The rattle, fashioned from cedar wood, is 33 cm long and consists of two parts joined together with cedar fibres. It is painted in red, yellow, blue and black. The ornamental design used here recurs among different tribes on the north-west coast and is of great magical significance. Similar Haida rattles in the form of birds can also be seen in the Natural History Museum in Vienna.   W.R

Illustration 13

Tsimshian Clapper · British Columbia · Length 26.7 cm

National Museum of Canada, Ottawa, Cat. No. VII-C-485, Neg. No. T 6165

This Tsimshian clapper is another example of the highly advanced art of the north-west coast Indians and their endeavour to produce perfectly formed objects endowed with magical powers. The two halves of the wooden clapper are bound together with a leather thong. When shaken, the instrument gives out a sharp percussive noise not unlike the clicking of castanets. Both sides of the clapper are ornamentally carved in the traditional Tsimshian style.

Shamanism, which is practised by the medicine men attached to the North American tribes, is of Asiatic origin and is particularly marked among the Siberian peoples. In America it is most evident among the Eskimo, living as they do in an Arctic environment. Mircea Eliade (820, p. 166) discussed the significance of shaman instruments and mentioned how in North America, as in most other areas, the shaman uses a tambourine or a rattle. When there is no ceremonial drum, this is replaced by a gong or a small bell. But they always use an instrument that enables them in some way to establish contact with the "spirit world". This term must be understood in its widest sense, as it embraces not only gods, spirits and demons, but also the souls of their ancestors and of the dead and of mythical creatures. This contact with the supersensory world is preceded by a state of trance, aided by the "entrance" of the shaman or magician in his ceremonial costume and accelerated by the ritual music.

In his publication on medicine men from the northern Pacific coast of America, Marius Barbeau (56) has published several photographs of shamans from that area, including a picture of a shaman from Bella Coola called Alec Kimsquit (text picture), holding a rattle in his hand. This photograph was taken in 1923 by Harlan I. Smith (National Museum of Canada, Ottawa, Neg. No. 58,525).   W.R.

12

13

Illustration 14

Wooden Kitksan Rattle · Skeena River, British Columbia · Length 30 cm

Museum of the American Indian, Heye Foundation, New York, Cat. No. 9/7998, Neg. No. 29,426

From an artistic point of view this shaman instrument of the Kitksan, belonging to the Chimmesyan linguistic family, is certainly superior to most of the rattles known to us, but its round, bulging shape is typical of the tribes of the north-west coast. The ornamental decoration represents a beaver's head, with its tail marked by hatching. A face is looking out of the inside of the beaver — an example of the human metamorphosis of which, according to these Indians, every animal is capable. The rattle consists of two hemispheres of cedar wood fastened together with two metal pins and tied with a thong. The other half is just as elaborately carved as the side turned towards the viewer.
In addition to the rattle the Kitksan also have a frame drum. A magnificent example with an artistically painted drum membrane is included in the private collection of Marius Barbeau (56, Illust. 48). A piece of elk leather was stretched over a round hoop of soft wood 63.5 cm in diameter. Like the rattle, this drum is a shaman's instrument.

W.R.

Illustration 15

Salish Rattle · Vancouver Island, British Columbia · Length 37 cm

Museum of the American Indian, Heye Foundation, Cat. No. 20/347, Neg. No. 29,427

As well as wood or hard fruit shells, material of animal origin was also used in the making of rattles, e.g., the shell of the turtle, which is thought to have magical properties. The rattle illustrated here, which was used by the Salish on Vancouver Island on the west coast of Canada on ceremonial occasions, is made from the horn of a mountain sheep. Before that hard substance could be fashioned, it had to be placed in boiling water. It is wound round with coarsely spun wool and the decorations on the handle depict Swaixwe (Xwai Xwai), a supernatural being with great magical power. The rattle is manipulated by the person wearing the mask which denotes that being in the ceremonies named after it.

W.R.

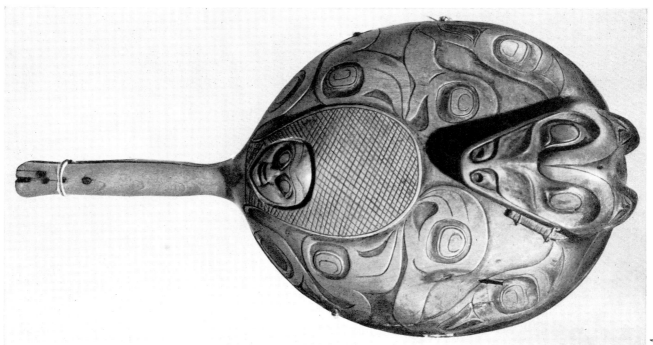

Illustration 16

Haida and Makah Reed Instruments · British Columbia and the State of Washington · Length 32—45.7 cm

Museum of the American Indian, Heye Foundation. New York, Cat. No. 19/3535, 10/649, 6/38

Wind instruments in which vibrating reeds set the air column in the instrument in motion are often described in the literature as whistles, although, scientifically speaking, this is not quite correct. The specimens illustrated here were made by splitting a length of cedar wood and hollowing out the core. A reed was inserted in this air channel and then the two halves of the tube were bound together again. Instruments of this type only occur in the north-west coast area of North-America. The shortest of the three wind instruments illustrated here was acquired by William Fitzhugh (d. 1925) from the Haida on the Queen Charlotte Islands for the Museum of the American Indian in New York. The slender mouthpiece is split lengthwise and a reed is wedged in between these two elastic lips and made to extend into the bore. The other two instruments come from the Makah who live near Neah Bay in the state of Washington. They were blown during the Tklokwali ceremony, which took place about the time of the winter solstice and lasted for several days. Because of the raucous sound made by these reed instruments without finger-holes and their indefinite pitch, we may wonder about their musical value, but this is outweighed by their magical significance. The importance attached to them by those Indian tribes is evident from the fact that they perform a vital musical role in masked dances and ceremonies and are used in particular by the leader of the dance as a signal to mark off the individual phases of the various dances.

Two reed instruments each with five finger-holes, found by Troup on the north-west coast in 1892 and handed to the British Museum in London, must be regarded as a separate and later form of the specimens without finger-holes that are illustrated here. In the same collection there is another instrument of this type from the Queen Charlotte Islands with four round finger-holes set at regular intervals. Experiments conducted by Francis W. Galpin showed that the better of the two specimens with five holes had a scale corresponding to the first five notes of a major scale starting on E flat. W.R.

Illustration 17

Vertical Haida Flute, Front and Side View · Queen Charlotte Islands · Length 42 cm

Übersee-Museum, Bremen, Cat. No. C 198, Photograph by Helmut Jäger

It is assumed that the Haida wind instrument reproduced in Illustration 18 and this one too were carved by George Gunya from Slate Creek near Skidegate about 1830. He had become well known for his delicate carved work in shells, ivory and argillite, which he sold to seamen. These instruments give us some idea of the very strong artistic sense of the Indians on the north-west coast — above all, the Haida — a talent also evident in their homes and household furnishings, as well as in their clothing, ornaments and ceremonial paraphernalia.

Illustration 18

Haida Wind Instrument · Queen Charlotte Islands · Length 18 cm

National Museum of Canada, Ottawa, Neg. No. 78,657

The national Museum in Ottawa was only able to give a limited amount of information about the origin and where-abouts of this instrument and the author has been unable to find out the museum or private collection where this valuable specimen is located. It is carved out of argillite, a soft stone that hardens with weathering, and measures 18 cm from one end to the other. The original photograph bears the legend: "Loaned by R. C. W. Lett, Vancouver, Photo, Leonard Frank, 1877, Vancouver." The instrument was dug up on one of the farms on the Queen Charlotte Islands and was said to be "so old that the Indians of today know nothing of it." The seven blow-holes matched to seven resonance chambers indicate that it is a kind of pan-pipe or mouth organ. But it is impossible to give any precise information without actually seeing the instrument. It is similar in shape to the familiar tobacco pipe heads that used to be made in large numbers from argillite by the north-west coast Indians. W.R.

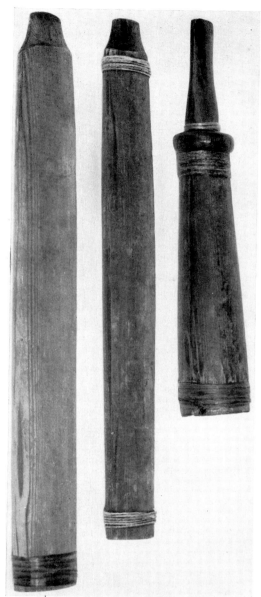

16

17

18

Illustration 19

Four-toned Kitksan Whistle · British Columbia · Length 44.5 cm

Museum of the American Indian, Heye Foundation, New York, Cat. No. 6/6279, Neg. No. 29,246

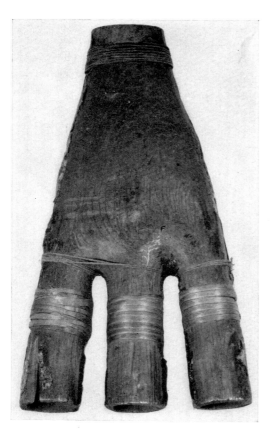

Like the reed instruments reproduced in the previous plate, the multiple-toned whistles illustrated here are only to be found in the north-west coast area of America. The four-toned whistle was acquired by G. T. Emmons from the Kitksan in Kispiox Village, British Columbia. It is 44.5 cm long and, when blown, the sound pattern is as follows: the pipe to the left of the mouthpiece sounds a clear f; the left front pipe is dead and does not speak in its present state; on the right front pipe we get a g and on the pipe to the right of the mouthpiece an f sharp of rather indeterminate pitch. The sound emerging from the three speaking pipes is therefore a dissonant chord composed of the notes f, g and f sharp.

The three-toned whistle in the text picture has been fashioned from a piece of spruce root with fibre bindings. It came from the Tsimshian on the Skeena River and can be viewed in the National Museum of Canada in Ottawa, Inv. No. VII-C-1610. Its dimensions are: length 25.4 cm, maximum breadth 14 cm, and diameter of the pipes 3.8 cm.

Elaborately carved Haida whistles with which the members of the totem associations invoked the spirits are exhibited in the Provincial Museum, Victoria, B.C. These are anthropomorphic in design, with the gaping mouth of human figures always forming the sound hole.

Francis W. Galpin, who has made a special study of the wind instruments of the Indians living on the north-west coast of North America (520, p. 115 ff.) draws a distinction between pipes without finger-holes that are stopped or open and between finger-hole flutes and reed instruments. He subdivides the group of pipes into instruments blown with the mouth and those in which the air supply is obtained by mechanical means, such as a bellows or animal bladder (similar to the platerspiel). One of the four-toned pipes studied by Galpin produces the notes a'—c''sharp—a''—c''' sharp. All these wind instruments have a magical and ritualistic function and are only used for certain ceremonies.

W.R.

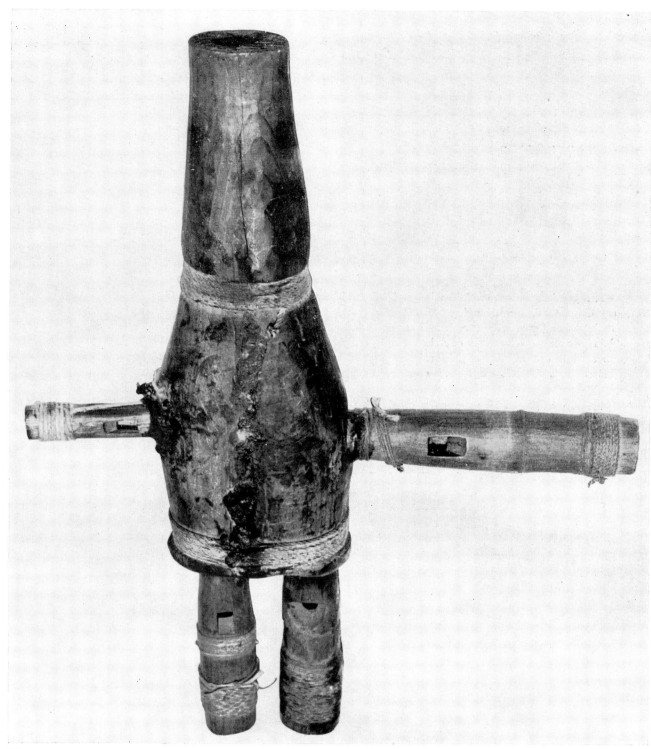

19

Illustration 20

Musical Bow of the Tlingit (Alaska) and the Maidu (California) · Length 152 cm and 200 cm

Museum of the American Indian, Heye Foundation, New York, Cat. No. 21/456 and 21/1645

The musical bow, which is one of the most ancient instruments, only occurs in a few places in America. The Tlingit bow from Alaska (on the right) is decorated with typical eye ornaments painted on in red and black. The bridge is not directly attached to the bow, but to a thin wooden span which only lies along the bow at both ends, but stands slightly away from it in the middle. This space serves to amplify the sound of the string. The text picture shows an

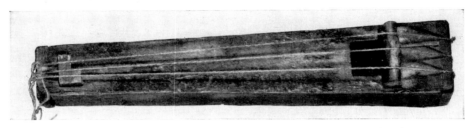

Eskimo stringed instrument exhibited in the National Museum of Canada in Ottawa (Inv. No. IV-C-783). It comes from the Central Eskimo belonging to Baffin Land and is built up from wood and sinew strings. The dimensions are: length 51.4 cm, maximum breadth 9.5 cm and maximum depth 8 cm. The bow with its fish-bone string is 26.7 cm long. This instrument is possibly of Asiatic origin or was influenced by Asiatic pieces.

The musical bow of the Maidu of California (on the left) has a bridge over which the string is held taut. The curvature of the instrument, which is 2 m long, is convex, in contrast to the far more usual concave bows. W.R.

Illustration 21

Musical Bow of the Yokuts from Fresno · California

Robert H. Lowie Museum of Anthropology, University of California, Berkeley, Cat. No. 1—10,789

This specimen, which S. A. Barrett obtained in 1907 in the Fresno area of California from the Yokuts, who call it *ma'wo*, represents the most primitive form of the musical bow. It is without the bridge and tuning pegs that we find in later versions and is similar in shape to the ordinary archer's bow. A sinew string is stretched over an elderberry cane into which pegs have been inserted from both sides, and to these the string is securely attached. When the instrument was being played, the musical bow was held in a roughly horizontal position in the left hand. The right end was raised to the open mouth and the string was plucked with a finger of the right hand or struck with a small stick. By changing the shape of the oral cavity the player was able to bring out the top tones of the fundamental note produced by the string. It is doubtful whether any phonograph recordings of the Indian musical bow are still in existence. W.R.

Illustration 22

Musical Bow of the Yokuts from Madera · California · Length 90 cm

Robert H. Lowie Museum of Anthropology, University of California, Berkeley, Cat. No. 1—10,427

This Yokuts musical bow with a tuning peg was obtained by S. A. Barrett in 1906 from the Picayune in the Madera area of California for the museum collection in Berkeley. The bow, 90 cm long, is made from a slender elderberry cane with a tuning peg stuck through one end of it. A string has been wound round one end of the peg.

Among the Maidu of California the musical bow is used by the shamans to establish contact with the spirit world. The Yokuts play it when mourning their dead. But the ritual character of the musical bow has not been so strictly preserved as among the Maidu, because the Yokuts also play it when they lie down to sleep at night.

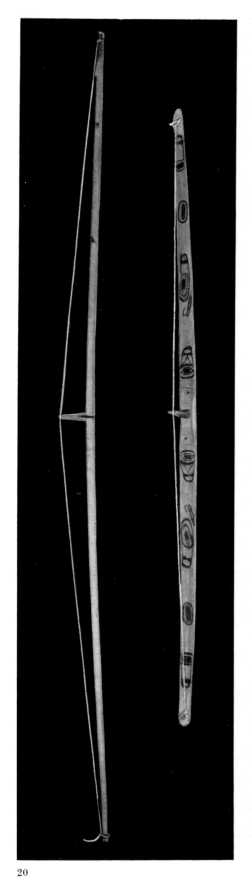

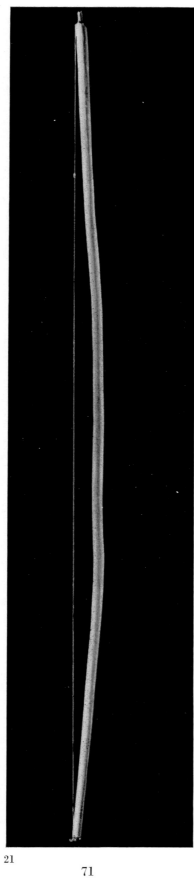

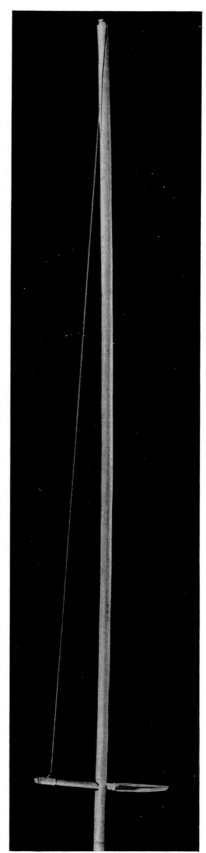

20

21

22

Illustration 23

Papago with Scraping Stick

Smithsonian Institution, Bureau of American Ethnology, Washington, D. C., Neg. No. 2775

Possibly before the beginning of our era predominantly long-headed tribes distinguished for their artistic plaited work advanced towards the south-west of North America as far as Arizona. They are generally termed "basket-makers". At about the same time or just slightly earlier the Hohokam arrived in the area (cf. p. 48). As they cremated their dead, we know nothing about their physical structure. Only two round skulls have survived. They irrigated their fields and created a very advanced civilisation and were, in fact, the forerunners of the present-day Pima and Papago.
The Papago squats on the ground and rests a slightly curved notched stick *(hiohkat)* on a shallow upturned basket which serves as a resonator to amplify the sound. With a smooth stick he makes a rasping, rattling noise by continuously stroking it up and down. Scraping instruments were used by the Papago to accompany songs originating from the sea coast, the purpose of these songs being to beg for rain and ensure a good harvest. They were also used in the Viikita ceremony. This photograph, taken by José Panco, was acquired by Frances Densmore about 1920.
The notched stick was already familiar to the Aztecs in the pre-Columbian period and is nowadays in widespread use, especially in northern Mexico and the south-western areas of the United States. According to Izikowitz (579, p. 160) this instrument only occurs in South America in a few tribes that have been culturally influenced by negro immigrants.   W. R.

Illustration 24

Hopi Scraping Stick · Arizona · Length 39.4 cm

Museum of the American Indian, Heye Foundation, New York, Cat. No. 6/2057, Neg. No. 21,007

This notched stick, used as a scraping instrument, was obtained by R. H. Mangold from the Hopi in Arizona. Unlike the Papago specimen shown in the previous illustration, it is quite straight. The notches are marked in white.
The Hopi of Arizona living in *pueblos* use scraping sticks in ceremonies connected with the winter solstice and also for the rites and dances of the Katčinas (cf. Illust. 31). Numerous authors have written in detail about the significance and essential features of the Katčinas, R. Bunzel being specially outstanding in this field. Alexander M. Stephen has given a fairly precise description of scraping sticks (188, p. 407). According to him, the end of the notched stick is rested on boxes lying on the ground. The player holds the top end of the stick in his left hand and a bone in his right and uses it to scrape over the notches. With rapid downward movements of the right hand grating, rattling noises are produced, keeping time with the singing. But for certain song cadences the player makes slow upward stroking movements, thereby achieving special sound effects.   W. R.

23

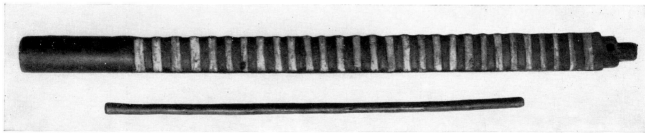

24

73

Illustration 25

Medicine Rites of the Sia-Pueblo · Jemez River, New Mexico

Smithsonian Institution, Bureau of American Ethnology, Washington, D.C., Neg. No. 2189

Photograph by M. C. Stevenson, 1888/89

According to Oskar Schmieder (832, p. 40), the most highly developed Indian civilisations in North America are located in the south-west of the United States. Here in a semi-arid area the Indians grow root crops with the help of irrigation. Their fields produce the same foods as the Indians in the east. But they live in houses built of stone and air-dried bricks and form large villages arranged in a honeycomb pattern, called *pueblos*. This cultural area too has had a varied past dating back to prehistoric times. Ruins and certain well-preserved cultural remains provide our only sources of information about the prehistoric cliff-dwellers and basket-makers. In prehistoric times there were direct connections running from the *pueblos* on the Rio Grande del Norte to the south-west to the outlying portions of the civilisations on the Mexican plateau. Among these Indian tribes a great number of rites and songs and dances are bound up with the fertility of the fields, the ripening of the crops, the desire for rain and certain seasons of the year, also with their awareness of the other world and the healing of the sick.

The picture reproduced here was taken by M. C. Stevenson in 1888 or 1889 during his stay with the Sia, a small tribe of Pueblo Indians belonging to the Keresan linguistic family. That tribe occupies one single *pueblo* on the north bank of the Jemez River to the north-west of Bernalillo in the state of New Mexico. In the *kiva*, a subterranean ceremonial chamber, a sick boy is sitting on a low seat and is being treated by members of the "Society of Giants", who are squatting on the ground opposite him. This men's association devotes itself to the healing of sickness and only a person who has already been cured of some ailment by its members is qualified to join. The Indians think that most diseases are caused by spirits which the medicine man tries to expel and drive away by magical songs or chants of supplication and special exorcising rites.

In this picture we can clearly see a line separating the patient and the "medicine men", who are singing and moving their rattles. The feathers they are holding in their hand and the idols and bears' paws lying in front of them are meant to intensify the magical effect of what they are doing. W.R.

25

Illustrations 26 and 27

Indian Water-Colour Paintings from the Pueblo of Isleta, New Mexico

Ritual in a Worship Chamber in the Pueblo of Isleta (Illust. 26)

"Hot Cornhusk Dance", One of the Dances Performed in Isleta on the Four Days after Christmas (Illust. 27)

For the originals see the Archives of the American Philosophical Society, Philadelphia

These water-colour paintings by an unknown Indian artist from the Pueblo of Isleta have a special ethnographical value because the ceremonies illustrated in them could never have been observed or photographed by a white man. Over a hundred of these interesting and artistic documents were obtained by Elsie Clews Parsons, an American expert on ethnology. They present a clear and reliable picture of the secret acts of worship and festivals held in one of the Rio Grande *pueblos*.

Although the Pueblo Indians were exposed to Spanish influence away back in the 16th century, they have retained essential features of their traditional civilisation up to the present day and are certainly among the most conservative Indian groups in North America. Sentries are posted in Isleta during the solstice ceremonies and they prevent strangers from approaching the village. Even the use of normally quite familiar Mexican expressions is forbidden to those taking part in religious festivals.

A great number of their ceremonies are linked with agriculture. For example, Illustration 26 shows part of a ritual intended to protect the harvest and save the fields from attack by locusts.

In all the religious solemnities of the Pueblo Indians the order and plan of events are most carefully laid down and observed. The drawing gives us some idea of this. We see the row of Town Fathers (members of a medicine society) sitting at the back and accompanying their song with gourd rattles, whilst the female members of the society are seated at the side. In the foreground the "Corn Chiefs" are saying prayers. The leaders of the seven ceremonial groups of Isleta are responsible for the carrying out of certain rites. These leaders (Corn Chiefs) and their helpers act as priests. In the middle of the picture we can see the altar of the Town Fathers. It is depicted by means of a tiered cloud symbol "painted" with maizemeal on the floor of the worship chamber. Important cult objects illustrated are prayer feathers, stone arrowheads and the "corn mothers" of the medicine society, placed in containers decorated with feathers and beads.

E. C. Parsons has pointed out the extent to which Catholic ideas and forms of worship had been assimilated by the inhabitants of Isleta (154, p. 207). The Hispano-Catholic influence can be detected in their prayers, religious songs, dances and "fiestas". But Illustration 27 also gives a clear indication of the link between Christian festivals and Indian religious customs. It shows one of the dances performed in the village square of Isleta in the Christmas season. The men and women have appeared in their traditional ceremonial costume, all ready to dance round in a circle. The women dancers are holding eagle feathers and the men have feathers and gourd rattles in their hands. They dance to the accompaniment of drums and singing, under the supervision of a "War Captain".   R. K.

26

27

Illustration 28

Green Corn Ceremony of the Pueblo Indians · Gouache Painting by Awa Tsireh (Alfonso Roybal) · Size: 49 × 70.5 cm

Museum of Modern Art, New York, Abby Aldrich Rockefeller Fund

Photograph by Soichi Sunami

This gouache painting depicts the green corn (maize) ceremony that is solemnly carried on up to the present day by the Tewa Pueblo Indians in the south-west of the United States. The male choir and the drummer on the right of the picture provide the music for the Corn Dance. The male and female dancers, who have formed up into a procession, are holding sprigs of evergreen and gourd rattles in their hands. Clowns, called *koyemši*, act as the masters of ceremonies and dance round the circle, indicating the direction to be followed by the solemn procession.

The painting has been executed in delicate yellow, brown, green and orange shades and can be regarded as typical of the south-west school of Indian art with its enchanting blend of stylised and realistic features. The artist came from the San Ildefonso Pueblo tribe and was a joint founder of a school of painting.

The Corn Dance, which we are about to describe here from an account by Laura Boulton (395), is an old and very lovely Pueblo dance in which Indian and Christian elements are blended together. Among the Pueblo Indians of the Rio Grande area the dances were set aside for particular seasons and the Corn Dance is, in fact, the most important summer dance. It forms part of a ceremony of supplication for growth and rain and is performed in most *pueblos* on the special day dedicated to the saint after whom the Spaniards named the settlement. If the saint's day falls in autumn — as, for example, in Jemez — the dance is performed when the harvest is brought in.

Nowadays most of the big dancing festivals are introduced by a Catholic ceremony. There is no connection at all between the Christian Mass for the saint and the old traditional ceremony inaugurated by the clowns. They come hurrying out of their *kiva* with wild leaps, indicating to the spectators with their painted bodies and their costumes made of maize cobs or corn husks and also rabbit skins that they are the spirits of death. They spend the whole day doing interesting burlesque turns. The dancers, male and female, come out of the *kivas* in magnificent costumes with rattles and little bells. Their leader carries a pole topped with a decoration of yellow feathers, which is a symbol of the sun luring the rain. A large group of chanters, beating out the rhythm for hours on end with their hands and feet, appeal to the supraterrestrial powers, pleading for clouds and rain as they sing and strike their drums.

The Zuñi, who live some distance away from the other Pueblo Indians, have retained their old customs and have only assimilated minor Catholic influences. Zuñi beliefs still remain very strong and ceremonial dances go on throughout the year. In the winter hardly a week goes by without some celebration. With the coming of spring all the Indians are busy planting, but in summer the rain dances begin.

The individual ceremonial groups form societies and associations. The Mudheads, or clowns, appear in practically all the dances throughout the year. Ritual life is dominated by the priests who are extremely powerful. The greatest power of all is invested in the sun priest. The Zuñi are divided into six groups, each of them with a *kiva*. This assembly house is built partially underground inside a residential block, so that it will not attract the attention of outsiders and will not even be visible to them. A *kiva* group of this kind holds two dancing festivals every year. Boys are taken into the *kiva* when they are eight years old and again when they are twelve, but girls are only admitted when they "have their dreams". The items in the *kiva* include certain masks. Zuñi masks are particularly elaborate. When he puts on a mask, the dancer becomes a supernatural being and has a certain influence with the powers that are in control beyond this human world.

W.R., L.B.

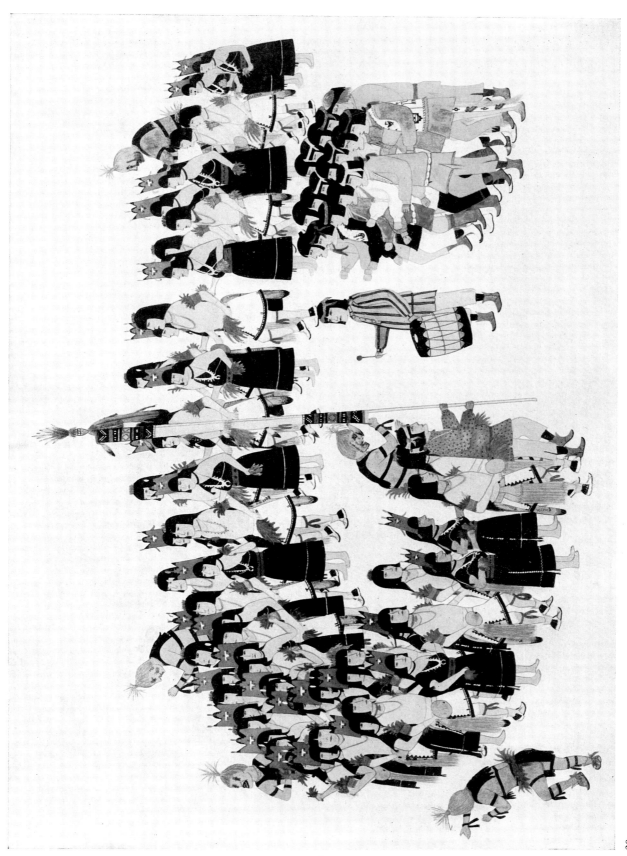

Illustration 29

Zuñi Clay Drum · New Mexico · Height 47 cm

Museum of the American Indian, Heye Foundation, New York, Cat. No. 10/8790, Neg. No. 21,008

This clay drum comes from the Zuñi of New Mexico, a tribe of Pueblo Indians known, amongst other things, for their clay water vessels, mostly painted in colour. The bent drumstick is similar to those used by the Navaho, who live near the Zuñi. The same type of instrument has also been unearthed at Neolithic excavation sites in Europe. As a general rule, they are encircled by knobs which help to stretch and attach the drum membrane. This principle is evident in the Peyote drum shown in the following illustration.   W. R.

Illustration 30

Peyote Drum

Museum of the American Indian, Heye Foundation, New York, Cat. No. 22/4435, Neg. No. 29,121

This Peyote drum consists of an iron cauldron filled with water. The question arising here is whether the water in the instrument is primarily of magical and religious significance or of acoustic value. This latter interpretation may be the right one, as dampness keeps the drum membrane supple and allows the tension and pitch to be altered. These drums are used to accompany Peyote songs, which are never sung by a group, but always by a solo singer. Before the act of worship starts, the drum is ceremonially corded. The pitch of the instrument can be altered by moistening the skin membrane or by lightly pressing the surface with one's left hand. It can thus be tuned to suit the song. We are therefore dealing here with instruments showing some of the characteristics of the kettle-drum.   W. R.

Tribes who originally had quite different cultures and languages became concentrated inside a single reservation area, so the individual ethnic groups gradually gave up certain of their cultural idiosyncrasies in favour of a hybrid "pan-Indian" civilisation. This led to the establishment of various social and religious movements which very soon found adherents, especially in the large reservations. These elements included the dream dance, the ghost dance and Peyote worship. The common feature shared by these new teachings and forms of worship was their syncretic quality, expressed in a combination of traditional Indian ideas with a number of Christian adjuncts. The so-called Peyote cult is today the most widespread movement of this type. It is bound up with the veneration and ritualistic enjoyment of an echinocactus *(Lophophora williamsii)* native to the Rio Grande valley and northern Mexico, the toxic components of which induce visions and hallucinations. This cult has its roots in certain ritual practices of the Indians of northern Mexico which definitely go back to pre-Columbian times. Towards the end of the 19th century this form of worship, which had adopted certain Christian elements in the meantime, extended very rapidly in a northerly direction, and Apache and some of the Texan tribes would have been the first to carry the Peyote cult to the Prairie tribes, among whom it was favourably received and widely adopted.

The Peyote cult spread among the North American Indians at a relatively late date, so we can attempt a fairly reliable reconstruction of this movement from oral traditions and written documents, the extent of which can be gathered from the detailed evidence presented by La Barre (120), Slotkin (172), etc. Students of ethnomusicology very soon began to concern themselves with this interesting phenomenon and the musical material available became a basis for testing the reliability of information about all the various practices that had been passed on to or borrowed from different tribal groups and cultural provinces. D. P. McAllester, the author of what is still the most comprehensive study on Peyote music (633), found, for example, that the music at a Peyote ceremony of the Navaho was clearly different from the "Navaho style" and showed similarities to the "Ute style". This is in complete agreement with the results of ethno-historical research, as the extension of the cult from the Ute to the Navaho is a definitely established fact. Even more remarkable is the distribution of individual songs or chants of the Indians of northern Mexico, such as the Canto del Peyote sung by the Tarahumara, which G. P. Kurath encountered both among the Navaho and the Cheyenne. The studies by W. Rhodes (704/705) are also very informative, as he traced the movement of a musical detail occurring in the Peyote complex (the opening song in the Peyote ceremony). B. Nettl (679), taking as his basis a number of Peyote songs, was also able to demonstrate the relevance of ethnomusicology for solving problems connected with the history of Indian civilisations.   R. K.

29

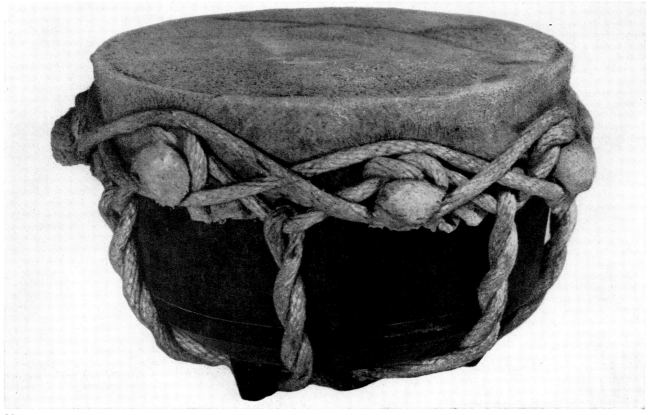

30

Illustration 31

Niman-Katčina Dance of the Hopi · Arizona

Smithsonian Institution, Bureau of American Ethnology, Washington, Neg. No. 42, 189-F

Photograph by A. C. Vroman, 1901

Among the Hopi each *pueblo* has organised religious associations, brotherhoods and men's societies, membership of which may be voluntary or compulsory for all the men in the tribe. The masked society of the Katčinas, whose members lived outside the townships in remote areas of the San Francisco Mountains, occupied a special position of power and respect. It was thought that these masked "ancestral spirits" had an effect on rain and the growth of seeds and that, until they made their appearance in the *pueblos*, they dwelt in a legendary lake in the realm of the spirits and the dead. Alexander M. Stephen, a Scot by birth, made a detailed study of Hopi life at the end of the 19th century and gave a vivid description of the entry of the Katčinas into the *pueblos* (188). He told how these masked men took up their position in line, one behind the other, and turned towards the four cardinal points. After singing for a time, they danced round the courtyard. Then they went into the *kivas*, the subterranean ceremonial chambers in the *pueblos*, ranged themselves along three walls in a double line and danced and sang, taking their lead from a man sitting at the fire. In the numerous festivals and fertility rites of the Hopi dancing, singing and musical instruments play a vital role. Painted calabash rattles, clacking turtle shells, scraping sticks, bullroarers, drums and flutes all help to create the sonic background for these magical performances. Their songs have been a source of interest to many investigators (526). Among the Hopi dances, the Snake Dance (text picture), which is held every two years, has become famous. The dancers grip live rattlesnakes between their teeth, but they are not bitten by them.

The Niman-Katčina dance illustrated here is performed after the harvest, when the Katčinas return home to the mountains from the *pueblos*. They wear leather masks adorned with feathers and painted symbols which cover their heads completely. The mask mystery is kept secret from the women. In their right hand they hold calabash rattles which they shake in time with the rhythm of the dance.   W. R.

31

Illustration 32

Papago Flute-Player

Smithsonian Institution, Bureau of American Ethnology, Washington, D.C., Neg. No. 2774

This photograph shows Sivariano García, one of F. Densmore's main Papago informants. We are indebted to Miss Densmore for the following description of the vertical flute used by the Papago and their method of playing it: "This instrument is made of cane, the outer septums removed but the middle septum retained. Two small holes are made from the outside into the bore, one on either side of the middle septum, and a groove or channel is cut from one hole to the other. The player places his index finger above this channel, its lower edge on a line with the lower face of the septum, thus forming a whistle. The finger, by a slight motion or adjustment, directs the air and thus forms a part of the equipment or sound-producing mechanism of the instrument. Three finger holes are made in the tube below the sound hole. The first finger of the left hand was held steadily above the upper sound hole and the various tones were produced by changes in the positions of the first three fingers of the right hand."

According to Frances Densmore, the Papago used four kinds of musical instruments — cane flutes, gourd rattles, scraping sticks and the so-called basket drums. Any basket of medium size could be used as a basket drum *(tamoa)*. It was placed upside down on the ground and was beaten with the hands. Often three or four men pounded a simple instrument of this kind simultaneously with their right hand, while a few men also held a gourd rattle in their left hand. The Papago made a very clear distinction between dances and songs that were only accompanied by one particular instrument (e.g., songs performed for the healing of sickness or in rain-invoking ceremonies), and others in which two kinds of instruments could be used (449, p. 3).   R. K.

Illustrations 33 and 34

Dance of the Deer · Dancer and Yaqui Musican with Flute and Drum

Photograph by Luís Márquez

Among the natives living in the south-west of the United States, an area formerly belonging to Mexico, numerous legends are sung, played, danced and recited, including the "Dance of the Deer". It occurs among the Yuma, Papago, Yaqui, Tepehuan and Cora Indians and the tribes living even farther to the south and forms part of a very old tradition which has survived, thanks to the care with which the natives have preserved their mythological tales. All these legends consist of a great number of single scenes and episodes in which various animals appear. The instrumental pieces contain characteristic peculiarities in melody, rhythm and form. The sung parts are couched in obscure and old-fashioned language, with the highly imaginative descriptive tales, in which the life of some legendary hero is recorded, serving as the connecting link. The choreographic presentation often depicts the action in highly realistic manner.

The Deer is a hero and sun symbol and scenes are woven about his person with the other cultural hero known as the Coyote and Pascolas appearing in them (cf. Illust. 35). Even the growing of the grass and the rustling of the bushes is reproduced in note form. This Dance of the Deer is performed four times a year, always at the beginning of the seasons, as a kind of fertility spell and may last for a whole night or even two or three. It always starts at sunset and ends at sunrise. The ancient Asiatic symbol of the Deer has a varying significance for the Indians. It represents the sun and the day also the maize god and symbolises fertility and getting one's daily bread. But it also represents the wizard with his magic powers. All the performers appear unclothed in the upper part of their bodies and wear the head of the animal they are portraying on their head. Coarse linen is wound round their legs from the thigh to the knee. They have a cloth or sash tied across their chest and this denotes that they are dancers. Round their hips they wear a belt decked out with little bells or deer's hooves and a necklace round their neck. They dance barefoot, but wear chains made from seed boxes of the mariposa orchid on their ankles and they hold rattles or small bells in their hands. The dancer playing the part of the Deer fastens a prepared deer's head, its antlers decked with ribbons and flowers, on his head (Illust. 33). The Deer, who personifies the day, is pursued and killed during the dance by the Coyote, representing the night. In "Yuman and Yaqui Music" (457) Frances Densmore gave quite a full description of this Deer legend.

According to it, the Deer comes from the sources of the Colorado and wanders to the Pacific Ocean. After various episodes involving fish and elks, he returns to Phoenix (Arizona). After giving his name to several mountain ranges he sends light streaming forth and then remains in darkness. The spider opens a path for him and, rising up to the light, he invites the animals to take part in a contest in which each will demonstrate his cleverness. Blackbirds, auras, cardinal birds, humming birds, nightingales, owls and hawks participate. When the Coyote is summoned forth, he throws up a little dust which he has picked off the ground and he begins to blow, so creating the stars and the rainbow. The nightingale announces the coming of morning and sunrise. In other interludes the wind and flowers and also the quail and a hedge-sparrow appear. The people speak, the bushes sing and the thicket stays resting under the trees. With the first summer rain the Deer sprouts his antlers and the maize flower spikes also appear. The sun rises and goes to seek out the clouds.

In an article from the periodical called "Ethnos", the Swedish author Gösta Montell enumerates the instruments needed to enact this legend and also gives the terms for them, translated from the Yaqui language into Spanish: *zenazo, cistrum* or *senassam* = a wooden instrument with metal plates used by the persons portraying the Coyotes and the Pascolas; *ténabaris* = seed box of the mariposa orchid; *temboin* = chains made from these seed boxes wound round their ankles; *rihuti* or *grijutiam* = belt on which small bells and deer's hooves are hung; *ajam* = gourd rattle carried by the person playing the part of the Deer; *jerucia* = a notched stick rested on an inverted dish (the player scrapes over the notches with another — thinner — stick); *cuzía* = bamboo whistle made from two parts, one inserted in the other; *cubahí* = a shallow tubular drum with two membranes that is accompanied by a flute.

The two last-named instruments are played by the Yaqui musician (Illust. 34) who accompanies the Dance of the Deer. V.T.M.

34

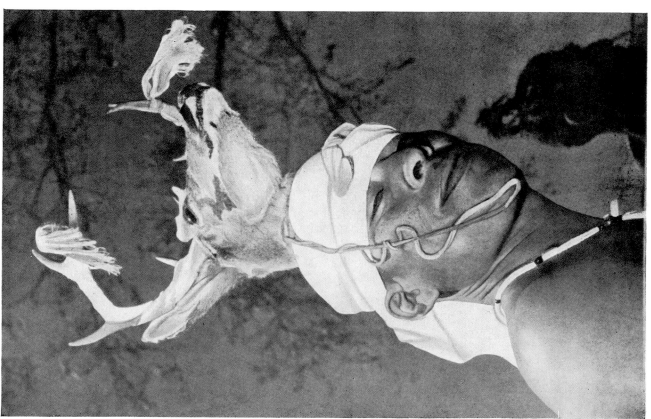

33

87

Illustration 35

Pascola Dance in Pascua · Arizona

Photograph from "Arizona Highways", January 1949

The Pascola Dances are performed by the eight conquered Yaqui peoples — the Cocori, Bacum, Tori, Vicam, Potam, Raun, Huiribi and Belem — and are connected with the ceremonies of Holy Week, i.e., the beginning of spring. They start up on the eve of Palm Sunday and last right through the night, but are not resumed until Easter Saturday. While the bells are ringing and fireworks are being let off, dances of the "Deer", "Coyotes" and "Pascolas" are performed in front of the church doorway. With the beginning of the Gloria these dancers turn, followed by the angels and all the assembled multitude, to a leafy bower erected opposite the church. Then the ritual dances begin. The costume of the Pascola is similar to that of the Deer and the Coyote, except in certain important details. For example, the Pascola has his hair tied at the back of his head with a coloured ribbon called a *vela*. The upper part of his body is naked and his face is often covered with a small black wooden mask with white crosses and zigzag lines painted on it and a beard and moustache and also eyebrows made from long white animal hair attached. During certain sections of the dance the mask is turned round towards the nape of the neck and the face is exposed. The dancers have a strip of coarse linen wound round from the hips right down over the knees. This is held together at the waist and above the knees with a long woollen cord. In addition they have a wide leather belt buckled round them, with small bells attached. Their ankles are encircled by chains made from the seed boxes of the mariposa, a species of Mexican orchid. The Pascola dancers hold a clapper made from a short wooden stick with round metal discs inserted in it. This instrument is played by striking it on the palm of one's hand.

These details, as well as the explanation of the word *pascola*, help us to interpret the role of the dancers more accurately and also what they are intended to symbolise. The actual meaning is unknown. The natives themselves pronounce the word *pahcola*, and the Europeans obviously linked it with Easter (*Pascua* in Spanish), the festival of the Resurrection. These dancers certainly play a very important part in the ritual dances of Holy Week, especially the ceremonies at the beginning of the Gloria on Easter Saturday. But the Pascolas also dance at quite different times in connection with the Deer legend. For example, they very frequently appear at the start of the summer rains and in August, and this would appear to justify the assumption that they represent the rain god, the Tláloc of the Aztecs, referred to here as Pahcoa — the secret meaning of this name being presumably "rain", the sound of which is imitated by persistent shaking of the *zenazo*. Further confirmation of this interpretation is supplied by the black mask, complete with beard, white eyebrows and ornamental symbols, as described above. The Pascola Dances interpolated in the "Dance of the Deer" present a clear contrast. Indigenous dances from the old days alternate with others showing an obviously European influence. In the former the accompaniment is provided mainly by the one-handed whistle and hand drum, dishes beaten on water, scraping instruments and calabash rattles, but in the latter instance violins, harps and the rattle referred to as a *cistrum* or *zenazo* are used. The Pascola Dance tunes are definitely of European origin and the rhythms were obviously borrowed from the Andalusian *guajira*, in which there is an alternation of $^3/_4$ and $^6/_8$ times. In this connection Francisco Domínguez comments that the music for the dances of the Deer and the Coyote are pentatonic and that of the Pascola is diatonic.

The Pascola repeatedly intervenes in the dance legend of the Deer. He hides, howls at the Deer like a Coyote and terrifies him. In the episode entitled "the Pascola preparing to dance" he is attacked by the Deer, who strikes him with his antlers. In the end the Pascola kills the Deer with arrows.

The Pascola Dance can be seen in Pascua, a Yaqui village in the state of Arizona, because the Yaqui war, fought in the closing years of the 19th century, resulted in the emigration of many members of that tribe to the United States. Between 1910 and 1920 some groups of Yaqui fled to Tucson (Arizona) in the wake of the insurrection, so Frances Densmore was able to make notes on dances of this type and the material was published by the Smithsonian Institution in Washington. But now, of course, the Yaqui are no longer persecuted. They are at liberty to carry on their old customs, including the Pascola Dance.   V.T.M.

Illustration 36

Apache with Stringed Instrument

Smithsonian Institution, Bureau of American Ethnology, Washington, D.C., Neg. No. 2580-b-4

This photograph, which A. F. Randall took roughly some time between 1882 and 1886, shows an Apache playing on a one-string Apache fiddle. This instrument is now almost completely obsolete and very few Apache would still be able to make or play one. The fiddle was not used to accompany singing, but for solo instrumental recitals of love songs. McAllester gives two of the Apaches' customary names for that instrument: *tsii'edo'ai* ("wood singing") and *kizh kizh dihi* ("buzz, buzz, sound"). The latter is an onomatopoeic name bringing out the special timbre of the instrument.

W. R.

Illustration 37

Apache Fiddle with Bow · Arizona · Length 54 cm

Museum of the American Indian, Heye Foundation, New York, Cat. No. 8/4561, Neg. No. 21,009

The origin of the Apache fiddle is a highly debatable problem among ethnomusicologists. As its distribution is confined to the Apache belonging linguistically to the Athabascans and also the Dieguenos of the Yuman linguistic family of southern California, it is generally regarded as a native version of the European violin, reaching there via Mexico. The instrument is made from the strong stalk of the mescal agave, from which a suitable piece has been cut and hollowed out with care. At each end 5—7 cm of the pith has been left to provide a proper hold for the tuning pegs and string pegs used to fasten the strings. Round, triangular and rhomboid holes are carved in the body of the stringed instrument to provide for emission of the sound. Strands of horse hair have been used for the bow string and fiddle strings. The specimen fitted with two strings is decorated with painted geometrical drawings and zigzag lines. It was discovered among the White Mountain Apache in Arizona. The instrument illustrated in the text is adorned with a yarn tassel and is about 40 cm long. It comes from the Chiricahua instrumental group of the Apache in Oklahoma and is also exhibited in the Museum of the American Indian in New York (Cat. No. 2/188, Neg. No. 22,462).

W. R.

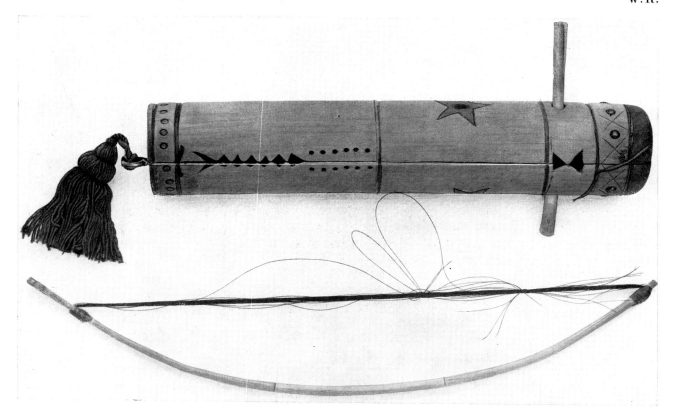

36

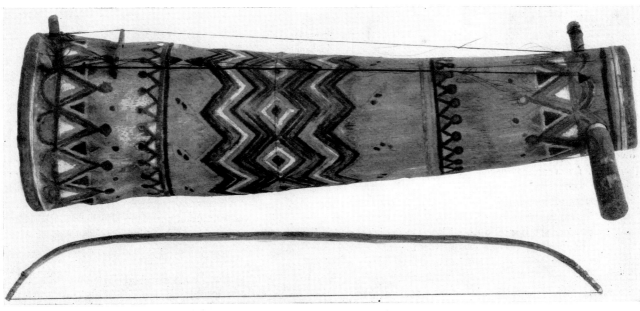

37

Illustration 38

Apache War Dance — Part of a Picture by George Catlin, 1855

American Museum of Natural History, New York, Neg. No. 324,939

The Apache belonging to the linguistic family of the Athabascans, who had migrated down from the north into the south-west, were the last tribe to submit to United States rule. This picture, painted in 1855 by George Catlin, who devoted himself entirely to making pictures of Indian life in the early and middle years of the 19th century, shows three circles of dancing Apache warriors before a fight with the Navaho. Each dancer is carrying a shield in his left hand

and a spear in his right. In the first circle a group of four men (four is the sacred number in which also the *manito* powers appear) are accompanying the singing with drums. This picture is of particular interest and value as a visual document from an eye witness, because it shows Apache singing and dancing customs before that tribe became subjected to outside influences as a result of contact with the white man.

In war, as in all their other enterprises, the Indians relied on assistance from supernatural powers. They invoked them with chants that were often derived from some dream vision. The war chants of the tribe also include the songs they sang before setting off on a military expedition and going on the warpath, or during the actual fighting or when they returned victorious or were performing the scalping dance. W. R.

The present-day Indian dances have often lost their original function, but they do reveal an amazingly marked tendency to retain old forms and traditions, especially among the Pueblo Indians. A particularly colourful scene is presented by the Comanche dance, as performed by the inhabitants of the Pueblo de San Ildefonso (text picture). The dancing is accompanied by the drummers standing in the foreground and a group of singers.

38

Illustration 39

Hidatsa Warrior with Deer-Hoof Rattle in the Dog Dance

Copper Engraving by René Rollet from a Painting by Carl Bodmer, 1834

From "Reise in das innere Nord-America in den Jahren 1832—1834" (Coblenz 1839/41), a Travel Book by Prince Maximilian zu Wied

This portrait of a Hidatsa warrior named Pehriska-ruhpa in the costume and pose of a Dog Dancer was painted by Carl Bodmer at Fort Clark early in March 1834. The warrior modelled for the artist for several days. The magnificent headdress, the calumet hanging on a strap, the actual costume, the bow and arrows and the animal hoof rattle have all been reproduced in clear detail. The "Dog Society", like other similar military associations, consisted in most of the Prairie tribes of all the braves fit for battle. The Indian illustrated here was a chief or war leader wearing a long strip of red cloth or leather as a token of his rank with a slit at one end through which he put his head. The other end hung down over his back and trailed behind on the ground.

The Hidatsa living in north Dakota and also the other northern tribes belonging to the linguistic family of the Sioux were farmers and bison hunters during the Prairie Indian period, but nowadays live mainly in reservations. Men's societies that were ceremonial in character and had military and police functions were a typical feature of these tribes. The members of the associations had special insignia in the form of feathered headdresses, draperies hanging down their backs, flutes and rattles. The warriors were divided up into age groups and different ranks, based on their exploits. Every military expedition was a religious act in their eyes, and they took medicine bundles along with them. These were the property of the clan and in addition to amulets often included musical instruments.

As we can see from the distribution of animal hoof rattles in America, they are among the most primitive instruments used by the ancient hunting peoples. They occur, for example, in South America in the Chaco and the Amazon area, also in western Mexico and California and among the hunting tribes in the Plains to the west and in the interior of North America. The nomadic peoples living in these last-named areas, especially the "Great Basin" of Nevada and Utah, also Oregon and California, have remained at a relatively low cultural level. The investigations of George Herzog (556) have revealed particularly archaic and elementary musical forms of expression in those regions. The music of these tribes has a reduced melodic compass and is tetratonic in structure with simple rhythms and a relatively mild and feeble mode of presentation. But the prime characteristic of the songs is their formal plan. Each part is repeated once, but the repeat versions are usually rather abbreviated, compared with the first phrase. The animal hoof rattle is one of the few musical instruments used. In southern California the rattle is a shaman instrument and is heard in mourning ceremonies, but among the Prairie Indians it is connected with the "Dog Society" rites.   W. R.

Illustration 40

Exponents of the Arapaho Sun Dance with Bone Whistles in their Mouths

Cheyenne, Arapaho Reservation, Oklahoma 1901

Photograph by George A. Dorsey, from G. A. Dorsey, The Arapaho Sun Dance; The Ceremony of the Offerings Lodge,

in: Anthropological Series of the Field Columbian Museum, Vol. IV, Chicago 1903, Pl. 86, Fig. 1

Some North American ceremonies, dances and songs are linked with the idea that sacrifice will enable one to live a better life or enter a better place in the next world. We come across this, for example, in the ceremony of the Sun Dance of the Prairie Indians which has a complex and varied ideological background and celebrated the revival of the sun's power, the stimulation of fertility among the bison and the admission of youths to full adult status. For the four days of the festival the youths, who had already fasted for four days, had the skin and muscle on their chests and backs pierced through. Pieces of wood were stuck through the wounds and cords were fastened to them. In this way the young braves were pulled up along a scaffolding erection that was sent spinning round. The main features of this ceremony are still preserved symbolically in the flying dances of the "Voladores" in Mexico and the Sun Dances of Peru, also in the *giradores* of Guatemala Among Prairie Indians, such as the northern Dakota and the Mandan, the youths were trailed round in a circle until the shields and bison skulls attached to their arms and legs had been torn off and the "dancers" sank down in a faint to the ground. In this ceremony the youths "died", then rose again as adults, to the accompaniment of drums and flutes. These two instruments were regarded as male and female and were essential for their rebirth to a new life. The Sun Dances were banned on grounds of cruelty, but they are still carried on in an attenuated form as a kind of symbol among some of the tribes.   P.C.

The significance and religious content of this ceremony have probably been open to greater misunderstandings among the earlier observers than any other of worship of the North American Indians (9, p. 651). It is not a "dance", but a very complicated rite taking up several days. As for the torturing of the young warriors during the Sun Dance (which was not done among the tribes of the southern and western Prairie area), this was not a compulsory test of male valour. It was, in fact, interpreted as a very urgent appeal to the supraterrestrial powers and some individual warriors were even prepared to submit to the ordeal more than once.

In the Sun Dance of the northern Prairie tribes (Dakota, Cheyenne and Arapaho) all the men who had undertaken to participate in the ceremony held a whistle made from the wing bones of an eagle in their mouths. They blew them unceasingly as they danced, with their eyes staring at the sun. According to the Dakota medicine man "Black Deer", the meaning of these whistles was explained to the dancers in more or less the following terms: "You all have whistles made from eagle's legs; a downy eagle feather must be fastened to the end of it. When you blow your whistles, remember that it is the voice of the spotted eagle; our ancestral father Uakan-Tanka can always hear it . . . ." (165, p. 100).

Bone whistles were a favourite instrument of warriors, as their shrill note made them particularly suitable for giving signals. Some military societies in the northern Prairie tribes adopted them as emblems. The instruments used in the Sun Dance had some eagle down attached to the bottom end.   R.K.

Illustration 41

Picture of an Episode from the Sun Dance · Indian Leather Painting (probably Dakota work)

Museum für Völkerkunde, Leipzig, Cat. No. NAm 3445

The Sun Dance scene illustrated opposite was painted on the skin of a mountain sheep. It not only reproduces part of what actually happened, but also shows the mythological relevance of the various cult objects (shields, bison skulls, a post, painted vessels for ceremonial equipment in the upper part of the picture and sun symbols down at the bottom) by means of the colouring and the added explanations (900, cf. also 78). In the middle we see the red-painted Sun Dance post from which a man, who has submitted to the hardest form of torture, has been suspended with straps. Hanging in a fork in the post is the sacred Sun Dance bundle, adorned with eagle's feathers. A medicine man with a feathered headdress has already undergone torture and is lying unconscious on the ground. Seven Sun Dance priests blowing bone whistles are standing round.   R.K.

96

41

40

97

Illustration 42

Arapaho Ghost Dance · Oklahoma

Pictorial Archives of the Smithsonian Institution, Washington, Neg. No. 35 (R)

Photograph by James Mooney, 1893

Between 1870 and 1890 the Indians had a great need for magic dances to express their spirit of revolt against the white men who had robbed them of their land. This led to the Ghost Dance conducted by the Indian prophet Wovoka of the Paiute tribe. Annie Dorsinfang-Smets (819, p. 117) has described the essential features of this dance, which contains strong Christian elements. It is closely linked with their belief in the end of the present world and the hope of a future life filled with bliss. In this better world people did not work or fast and they never suffered hunger or grew old, but there was also a relentless urge to destroy the white man and a longing for an idyllic way of life which was to be the exclusive prerogative of the Indians.

The success of the Ghost Dance and its spread among numerous Prairie tribes were due to its uncomplicated character. There are no initiation rites and everyone takes part. After they have danced for four or five days, the medicine man or one of his authorised representatives puts some of the participants into a state of trance. The people "possessed" in this way are thought to restore the old link with heaven that existed away back in the early days.

Alexander Lesser (826) describes in detail the whole sequence of the Arapaho and Pawnee Ghost Dance. Their very lengthy dancing festival began with a smoke offering, in the course of which pipe smoke was blown towards the four corners of heaven. The dancers formed themselves into a circle and the women gradually joined in. As the dancers circled round in a clockwise direction, holding one another by the hand, the Ghost Dance songs were sung. But these include songs and chants for which there was no dancing. It is difficult to estimate how many there were. The seven leading singers, with crow's feathers on their heads, started up the melody and the others then joined in. A few "hypnotists" moved about inside the circle of dancers, then stopped in front of certain individuals and tried to put them into a trance. If they succeeded in hypnotising one of the dancers, he was laid down on the grass, on waking up from that state, he described the "pictures" he had seen and sang the songs that he had allegedly learned during that twilight period.   P.C.

42

Illustration 43

Vertical Dakota Flute

Museum of the American Indian, Heye Foundation, New York, Cat. No. 8/3237, Neg. No. 21,007

The flute was a particular favourite among the Indians and was mainly used for playing love songs and when courting. The end-blown wooden flute illustrated here with six finger-holes comes from the Dakota, a tribe belonging to the linguistic family of the Sioux. It is 57.8 cm long and is decorated with ornaments and also with pendant rawhide thongs.

The prehistoric aerophones that have been unearthed in settlement areas belonging to members of the Hopewell civilisation reveal connections with the civilisations in the south-west and in Mexico. To-day we find end-blown flutes among the majority of Indian tribes, either in the form of notched flutes or split whistles. There is no standard tuning and the scale patterns differ not only from tribe to tribe, but also from instrument to instrument within the tribe. For acoustic reasons, however, it would appear that the scales used are similar to our Western diatonic system.

P.C.

Illustration 44

Mandan Warrior Decked in Wooing Finery · Upper Missouri

From "Reise in das innere Nord-America in den Jahren 1832—1834" (Coblenz 1839/41), a Travel Book by
Prince Maximilian zu Wied, Illust. XXIV

Among the melodic instruments of the North American Indians the finger-hole flute with a movable adjuster was one of the most advanced. It was, as a rule, 60 to 65 cm long and was fashioned in two halves from soft wood. The two parts were hollowed out until only a massive core was left, separating the upper "wind chamber" from the lower portion, which was hollow. Above and below this division rectangular openings were cut in one of the longitudinal halves and the finger-holes (usually six in number) were burnt into the wood and the pieces were glued together. The distance between the finger-holes was determined by the finger size. A movable device was placed over the rectangular holes. Its inner surface had a groove through which the air current was taken out from the top opening and brought round against the sharp edge of the bottom one. This device has been described by Curt Sachs.

The finger-hole flute — American ethnographers call it a flageolet — was in widespread use among the Lakeland and Prairie Indians, often for courting purposes. The Mandan warrior painted by Bodmer for the volume of illustrations which accompanied the travel tales of the Prince zu Wied shows by the way in which he is decked out that he is preparing to meet the maiden of his choice. His equipment includes a flute, the adjusting device on which has been made from a piece of raw hide. The flute is adorned with strips of skin, which were replaced in specimens from a later period by brightly coloured ribbons.

R.K.

Illustration 45

Whistle Language in Courtship (demonstrated by a man from the Mexican Kickapoo group)

Milwaukee Public Museum, Milwaukee, Wis.

Photograph by Ritzenthaler/Peterson

In a central Algonkin group, the "Mexican Kickapoo" living in Coahuila (northern Mexico), the traditional form of wooing with a flute was superseded about fifty years ago by quite a different mode of communication. The young men and girls use "whistle language" to reach an understanding and it actually imitates the pitch, stress and rhythm of the Kickapoo language. Ritzenthaler and Peterson have described the whole technique of "courtship whistling". Both hands are placed together in such a way that three fingers of the right hand lie on the base of the index finger of the left hand. The lips are placed against the thumb knuckles for blowing and the note is altered by opening and closing the fingers of the left hand (161, p. 61).

R.K.

43

44

45

Illustration 46

Osage Song Record Stick

Box Cover with Pictographic Song Records of the Chippewa (Ojibwa)

Museum of the American Indian, Heye Foundation, New York, Cat. No. 2/891 and 10/6938, Neg. No. 21,033

Among the Osage a song record stick was used to aid the singer's memory in the artistic rite of the night vigil, a ceremony of supplication to the supraterrestrial powers, and also on other special occasions. It shows the arrangement of songs in groups and classes. Each notch signifies a song or chant. The fairly considerable intervals between the indentations indicate the individual groups. The underside of the stick is marked in the same way. When the singer has reached the end of the stick, he turns it over and continues on the other side. These are, in fact, long song cycles.

The songs of the Midéwiwin ("Grand Medicine Society"), a secret religious association of the Ojibwa (Chippewa) living in north Dakota and to the north-west of Upper Lake, are estimated at a few hundred. They are all written down in the form of mnemonic signs on strips of birch bark, with pictograms representing the essential ideas in each song as an aid to the memory. Certain ceremonial songs are combined in series of eight or ten, and the members of the Midéwiwin danced during the second half of these song groups. The old tribal myths and teachings are perpetuated in the texts of these songs. The picture writing shown in the illustration was developed to a high degree by the Ojibwa and marks the nearest approach to an early form of writing. (We find something quite similar in the sacred tribal chronicle of the Delaware, the "Walam Olum", an account in carved picture writing extending from the Flood up to quite recent times.)

The tunes of the Midéwiwin songs, mainly built up from small melodic progressions, are supposed to prolong life and heal the sick by magical means. But there were also lengthy rites with singing and dancing when the shamans initiated new members of the medical society. In order to be admitted, the candidates had to undergo a ceremony of killing and resuscitation. The instruction received by each applicant is interesting and has meant that the songs have been handed down unaltered through the years. Diamond Jenness has given a detailed description of this period of preparation (824, p. 71). Any young man wanting to enter the "Grand Medicine Society" approaches a member who introduces him as a candidate during a festival held either in the spring or the autumn. He is then given a teacher to whom he attaches himself for several weeks or months in order to receive the neccessary instruction. During this time the youth either leaves his family and lives with his teacher, or the two families move in together and camp immediately alongside one another, which is what usually happens. He receives his training in the daytime in the solitude of the forests or at night in an empty wigwam where no-one can listen to their conversation. He supplies some tobacco for every lesson so that his teacher can begin it with a smoke offering to the various *manidos*. He blows the smoke towards all the four corners of heaven. After these preliminaries the actual instruction begins. For this a water drum (cf. p. 80), rattle and other percussive instruments regularly used in the medicine huts are brought into service.   W. R

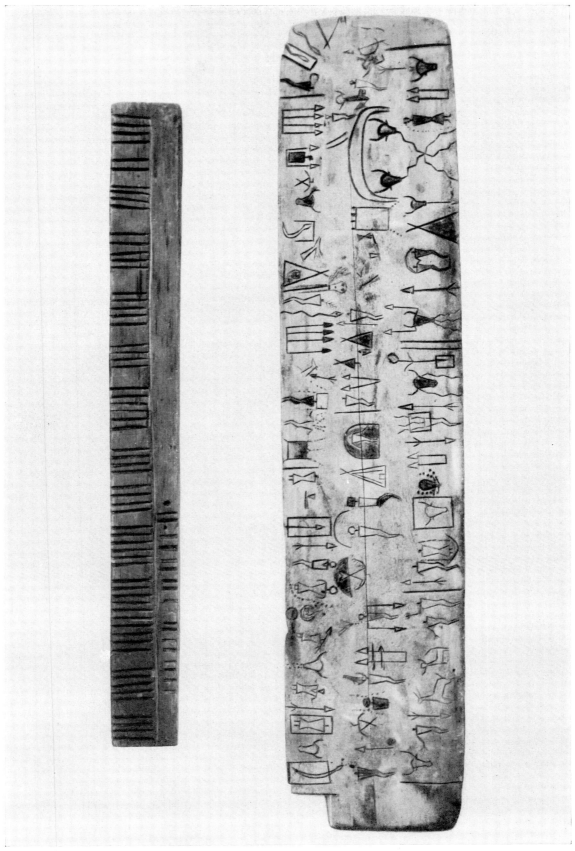

46

Illustration 47

Delaware Deerskin Drum with Beaters · Length about 100 cm

Museum of the American Indian, Heye Foundation, New York, Cat. No. 2/1087. Neg. No. 21,006

The deerskin drum of the Delaware is quite unique, as the more usual Indian drums are round and sometimes even rectangular in shape. The deer skin is folded several times and is secured with long rods that are bound with ropes. The flat beaters with their V-shaped notches are also unusual. Because of its structure, this instrument would appear to be a survival from an early period, when the making of drums was still unknown and animal skins were beaten as percussion instruments. W.R.

Illustration 48

Seneca Turtle-Shell Rattle · Length 57.5 cm · Cattaraugus Reservation, New York

Museum of the American Indian, Heye Foundation, New York, Cat. No. 20/5535, Neg. No. 29/20

Just as the frame drum was very closely connected with the activities of the shamans in Arctic and sub-Arctic America, other musical instruments served as symbols or essential features of various social and religious institutions among the Indians.
These include a rattle manufactured from the shell of the North American snapping turtle *(Chelydra serpentina)*. Together with grotesquely carved wooden masks it forms part of the characteristic ceremonial equipment of the Iroquois False Faces. This well-known masked society of the Iroquois, which in olden days had all the special features of a secret religious society, has survived up to the present time in five conservative communities living less than a day's journey away from the city of New York. These are the "pagan Seneca" from the reservations of Tonawanda, Cattaraugus and Coldspring (near Buffalo City), also the Onondaga, whose reservation is close to Syracuse, and the Iroquois of the Six Nations Reserve in Canadian Ontario. The False Face masks are images of wood sprites, demons of disease and wind spirits, who are regarded as the divine patrons of these confederations. Their leader is Shagody-owéhgowa, the Lord of the Storm Wind, who passes over the earth after the sun.
As the masked members represent these evil beings, people turn to them mainly to ask for diseases to be cured. Their secret rites are held in the traditional longhouses. Apart from private healing ceremonies, the masked figures appear in public three times a year in order to expel the spirits of disease. In the spring and autumn they go through the houses with their rattles, sweep the floors with spruce twigs and blow ash over the sick. These exorcising operations form the focal point of the New Year festivities, in which the spirits of disease are requested to take away the diseases that they have inflicted on human beings in the past year. R.K.

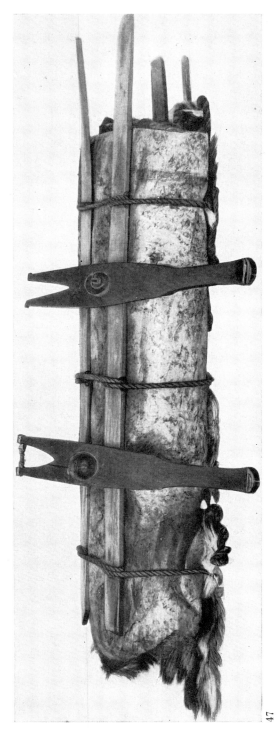

47

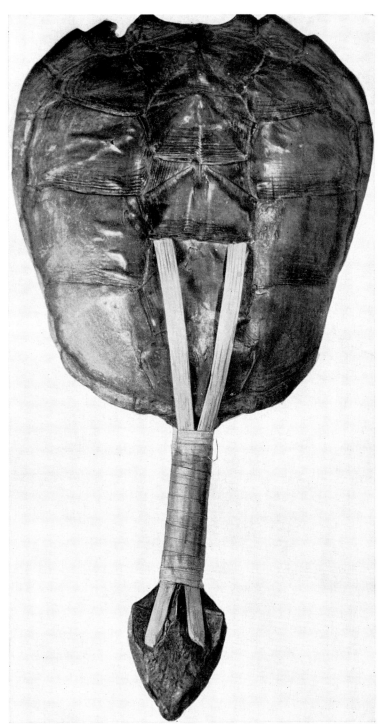

48

105

Illustration 49

Big Drum of the Shawnee

National Film Board, Canada, Neg. No. 97,146

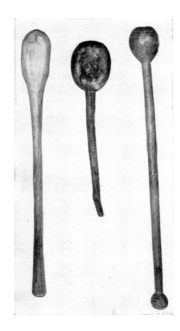

The big drum is in widespread use among the Indians of North America. In their study of the Flathead Indians (828) Alan and Barbara Merriam mention that two types of drum are to be found among these tribes at present — the big war drum and the small hand drum. The former is very often a large drum originating from Europe, both heads of which have been replaced by deer skins. The drumsticks or beaters for both instruments are made from wood that is readily available, preferably wild cherry. Cloth is wound round one end of the stick and tied with a cord. Occasionally the instrument is beaten with club-like sticks that are not padded. Three specimens of this kind, made by the Tsimshian in British Columbia, are shown in the text picture. They are exhibited in the National Museum of Canada (Neg. No. T 9326).

According to the authors mentioned above, the war drum (big drum) is always played by at least four men who sing and beat it simultaneously. The stick is held fairly loosely, but can be brought down with considerable force when necessary. In certain types of dance — for example, the War Dance — the performers kneel or sit round the drum, which is placed on the ground. In other dances (e.g., the Owl Dance) the musicians hold the drum with their left hand and stand manipulating the drumsticks with their right.

The Shawnee, who, together with other hunting tribes, had pushed far on to the south, away from their northern forest home, have also retained many of their own special features in their new agrarian habitat. Apart from drums, they use calabash and deer hoof rattles, also flutes and whistles. Judging by old reports, the wind instruments mentioned here were originally blown only by the braves as they were setting out to do battle. Flutes and whistles no longer have this function, of course, but even today they are not used for dancing or games. Their music has become adapted to a large extent to suit particular occasions.   W.R.

49

Illustration 50

Iroquois Rain Dance

National Museum of Canada, Ottawa, Neg. No. T 3151

The Iroquois, who live near Lake Ontario, but are also scattered about in other areas of south-east Canada and the north-east of the United States, had already joined together to form a state confederacy in the 16th century. They go in mainly for root crops and maize-growing plays an important part in their lives. The success of their field work, which is done by the women, is largely dependent on the weather, so special importance is given to rites connected with vegetation and rain.

According to Gertrude Prokosch-Kurath (598) a great number of "social dances" of a ceremonial nature are perpetuated in the Iroquois traditions and are used to terminate the meetings of the "Six Nations". They have "Food Spirit Dances" performed for entertainment, also pair dances named after birds and other creatures. They always go in for group dances, often led by one dancer. Every kind of dance ceremony is accompanied by a special song or chant that is so typical of it that it would be quite impossible to mistake it. The various song cycles are differentiated from one another by the compass and structure of the melodies with their particular motifs, length of phrase, tempo, mode of presentation and voice technique on the part of the singer. For example, there are shaman songs of restricted compass for healing the sick and the vast, sweeping melodies for some women's dances, the emphatic staccato beat of the Bear Dance songs and the sustained melodies accompanying the Corn Dance. Some of the song cycles are presented in the form of alternating chants, either on a single note, as in the Bear Dance, or with short melodic phrases. In the Bear Dance songs of the Onondaga-Cayuga the male dancers answer the leading singer, who is seated. The choir usually repeats the song sung by the leader of the dance. In all these tribes singing is the prerogative of the men. But the women sometimes sing too, e.g., in the festivals of the dead, the female planting rite and the bush-shaking dance.

Among the Iroquois musical instruments provide a background of sound for singing, except in the case of the whistle used in the "Small Water Medicine Ritual" and the vertical flute with six finger-holes associated with courting songs. The shamans mainly wield calabash rattles. The singers involved in the Corn Dance and various other dances shake cow-horn rattles as they lead the line of dancers. A small water drum is beaten during the War Dance and a big drum during the ritual for the dead. Drums are used in conjunction with rattles for the "Dark Dance", the "Eagle Dance", the "Women's Dance" and the "Fish Dance". In the "Big Feather Dance", as in the masked dance of the False Faces, percussive idiophones made from turtle shell are in evidence.

50

Illustration 51

Eagle Dance of the Iroquois

People who have large birds as "familiars" or have dreamt of large birds or been healed of the "eagle sickness", a nerve complaint affecting the shoulders, back and legs, join a society called the "Fan Strikers" *(hadine'gwa'is)*, which is subordinate to the medicine men. A special ceremony is enacted by the members of the "Eagle Society", with as its focal point the "Eagle Dance", or "Striking Dance". It is in honour of their tutelaries, a kind of giant eagle existing in their mythological phantasy and wheeling up in the clouds under the dome of heaven. The Seneca call them dew eagles or "cloud dwellers" *('o'shada'ge'aa')* and credit them with the power to revive withered plants and dying persons. Among the Cayuga and the Onondaga the term for this giant bird is the *ha"guks*. The Iroquois believe that the "Eagle Society" was founded in early times by a youth who was said to have been carried off through a hole in the sky. He lived for a generation in a large bird's nest, then finally, sitting astride one of the young birds, he returned to earth. The song that he brought back with him bears the title "Striking a Fan Song" and the dance appears to be a survival of the old calumet dance with which the famous Jesuit father Marquette was greeted by the peoples to the south of the five Great Lakes.

The Iroquois appropriated a variant of the calumet ceremony in the 18th century and the Eagle Dance dates back to this ancient tradition. To the accompaniment of drums and horn rattles the men or youths take a few steps towards the middle in pairs in a bent posture, leaning so far forward that they are almost touching the ground with their faces. Some of the dancers can bend so far down without supporting themselves on their hands that they can actually pick up a coin between their teeth. As they do so, they hop sideways and imitate the motion of birds feeding. Shortly before the end of the dance a speaker, usually an old man, beats on a stick and interrupts the singing to say a few words in praise of the tribal warriors or to commend the dancers and sometimes gives a brief account of his own exploits or tells a humorous story.

According to Gertrude Prokosch Kurath (600, p. 248), the music of the Iroquois remains their most important cultural form of expression. The songs belonging to the Eagle Dance are no exception. Fortunately, the three most important tribal versions have been recorded, and these agree with descriptions of the dance and can be studied more accurately than dances which have had to be transcribed from memory from notes made on the ritual and from descriptions.

W.N.F.

110

Illustration 52

Song of the South-Eastern Algonkin with Rattle Accompaniment · Drawing by John White, 1585

Photograph from the Smithsonian Institution, Bureau of American Ethnology, Washington, D.C., Neg. No. 18,717

In 1585 John White made the water-colour drawing shown opposite. This early picture comes from the area of the Algonkin living along the coast of the present state of North Carolina. Grouped round the fire, the men and women are singing to the accompaniment of rattles. To make these instruments calabashes filled with seeds or small stones were used.

There are several quite old accounts of the music and dancing of the Indians in the eastern portions of North America. Robert Beverley gave a description of his impressions ("The History and Present State of Virginia", London 1705, V, 53f.). Their singing was not among the most agreeable he had heard. It was distinguished, above all, by breaking of the voice and was filled with a kind of slow melancholy. But he could not deny that their music contained certain wild notes with a pleasing sound. Descriptions of their dances refer to various forms. While some are dancing, the rest sit in a circle on the ground, "singing lustily and shaking their rattles". The dancers sometimes sing or wear a threatening or horrible expression on their faces and stamp furiously on the ground with all kinds of grimaces and contortions.

W. R.

Illustration 53

Natchez Dance · Lower Mississippi

From Illustration in Antoine S. Le Page du Pratz: "Histoire de la Louisiane", Vol. II, p. 376, Paris 1758

Our knowledge of the Indians of the Atlantic coast of North America and present-day Lousiana is particularly poor because, apart from some groups who have managed to survive, the Indians living there were annihilated or assimilated away back in the 18th century. For these areas we have to rely almost entirely on accounts from travellers, missionaries and officers of the European colonial powers, which, like most ethnographical reports of many years ago, only occasionally contain references to Indian music and musical instruments.

Le Page du Pratz is one of the most important authorities on the interesting Natchez civilisation. His drawing illustrates their harvest ceremonies and shows the nocturnal dancing festival which took place on the eve of the ceremonial ball game. The green corn festival and the harvest festival were the most important agrarian rites celebrated by the farming peoples in the south-east of North America. They were held when the maize was ripening and being harvested. The focal point of the Natchez harvest festival was the communal rite of consuming the freshly harvested maize.

The text by du Pratz provides no information about the dancing that took place afterwards. He merely mentions how at the beginning of the ceremony a man got down in the middle of the dancing area and started to beat out the rhythm on a pot-like drum containing some water. First of all, the women formed a circle round the drummer and were in turn surrounded by a circle of male dancers. These held gourd rattles *(chichicois)* in their hands and used them to accompany the steps of the dance. The circle of female dancers moved from left to right and the men went in the opposite direction. Indeed, du Pratz was amazed at the precise way in which the Indians managed to keep time.

R. K.

53

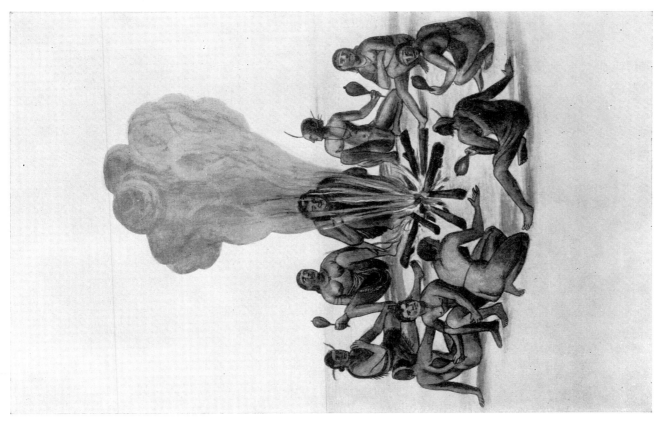

52

113

Illustration 54

Teponaztli (Wooden Drum) from Tlaxcala

Mixteca-Puebla Civilisation · Pre-Cortesian · Walnut · Length 60 cm

Museo Nacional de Antropología e Historia, Mexico

Photograph by Irmgard Groth Kimball

The archaic traditions and ancient instruments that we come across in Mexico do not merely arouse our interest from a musical point of view. The musical instruments that have been unearthed in the area occupied by the advanced Aztec and Maya civilisations are often impressive works of art bearing decorations that can be directly connected with religious symbolism. The *teponaztli* illustrated here, a lavishly adorned wooden tongued drum that can be classed among the idiophones, is one of the instruments of that kind that has survived from the pre-discovery period. It shows a man lying on his stomach. The feathers symbolise the quetzal bird and the spirally wound cords represent two entwined coatl snakes, abstractions of a motif commonly occurring among the Mexicans of old. The two combined symbols are an invocation to the highest god, Quetzalcoatl, the "feathered serpent".

The instrument illustrated here comes from the Mixteca-Puebla civilisation. The Mixtecs lived to the south-west of present-day Mexico City (Tenochtitlan) and the Xochicalco district. Their western neighbours were Toltecs, the eastern Zapotecs. Since the Conquest by Cortés in 1519 the artisan products of the Mixtecs have been famous for their beauty and have excited the admiration of Europeans down the ages. It can be assumed that the Mixtecs represented the peak of Mexican culture at the time of the Conquest. Their civilisation radiated out towards Tenochtitlan, Monte Alban, Oaxaca, Puebla and Tlaxcala.

The typical feature of this percussion instrument carved from walnut and hollowed out inside is the H-shaped slot on the top side, separating two wooden tongues. The tongues, which differ in length and emit notes that are tuned to one another (in the case of the instrument from Tlaxcala illustrated here the interval is a minor third), were beaten with clapper-like devices, the ends of which were covered with rubber. The Aztecs called them *olmaitl*. By changing the striking place it was possible to produce two notes on each of the two tongues, also double sounds by simultaneously striking both tongues. The cavity inside the instrument serves as a resonator.

In the Museo Nacional de México there is a stone statue presumably coming from the Olmeca civilisation (800 B.C.). It displays two musicians, one of whom is playing the *teponaztli*. The Museo de Arqueología in San José, Costa Rica, contains three proto-*teponaztli* carved out of tree trunks. They have only a single tongue and their style and decorations reveal Polynesian characteristics (text picture). In this connection it should be borne in mind that cultural relations evidently existed between Central America and the peoples of south-east Asia during the classical period. An amazing Asiatic influence is evident in ceramics and dancing and also in some of the paraphernalia linked with magic in the Mayan area of Central America and on the coast of Ecuador. This emerges clearly from the studies by Emilio Estrada, Caamano, Evans, Ekholm and von Heine-Geldern. ·   S.M.

114

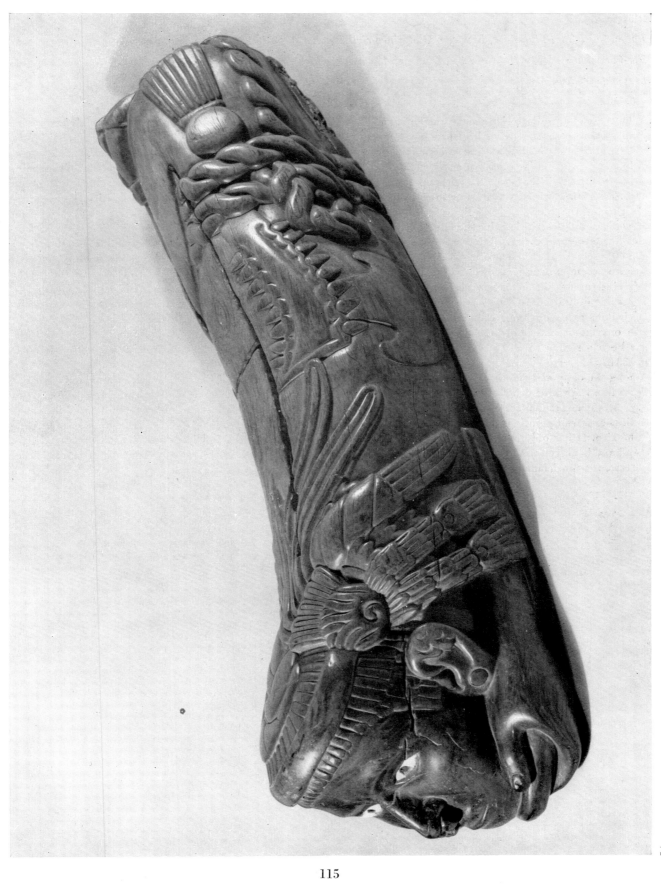

Illustration 55

Panhuéhuetl from Malinalco, Mexico · Matlazinca civilisation

Pre-Cortesian · Wood · Height 97 cm, Diameter 42 cm

Museo de Toluca, Mexico

Among the old pre-Cortesian membranophones of Central America the dominant instruments are clay drums with a simple membrane and cylindrical or kettle-shaped, also the *huéhuetl*, the tubular drum made from a hollowed-out tree trunk. The *huéhuetl* is used as an instrument of worship or for signalling purposes, either as a small portable drum or in a large version (*panhuéhuetl* or *tlalpanhuéhuetl*) standing upright on the ground or on a frame. The top opening of the wooden cylinder is covered with a parchment membrane made of jaguar skin that is securely glued to the outer edge. The skin was held over a flame to make it taut. This drum was beaten with their bare hands, with the fingers or the palm of the hand.

In codices and descriptions by the chroniclers the *huéhuetl* is in most cases mentioned in conjunction with the *teponaztli*, the tongued drum. Both were predominantly ritualistic instruments. Acosta, for example (817, 1940 edition, p. 508), reported that the two instruments agreed so well together that they produced quite good harmony and were used to accompany a great variety of chants and songs . . . . The people all sang and danced to the sound and beat of these instruments in such perfect order and unison with both feet and voices that it was a pleasing sight to watch.

The splendidly decorated *huéhuetl* illustrated here comes from Malinalco and is of Aztec origin. It was made with meticulous care from the trunk of the savin-tree *(ahuéhuetl)*. The illustration shows a priest of the god of dancing, also one member each of the order of the jaguar and the eagle. The symbol of war (*atl-tlachinolli* = water and fire) has been assigned to these "knights". In the middle appears the calendar sign *nahuí-ollin* = 4 motion (cf. 652, p. 133 ff.).

Among the old percussion instruments still used by the present-day natives of Central America there are interesting types like the gourd drum of the Yaqui, the turtle-shell *áyotl* so much in favour among the Maya-Quiché and the *kayum*, a drum made from fired clay with a decorated sound opening. This last instrument can be seen in Mayan codices and wall paintings and is still used today by the Lacandon in the primeval forests of the province of Chiapas in Mexico. It has only one membrane and, like the *huéhuetl*, rests on a wheel plaited from lianas or a three-legged stand and is played with the fingers or the palm of the hand. By playing it in this way, without using drumsticks or beaters, the musicians can achieve greater variety of sound and effect.   S.M.

Illustration 56

Teponaztli · Pre-Cortesian · Tepoztlan, Morelos, Mexico

Photograph by Bodil Christensen

The *teponaztli* is in existence even to-day, as is shown by a number of specimens still in use under various names: *tun-kul* in Yucatan, *tinco* and *teponahuaztli* in Chiapas, *quiringua* in Michoacan, *tepenahuasqui* in Jalisco and *teponaztli* in Tepoztlan (Morelos), Xico (Sierra de Puebla), San Juan Atzingo (Mexico) and Huehuetla (Hidalgo). These instruments are regarded as common property, i.e., they are never loaned out or sold, and the men in charge of them watch jealously over them and make sure that they are kept safe. These custodians have the task of playing them on festival days and ensuring that they remain in good condition. The people living in places where such instruments are still to be found will often protect them at the risk of their own lives. The instrument from Tepoztlan that is illustrated here displays decorations similar to the pre-Cortesian specimen from Tlaxcala (Illust. 54).   V.T.M.

Illustration 57

Teponaztli-Player · San Juan Atzingo, Mexico · Length 55 cm, Breadth 20 cm, Height 18 cm

Photograph by G. Mohedano

The *teponaztli* of San Juan Atzingo remained unknown until 1938, when it was discovered by Laurence Eckart. It was later photographed by Rodney Gallop, who published his pictures in his "Mexican Mosaic". The instrument shows a dog lying on its belly. In the Aztec soothsaying calendar *tonalámatl*, a sacred book in which the ritual calendar *tonalpohualli* was recorded amongst other things, the dog symbolises a calendar day and occupies the tenth place within a twenty-day period. According to Mexican mythology, the dog was the leader of souls and helped them to cross the nine rivers of the underworld by carrying them on its back. So natives in the pre-Spanish period kept dogs and looked after them, especially ones that were coloured like lions. They were sacrificed when their masters died so that they could accompany them on their journey into the other world. But in the field of musical instruments the dog was more connected with calendar festivals than with journeying into the other world. Nowadays the instrument is only played on 24th June during the annual festivities commemorating the day of John the Baptist. This extract from the original photograph shows that the *teponaztli*-player sits on the steps in front of the church doorway.   V.T.M.

Illustration 58

Cenobio López de Juchitlán and Two of his Accompanists · Isthmus of Tehuantepec

Photograph by Yáñez

Before we can understand this illustration and the significance of the small group of musicians consisting of Cenobio Lopez and his two accompanists, the following explanation is necessary. López is blowing a vertical flute made from bamboo cane with five finger-holes. The young man on the left of the picture is beating a drum of the old Spanish type, which is resting horizontally on his knees. A boy barely thirteen years old on the right of the picture has a turtle shell about 30 cm long hanging on a strap round his neck and is using two branches from a deer's antler as drumsticks. The creator and leader of this group was Cenobio López himself, "blind Cenobio", who not only kept old melodies in his memory and handed them down, but also composed new pieces with a special flavour of their own owing to the insertion of cadence forms obviously derived from Spanish music. In spite of the remoteness of this area, the native Indian music has disappeared almost entirely and has been replaced by the music of the Spanish conquerors. During the four centuries of Spanish rule the indigenous melodies and rhythms and the old traditional instruments were forced into the background and Iberian music was introduced. Both types became amalgamated and adapted to each other and so, in the end, a new and definitely *mestizo* form of music came into existence.   V.T.M.

118

56

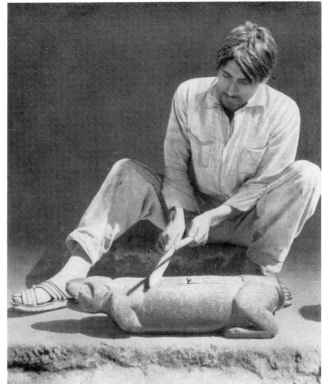

57

58

Illustration 59

Three Musicians with a Small Drum, Tlalpanhuéhuetl and Chirimía

San Juan Teotihuacan, Mexico

Photograph by Don Leonard

At the same time as the Aztecs and before them there were other ancient civilisations who had reached an extremely high level of cultural development and whose knowledge and skill in agriculture, pottery, painting, architecture, astronomy, music, poetry and dancing had been taken over by the Aztecs. Although Tula, the capital city of the Toltecs, and also Teotihuacan had been destroyed long before the discovery of America, many cultural remains have survived from that period of brilliance that was obliterated by the Spanish *Conquista*. These include a few musical

instruments and remnants of an ancient costume. This form of clothing is only worn by the present Indian population of Teotihuacan on the patronal saints' days, the most important being San Juan (John the Baptist, commemorated on 24th June), after whom the home of these three musicians was named. It is the day of the summer solstice, which the natives introduced into their new religion in order to keep the old sun cult alive. Of course, the sun was the supreme deity of the agrarian peoples.

For these festivities the musicians accompanying the acts of worship are dressed in almost the same way as those described by Muñoz Camargo in his "History of Tlaxcala". "They take out the appropriate emblems of rank, insignia and costumes with lavish feather decoration, also their clothing with all its rich and strange adornments. They fasten jewels of gold and precious stones on the joints of their arms and hands and wear hoops of fine gold on their arms and the calves of their legs and little gold bells on their ankles." There is no longer any glitter of gold to be seen, but they try to preserve the priestly dignity of the old musicians who were famed as teachers of music and dancing and the art of poetry in the *cuicalli* ("House of Song") and they go on wearing the costumes of their professional predecessors, as shown in the old codices. The same thing applies, in the case of the present-day musical instruments, some of them being survivals from the pre-Spanish period and others degenerated versions of the types imported by the Spaniards. The middle instrument standing on the ground is the *tlalpanhuéhuetl*, a vertical drum with one membrane. It has undergone no changes either in the resonance system, membrane or mode of tuning. When the skin loses its tautness because of the cold, damp night air, they hold the instrument to the fire or put a burning torch of resinous stone pine into the resonator from underneath and so the inside of the drum often becomes blackened with smoke. Warming makes the skin taut and it acquires a clearer sound. The ancient rhythms must have been very lively and varied since, as can be seen in the codices, this instrument was beaten with the fingers. In recent times it has been played with clenched fists or with large drumsticks covered with leather (text picture).

The *teponaztli* has been replaced here by a drum of European design. Although it has gained in rhythmic brilliance and mobility, it has lost some of the characteristic colouring peculiar to the pre-Spanish instrument. The marimba-like timbre of the *teponaztli* is undoubtedly much better adjusted to that of the *huéhuetl* than the shrill sound of the small European drum. The *chirimía*, which replaces the old beaked flute of fired clay with four finger-holes, differs in various respects from the early types. It has been reduced in length, but the diameter of the tube has increased, so this wind instrument has become difficult to play and the player is obliged to bind his abdomen in order to avoid a hernia. Musical changes are evident from the six finger-holes and the use of diatonic scales in place of the old pentatonic system. But a noble cultural heritage has at least been preserved in the form of these groups of musicians, hybrid though they may appear, who have managed to survive here and there in the various native settlements.

V.T.M.

59

Illustrations 60 to 62

Dance and Sun Ceremony of the "Voladores" (Flying Game), Accompanied by a One-Handed Flute and Hand Drum

Pahuatlan, Puebla, Mexico

Photographs by Bodil Christensen (Illusts. 60 and 62) and Luís Márquez (Illust. 61)

The dancing game of the "Voladores", which has survived up to the present time with only slight modifications, probably gives us one of the most striking glimpses into the ancient civilisation of Mexico. In modern Guatemala these dancers are called "Giradores" (revolving dancers). This custom is supposed to be a visual representation of the sun's course, as described in detail in the ancient myths collected by 16th-century chroniclers from the accounts of survivors from the city of Tenochtitlan. When the sun appears daily on the horizon, he is accompanied by numerous warriors who have fallen in battle. They bear the golden chair of the sun god Tonatiuh and, with this burden on their shoulders, they rise up to the zenith. On reaching the highest point at noon, they hand over the chair to the "female warriors" — women who have died in their first confinement or have caught an enemy warrior and so are classed as heroines. The women accompany the sun until he sets, dancing as they go, while the men climb down to the earth with whirling movements in the form of humming birds, butterflies or eagles, according to the season. In this myth the denizens of the underworld take possession of the golden chair as dusk begins to fall and they escort the sun back again to the point from which he rises.

The unique performance of the "Voladores" thus represents an old sun ceremony in the form of a dance. In all probability it was held at the time of the seasonal festivals and also in a special ceremonial form whenever the 52-year

cycle came to an end and a new time reckoning began. In the ancient Mexican civilisation every detail of this ceremonial act was of significance — the planting and tending of the tree serving as the axis for their rising and falling movements, which marked the beginning, the number of "Voladores", their costume and the greeting which each of the participants had to send out to the four corners of heaven from the top of the mast. The date of this festival in the Sierra de Puebla and in Veracruz often falls on 24th June, which marks the beginning of summer and the day of John the Baptist. In Pahuatlan six "Voladores" take part, in Papantla four and in Guatemala two. There are also instances of the dance being performed in Nicaragua and Brazil.

Illustration 60 shows the "Voladores" shortly before their downward flight. One of them is standing on the highest point of the giant tree trunk and bowing and sending out his supplications to the four corners of heaven with his right hand raised. Illustration 61 shows the climax of the whole event. The participants are floating down to earth, head downwards and circling round the mast on cords. During their flight the "Voladores" play on a one-handed flute and beat out the appropriate rhythm on a small hand drum (Illust. 62). The instruments used to-day are undoubtedly of Spanish origin. The small drum, 18 to 20 cm in diameter and 12 to 15 cm high, is fitted with two tightly stretched membranes and is fastened to the player's left hand with a cord. Simultaneously he is holding in the same hand a one-handed cane flute with three finger-holes (text picture). While the "Voladores" are whirling from the top of the giant mast, the men assembled down below (in some regions of the Mexican state of Veracruz) dance round the mast, shaking their *sonajas*, rattles made from calabashes. From sound recordings made in Huehuetlilla in the Sierra Norte de Puebla, Kurt Reinhard (701, p. 59 ff.) has made a study of the music for the "Juego del Volador".

The tradition of this flying game, which appears to be confined essentially to the ancient folk tribe of the Totonacs, can be traced very far back, and there are hints of it in the Sun Dance of the Prairie Indians. In the Stendahl Collection in Hollywood a terra-cotta object 35 cm high from the Mexican state of Nayarit (Ixtlan del Rio region) and dating from the pre-Cortesian era illustrates the flying game. It takes the form of a group of clay figures modelled on a round pottery disc. A mast is standing in the centre of a square surrounded by houses. A "Volador" is balancing on it and other dancers can be seen squatting on the ground round it. A similar illustration appears among the pictures in the Porfirio Díaz Codex.

V.T.M.

60

61

62

Illustration 63

Quetzal Dance · Huaxtecs · Cuietzala, Puebla, Mexico

Photograph by Luís Márquez

This is a Huaxtec dance common in the states of Puebla, Hidalgo and Veracruz, where it is known by the following names: Dance of the Sun's Gleam, Dance of the Quetzals (sacred birds of the Aztecs), Dance of the Cuetzalines, Lacas and Aras. In the Huaxtec language this dance is called *comelagatoazte*. It is shown pictorially in the Selden II Codex and so dates back to the pre-Spanish era. The performers are dressed in a kind of smock buttoned up to the neck and covered with geometrical figures, three-quarter length trousers trimmed with fringes in a different colour, a small apron dipping to a point at the front, a cloak worn over the shoulders — all in red and embroidered with large and small glass beads and spangles — and a conical pasteboard cap covered with linen and with a disc made up of thin rods and coloured ribbons at its apex. The rods are stuck in a small wooden disc decorated with a cross and are decked at the end with ribbons or tufts of feathers. This gigantic headdress is fastened on the head with a ribbon tied under the chin. In one hand the dancers carry rattles adorned with bright feathers and in the other small sun wheels similar to those on the headdress. Everyone taking part in this colourful scene represents a quetzal with an enormous feather ornament. Pictorial evidence shows that a magnificent train made of large pheasant feathers was worn in the early days.

Choreographically speaking, this dance is based on gracefully elegant and even majestic movements and side turns. The dancers take little jumps, raising one leg at a sharp angle while the rest of the body remains almost motionless. The groups generally consist of twelve or occasionally even sixteen dancers. The dance begins in front of the church building with a greeting to the Christian church. When they have taken up their positions, the dancers make a cross on the ground with the tip of their right foot. Thereupon the dance proper gets under way with all its multiplicity of figures. After it ends, the cloaks are taken off and the small suns they have been holding in their hands are put down at a certain place. Now they turn to the *girador*, a kind of revolving device. It is shaped like a cross with equal arms, revolving horizontally on its axis. All the participants have taken up their position facing the same way and, swinging up on the wooden cross, they set it whirling giddily round, until a bright glittering ball appears like the sun itself on the spectator's retina. Sometimes four such devices are used simultaneously. If there is only one *girador*, the remaining dancers move in time to the sound of their rattles and follow the rhythm of the musicians with their flutes and drums and the melodies prescribed for the individual figures.

The significance of this dance ceremony can be summed up as follows: This is a ritual dance in honour of the sun, which is performed by dancers disguised as quetzals, lacas or aras. Its theoretical basis is as follows:

1. All birds which have given their name to the dance are related to the sun or to the sun god.

2. The headdress of the dancers, which originally only represented the bird's feathered crest, nowadays symbolises the sun and, like light, contains all the colours of the rainbow.

3. The sceptre they hold in their hands is also a copy of the sun.

4. The day on which the dance game takes place, 24th June, commemorates John the Baptist and is for all the peoples in the northern hemisphere the point at which the sun runs its longest course.

5. The area in which the dance is still performed, i.e., the three Huaxtec states of Hidalgo, Puebla and Veracruz as far down as Nicaragua, corresponds to the area where sun worship is practised. This is the same region where the game of the "Voladores", also linked with the sun cult, is indigenous.

6. The acrobatics performed at the end of the dance, which are not altogether safe, give the idea of a large revolving sun in vivid colours.   V.T.M.

63

Illustration 64

Dance of the "Concheros" · Mexico

Photograph by Raul Estrada Discua

This dance owes its name to the instrument played by the dancers. It is made from a *concha* (shell) or an armadillo's carapace, and its bulging shape provides a very suitable resonator base for a plucked instrument of the mandoline type. A flat wooden cover with a round sound hole is attached to the animal's shell with resin. The instrument has a fret-board and five strings. The costume of these musicians ranges from very simple and plain outfits to the aristocratic-looking *tlatoani*, consisting of a splendid headdress decked with ostrich feathers, a collar or stomacher, a belt widening towards the front, sandals or *huaraches* with thick soles, also a regal mantle. Everything is embroidered with coloured spangles. This particular dance and the instrument too are to be found all over the centre of the country. Here we find names like the "Dance of the Concheros of Great Tenochtitlan", "Dance of the Great Conquest of Queretaro" or in Tlaxcala "Concheros of Death". These dances are performed as a central feature of the festivities at the beginning of the seasons. They are also danced in the course of rites dedicated to the "Four Winds", in which both Catholic Masses for the dead and heathen wakes are celebrated. This type is called "Concheros de los Cuatro Vientos". The origin of the dance goes back to the 16th century — in fact, to 25th July 1522, the day of St. James the Apostle, when a famous battle was fought between the Otomi and Spaniards on the one side and the Chichimecs on the other on the Hill of Sangremal in the Queretaro ravine. There the Chichimecs were defeated and accepted the new religion. Women and children can take part in the "Dance of the Concheros". An old man, an old woman, death and the devil appear as leaders, jesters or figures of fun. The people taking part in these ritual festivals form a kind of military organisation, including all ranks from the ordinary soldier to the general and also leaders of the conquest expeditions, ensigns, first and second "concheros" and trumpeters. They call themselves "Conquistadores" (Conquerors). The members of this organisation pledge themselves to belong to it for a definite period or perhaps throughout their lifetime in order to fulfil a vow taken during some moment of danger. V.T.M.

Illustration 65

Dance of the "Sonajeros" · Tuxpan, Jalisco, Mexico

Photograph by Luís Márquez

The performers of this dance are now called "Sonajeros" after the instrument that they hold in their hands. In the pre-Spanish era this rattle stick was called a *chicahuaztli* and was a symbol pertaining to the god of seed-time, "Our Lord, the Flayed One", Xipe-to-tec (Totec-chicahua). He was connected with the gods of fertility. Several round metal discs are incorporated in this artistically carved angular wooden stick and these cause a deafening noise when the instrument is shaken or hit. During the dancing wild cries and howls are uttered from time to time and the people stamp violently on the ground. In short, this is a vigorous masculine dance. It dates from the pre-Spanish period and is performed during the second month of the Aztec calendar (*tlacaxipehualiztli* — from 22nd February to 13th March), which precedes the start of spring. It is meant to shake the earth into activity and life and prepare for its fertilisation. The dancers wear everyday clothing in the Spanish style: knee breeches in a dark colour, open at the gusset and embroidered down below, a white shirt decorated with multicoloured oval shapes, the typical wide hat of the Jalisco people, made of coarse straw, a wide red belt or sash, a neckerchief, the inevitable stout shoes *(huaraches)* with their thick soles — and, of course, they carry a sounding stick, hence the name "Sonajeros". V.T.M.

64

65

Illustration 66

Martín Ruíz, Drummer of the Mariachi · Tlapehuala, Guerrero, Mexico

Photograph by Luís Márquez

Hispano-European instruments were introduced to Mexico by Hernando Cortés. In Cuba, shortly before his expedition to the coasts of Yucatan and Tabasco, the conqueror selected the soldiers who were to accompany him and also assigned musicians to join them. The latter were present at the invasion and subjugation of the mighty Tenochtitlan and also took part in the expedition to Hibueras (Honduras). So there has been military-type music in Mexico from those days, based on trumpets, transverse flutes (fifes), shawms and drums of the same type as those used by the Spanish troops in Flanders or the ones which travelled with the Emperor Charles V on his Italian campaigns. In the 16th, 17th and 18th century trumpets and kettle-drums were heard in Mexico when official proclamations were being issued and during the celebrations in connection with the church banner procession held on 13th August every year to commemorate the fall of the city. The *Conquistadores* certainly brought military musicians with them in the 16th century. For example, a drummer or drum-major accompanied Pánfilo de Narváez and Cristóbal de Tapia, and Hernando Cortés took several musicians along with him on his expedition to Nicaragua. They included five shawm-blowers, four of whom perished. It is also said that Diego Martín, a soldier nicknamed "Canillas" and Benito Bejel went with him. They had already served as drummers with the armies in Italy and later in Mexico. As trumpeters he brought Sebastián Rodríguez and Cristóbal Barrera. Others who followed him were Cristóbal Rodríguez Dávalos, a "very red-haired" soldier called Porras, the great musician Alfonso Morón and, above all, "Ortiz the Musician", who played the guitar, viola and lute and was also a dancing master. As regards the European musical instruments used in "New Spain" during the three centuries of Spanish rule, chroniclers mention the following: the *guitarra de arco, violín, rabel, vihuela, arpa, salterio, orlo, dulzaina, bajón, órgano, corneta* and *laúd*. It is also a known fact that a nun without private means would be admitted to a convent if she had a good voice or could play the clavichord, organ or violin. By order of the king, church choirs and orchestras were reduced during the period of Spanish rule in Mexico because the number of singers and musicians playing the multiplicity of instruments then in use was thought to be unnecessarily large.

The lansquenet drum, which replaced the *teponaztli*, retained the drum roll used in war marching and military parades. In Teotihuacan, Tlaxcala, Cholula, Guerrero, Tehuantepec, Oaxaca and Chiapas the drum was also beaten for religious music. It also gradually replaced the turtle shell, which was dedicated to the rites of Mother Earth, the mother of the gods, although the drum and turtle shell occasionally occur together, for example, in the Cenobio López group from Tehuantepec (Illust. 58). In this way the old lansquenet drum was handed down to us via the 19th century. Martín Ruíz, illustrated here, offers an interesting example. He not only retained the military drum of the 16th century in its pure, unadulterated form, but undoubtedly preserved a good number of old Spanish rhythms. With his deep-sounding drum that native musician accompanies the tales of the "Victorious St. Augustine", the tango "La Tortolita" and the Chilean Cuecas originating from the gold-diggers who came from Valparaiso around the middle of last century and merely touched Acapulco as they went on their way to California. The beating technique used by Martín Ruíz is worth describing here. He plays with two kinds of drumsticks. One is of the usual type and is made from hard wood. The other is short and broad and is padded with chamois leather. But the most interesting thing of all is to hear him at work and observe how he changes the drumsticks around and beats them both on the membrane and the rim to Hispano-Castilian rhythms based on $^5/_8$ or $^5/_4$ time.   V.T.M.

129

Illustration 67

Old Peruvian Musical Instruments (Aerophones)

American Museum of Natural History, New York, Neg. No. 38,827

Curious to relate, among the excavation finds made in the south of Central America and in South America the *teponaztli* and the plain and triple and quadruple flutes with a beaked mouthpiece are completely absent, although they frequently occur in the north of Central America. On the other hand, in the Chibcha area, in Tumaco (Colombia), which borders on Esmeraldas (Ecuador), many gold and ceramic objects and musical instruments have been discovered, bearing unmistakable characteristics of the Mayan civilisation. Although no actual ducted whistles have so far come to light, the whistling jars or vessel flutes found sometimes have whistle mouthpieces and a few of them produce diatonic and others chromatic scales. These are possibly objects coming from Mayan colonisers or from fugitives. As regards the Andean civilisations, the oldest named one, the Chavin culture (existing according to Trimborn back in the 8th century B.C.), had evolved advanced artistic forms. We must bear in mind that the prehistoric objects discovered belong to a wide variety of periods and that the Empire of the Inca dynasty was a late development, not founded until the 14th/15th century, and did not add anything new to the old civilisations preceding it

from an economic and artisan point of view. In Peru and Bolivia, which, together with Ecuador and the north of Chile, formed part of the *tiwantansuyo*, or Inca Empire, the traditional instruments include the *tinya*, a hand drum with membranes, drums similar to the Aztec *huéhuetl* with only one membrane, kettle-drums made of clay, whistling jars or vessel flutes (ocarinas) made of shells, clay or gourds, the notched flute known as the *quena*, also pan-pipes, which are thousands of years old. Interest has been shown in the artistic *silbadores* and also the beautiful flutes and trumpets from the Nazca civilisation and the numerous clay trumpets from the north coast of Peru, which was inhabited by the warlike Mochica, contemporaries of the Aztecs. In Cajamarca (Peru) and Cuenca (Ecuador) long cane trumpets are still in use. These are referred to as the *clarín* or *bocina* and are sometimes up to 2 m long. These instruments are attributed to the Inca and make a terrifying sound. They are normally played in pairs, being blown alternately in most cases. A related kind is to be found among the Araucanians in Chile under the name of *trutruka*. It too is played in pairs or groups.   S.M. Illustration 67 shows a collection of old Peruvian instruments from the American Museum of Natural History, New York. The wind instrument in the top left-hand corner is an endblown bone whistle with three finger-holes, now no longer played in Peru. But it has been found in numerous tombs on the coast and in the neighbourhood of Lima. The instrument illustrated here comes from Pachacamac (Lima) and is typical of that region. Beside it comes a *quena* with six finger-holes, then a whistling jar, or vessel flute, with four finger-holes, made from the fruit of a bottle gourd. This latter instrument belongs to the *canella* type (579, p. 286). Underneath these instruments there is a clay figure representing the player of a set of pan-pipes

with three pipes. Alongside it we see a bone pipe adorned with a bird carving. In the middle of the picture there is a set of bamboo pan-pipes with eight pipes in a row securely fastened to a bamboo rod running across them. On the right is a plain trumpet with a bent tube made from fired clay. This instrument is typical of the Colima region. The mouthpiece is also modelled out of clay. The slightly conical bell-mouth is often decorated with an animal's head, preference being given to the jaguar, as in the text picture. The instrument in the text picture is, in fact, a clay trumpet in two colours from Mochica dating back to the 4th century A.D. and exhibited in the Museo Nacional de Antropología in Lima. The lovely wooden vertical flute on the extreme right of the picture is decorated with a human figure and comes from our own period. We are struck by the fact that aerophones predominate among the instruments of old Peru and chordophones are completely absent.   P.C.

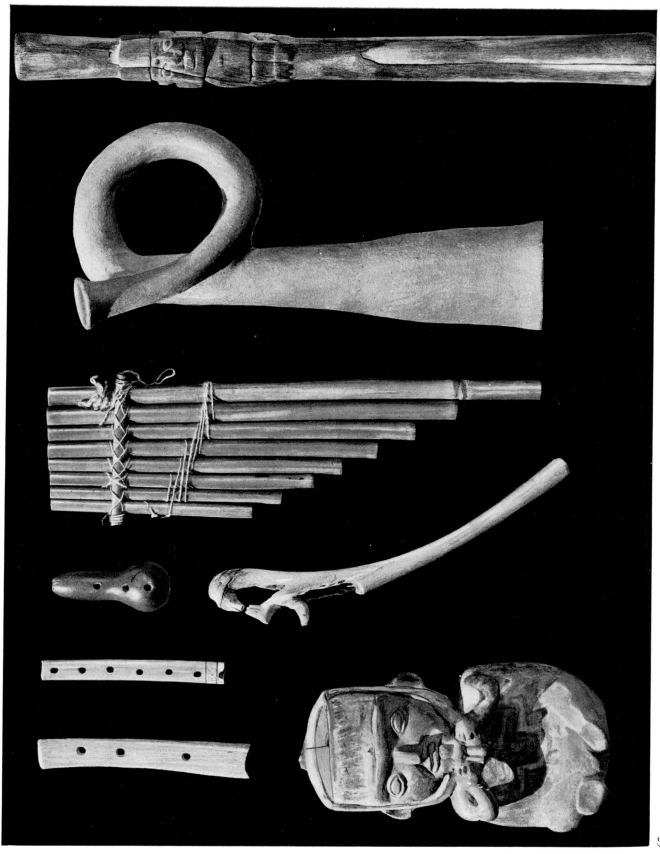

Illustration 68

Notched Flute Player at the Festival of St. Peter · Tiahuanaco, Bolivia

Photograph by Vicente T. Mendoza

This is an interesting illustration as it shows that notched flutes *(quenas)* do not only appear as solo instruments, but are also played in groups on certain occasions. Our photograph shows two *quena*-players performing together during the festival of St. Peter in Tiahuanaco. Note the costumes worn by the musicians with their large "wings" and striking hats with a high hooped device. V.T.M.

Illustration 69

Ayarachi, Dance of the Condors, Accompanied by Pan-Pipes and Big Drums · Cuzco, Peru

Swiss-Photo, Lima

Two mighty drum beats and a solemn, old-fashioned melody played on large pan-pipes are suddenly heard and a group of dancers appears as if by magic. They wear a huge feathered headdress and are draped in black and white cloaks. With the dignity of priests they stride with measured steps from one side to the other, playing the syrinx and beating big drums. This sombre music, with its note of wistful, melancholy longing, seems to send out a cloud obscuring the sun's light, and the procession of people seem about to be engaged in secret rites expressing both love and fear for their primitive deity Pachamama, Mother Earth — referred to as *toci* ("Old Grandmother") by the Aztecs and also present in rather similar forms among the Indians of North America.
Paratia or Parajj-tianan ("Dwelling-place of the Rain") is a place situated on the peaks of the Andes and it has remained in virtual isolation from before the days of the Inca up to the present time. We cannot say whether this is because of its geographical position or its harsh climate or the strong individuality of its inhabitants. High peaks, steep mountain slopes and eternal snows surround those hidden wastes like insurmountable bastions, with the Urpaccocheros or Alpaqueros sheltering in their midst. They are the remnants of a very ancient civilisation, as is evident from the woven fabrics and textiles and the music that has been handed down to us. Arturo Vizcarra de Lampas writes of this community as follows: "It was only logical that they should worship the god of the peaks in those surroundings and identify themselves with him. And so the Dance of the Condor came into existence — subsequently called the *ayarachi* because of its association with funerals. The *ayarachi* music is an expression of life and of man's ties with the earth. It is marked by a great wealth of different motifs and a very varied repertoire. This harmonious music with its well marked rhythm and slow movements is performed on pan-pipes in three different sizes which produce a harmony based on fifths and octaves. The accompaniment is provided by big drums. Twelve dignified dancers playing twelve sets of loudly sounding pan-pipes and twelve big drums with a muffled thunderous beat make the *ayarachi* a solemn, virile and deafening form of music." V.T.M.

69

68

133

Illustration 70

Pan-Pipe Players with Big Drums · La Paz, Bolivia

Photograph by Z. Jiménez

The Aymaran living in Bolivia and Peru occupy a large part of the Titicaca basin. Great musical awareness and a preference for instrumental combinations are highly typical of these people. Apart from the notched flute made from cane and held almost vertically and possessing five or six finger-holes, the main musical instrument is the pan-pipe, consisting of one or even two rows of stopped tubes. We often come across pan-pipe ensembles here, involving up to forty players. The instruments are of different sizes in order to provide the entire compass needed for the melody.

Our illustration shows four pan-pipe players simultaneously beating big drums. The first pipe from the left is the shortest and the two on the right are the longest, the second from the left being of medium size. The individual instruments are tuned to one another. For this purpose they have tuning devices for altering the tube length — pegs that can be stuck into the pipe openings from underneath. This appliance can be clearly seen on the longest tube, which comes on the second set of pipes from the right. The player sometimes pours sand or water into the bamboo canes, closed below by the septum, in order to raise the tone. Three or four sizes of these instruments are generally used. They are blown in pairs to form the melody and sound together in pure octaves or fifths. The large instruments, called *sicuris*, may be up to 80 cm long. The smaller instruments are termed the *ayarachi*, *morenos* and *twaillos*. If only a few pan-pipe players have assembled, each of them uses two instruments simultaneously, one of them being tuned a fifth lower than the other. The music of these ensembles is thus a simple type of organum. The melody is presented in parallel octaves or fifths.

The cylindrical tube drums of the Aymaran are strikingly large in diameter and have skin stretched over them from both sides. Only the front membrane of the drum, which is hung over the shoulder on a strap, is beaten. A leather strap is stretched over the rear one and short rods are attached to it. When the drum is beaten, these rods produce a rattling noise on the rear membrane.

As a stringed instrument the Aymaran often use small mandolines to accompany their songs. They have a bulging shape because they are made from the dried carapace of the armadillo. These are obviously copies of instruments imported from Spain.

The text picture shows an Aymaran singer and a musician who is blowing a *quena* and is wearing a high flower hat decorated with mirrors. He also wears a grass fibre skirt. All these symbols of fertility form part of the spring rites connected with sowing.   P. C.

Illustration 71

Women's Dance · La Paz, Bolivia

Photograph by Corderoy

The basic form of this dance for women is the quadrille in which dancers change places. According to Curt Sachs (721, French edition, p. 113), these dances are based on primitive models in which the turning movements act as a kind of fertility spell. Incidentally, these dances for four young girls in a quadrille form, such as we find in Bolivia, occur in a similar version in Indonesia, especially in Sumatra. A particularly interesting feature of these dances is the changing of places among the dancers, which evidently symbolises plaiting and weaving.   P. C.

70

71

135

Illustration 72

Diablada Dancers · La Paz, Bolivia

Photograph by Corderoy

Among the Aymaran and also among other Indian tribes in Bolivia and Peru there are a great many dances that are performed in different ways in the different places. An opportunity is provided for all kinds of dances by most of the church festivals, days of personal celebration, for example, weddings or the bringing in of the harvest, the mating season and shearing of the llamas and, last but not least, the ceremonies connected with the dead. In the masked dance, demons are presented in visible — often animal — form. The terrifying masks worn by persons portraying the devil during the dancing festivals are possibly of Spanish origin. The strange headdress of the *diablada* dancer illustrated here is made up of spirally coiling horns and leaves, blossoms and birds with outstretched wings.

P.C.

Illustration 73

Masked Dance · La Paz, Bolivia

Photograph by Linares

Dances with animal masks are as a rule the prerogative of men. They are often disguised as women and wear a mask with bison horns. These dances are based on a variety of ideas. The one shown here is predominant among the agricultural peoples and bears no reference either to hunting or stock-rearing. Certain animals are endowed with magic powers. Among these the Indians include the bison, which can bring both rain and fine weather.　　P.C.

Illustration 74

Sun Dance · La Paz, Bolivia

Photograph by Corderoy

The performers of the Sun Dance wear a hat with gigantic feathers and their clothing is decorated with sun emblems. They turn as they dance round their own axis and shake rattles of the *maracas* type. But the circle of dancers as a whole turns in a clockwise direction. This is the typical form of the Sun Dance. By imitating the sun's movement the men try to guarantee its regular motion, which is necessary for growth and life.

The myth of the bird symbolising the sun and the rain fertilising the earth forms the basis of a dance performed in Calapuja, a small place in the Puna region in the centre of Indian Peru. It is called *tika tikas* ("Flower of Flowers") (text picture). The dancers wear conical tufts of feathers on their heads and clothing made from large leaves. Their great leaps and strides and all their movements, in fact, are alive with radiant joy. In the middle of the group a dancer dressed as a bird receives slight bows from the other dancers. Each one of them carries a small drum *(unucaja)*, the membrane of which is moistened with water from time to time "so that it will sound better". A group of pan-pipes and a big drum accompany each figure with a persistent rhythm. The legend recorded at the same place by Pablo Dazo reports that the majestic *inquinito*, a proud and mysterious bird with gleaming plumage, made its appearance one day. In a ravine near the township, where there is an abundance of wild plants called *tikatikas*, it was taken unawares by a thunderstorm. The magic bird became entangled in the thorny branches of the *tikatikas*, which it changed into brilliant colours with its plumage. The people then realised that this was a divine being and began to dance round the bird in a circle and venerate it "with songs of admiration, joy and triumph".　　V.T.M.

136

72

73

74

137

Illustration 75

Sun Dance · Huyala, Peru

Photograph by Vicente T. Mendoza

The *inti tussoc* ("Sun Dance") is performed after plants, food and drinks have been presented as offerings to the sun god, his consort the moon goddess and the stars for the benefits of light and warmth that they have conferred on man. According to José Carpio Cabrera de Huayta, this dance is also called the *chullche*, because the participants wear gaiters with bells of different sizes on the calves of their legs and these ring out as they stride along in time to the music. The dancers' heads are covered with white linen cut out in the shape of rays. The person representing the sun wears a brass diadem and a black velvet jacket with ribbons and wide tulle sleeves and he also has a smiling mask. The two other performers, symbolising the moon and the stars, are masked as well. Everyone taking part has a staff in his right hand with an imitation of the sun, moon or a star attached to the tip. This is a ritual dance. The three performers dance in line with measured steps and lift their feet and stamp vigorously on the ground so that the little bells ring out. At a certain point in the ceremony they leave the centre of the dance area and turn to the four corners, where they then dance in a livelier manner. The dancers are accompanied by a *quena* and also by a large and a small drum. The musicians are not in costume. They follow the dancers as they perform the various figures. As a rule, the natives perform this dance on Corpus Christi Day and in exceptional cases (for example, in Lampa) on 8th December too.   V.T.M.

Illustration 76

The Ribbon Dance · Canteria, Peru

Photograph by Vicente T. Mendoza

This dance was performed in a bare, dusty field near Canteria. No rain had fallen there for years and all the inhabitants of the township had assembled for a lively and very ostentatious dance consecrating the Andean spring. This is undoubtedly a rustic fertility rite, a "tribute to the earth" *(ayriway)* — an all-embracing ceremony celebrating the the people's renewal of faith and hope. To the sound of several transverse cane flutes *(pinquillos* or *pinkullos)*, accompanied by the beating of drums *(tinya* or *curaj tinya)*, a great crowd of dancers noisily went into the field. Those who did not have special costumes appeared in their holiday finery with the striking *huarakas* or the slings pertaining to the ceremony. The group were led by a *macho* (steer), a youth who was all dressed up and was carrying a *llipi*, a pole decorated with fruits and bright ribbons and covered with blue paper. The blue colour symbolises the water or the small lake where the *ajoyas*, aquatic birds with black plumage, have their nests. They provide the natives with a part of their livelihood and "protect the llamas". Standing beside the *macho* was the sacred llama, laden with sacrificial offerings of silver as a token of abundance and led by an old woman, symbolising the *pachamama*. Jumping up all round it were its traditional enemies or "opponents"—the cunning wild cat *(oscollo)*, the gigantic, but artless black bear *(uku uku)* and the majestic condor. But the llama was protected from its enemies by the people and by the jesters *(chunchos)*. In the meantime, comical hybrid beings, half animal and half *chuncho*, presented in admirable pantomime, took it in turn to appear on the fringe of the dance. Only the llama and the condor, i.e., the earth and the sun, preserved their accustomed dignity in the midst of this tumultuous carnival. While all this was going on, the plaiting of the ribbons fluttering from the top of the *llipi* was begun. The dancers started in pairs, each taking a ribbon, and proceeded to plait a waving multicoloured cord and then let it go again. The dancing was always accompanied by music.
In these ceremonies we are inevitably reminded of the ancient May dance of fertility from Asia and Europe and also of the Mayan *chohom* dances. The Ribbon Dance described by Landa and Clavigero is similar too, and so are the joyous *xocotl huetzi* of the Aztecs, the Dance of the "Voladores" still performed in Mexico at the present time, and the Sun Dance of the Prairie Indians.   V.T.M.

138

75

76

Illustrations 77 and 78

"Wiffalas" Dance · Asillo, Peru

Photographs by Vicente T. Mendoza

In the picturesque township of Asillo, which possesses one of the most impressive churches in the country — to-day, of course, it stands in ruins — the ancient *Wiffalas* dance is still kept alive. This is obviously a fertility dance of the alpaca shepherds and is made up of three parts: *Passacaglia, Guerra* (War) and Carnival. In the first part the dancers

arrive on the scene, in the second the men are ritually whipped by the women and in the third an abundance of lively figures and scenes of joy are offered to the spectator. During the whipping operation in the middle portion of the *Wiffalas* the women strike the ankles of the men with all their might, but never stop dancing. This often goes on until the ground is bespattered with blood. The male and female dancers are tirelessly urged on by four *quena*-players and four drummers (text picture).

A similar dance, called the *wappululo*, is performed in Lampa. A large crowd of young men and women take part. Their dance outfit consists of black *olleras* trimmed with silk ribbons in different colour combinations — red and white, light blue and white, or green and white — and garish linen smock-like garments. On their heads they wear cloth caps and round their shoulders an *illijlla*, a cloak woven from coloured wool. In their hands they hold *huaracas* made up of bright, gaily coloured remnants of material. The men are dressed in linen trousers and shirts and straw hats and carry decorated whips called *huichihuichi* in their right hands. Both men and women have silk ribbons and serpentine stones hanging round their necks as ornaments. They dance to the beat of brilliant music produced by several *pinquillos* and the *machu quenas* (= big *quenas*), sometimes also by *tok'oros* (recorder-type flutes made of wood and of European origin). This is a group dance for couples arranged in various ways and is basically confined to the Carnival period. Up to four hundred couples take part and this can be regarded as a proof of its deep roots in the past. The individual dance figures vary and often have quite a theatrical effect, irrespective of whether they are danced in rows or in cross formation, entwining the *huaracas* or spinning "like tops", while the women sing a song of defiance. It is obvious that the *wappululo* of Lampa is an urban Carnival version of the old *Wiffalas*, which has survived in a remarkably unadulterated form in Asillo.   V.T.M.

140

77

78

141

Illustration 79

Paez Instrumental Ensemble · Caldenas, Tierradentro, Colombia

In Colombia there has been considerable mixing between the natives and immigrants, especially negroes. But there are still tribes who have preserved their Indian traditions, for example, the Kansa and Inga on the upper Putumayo, the Paez and Guambiano from Tierradentro, the Cuna and Goajira from the Atlantic coast and also a few groups in the Sierra Marta. These are partly descendants of the Chibcha, who had evolved an advanced civilisation between the cultural areas of the Maya and the Indians of the central Andes area before the Spaniards occupied Colombia in the 16th century. The oldest evidence of Chibcha music is provided by the gigantic stone figures of San Agustin, obviously depicting divine beings. One of the figures is blowing a flute, another a shell horn and a third a kind of anthropomorphic whistling jar.

The typical instrumental ensemble of the Paez musicians consists of three bamboo flutes about 60 cm long (one of them is actually slightly longer and serves as the bass instrument), a flat drum with two membranes, a set of pan-pipes of presumably Ecuadorian origin with sixteen pipes 3 to 10 cm long, a few rattles made from seed boxes and a big drum. In our illustration we can see a player with a triangle behind the flautists. In earlier centuries there were also a large conch shell *(fotuto)* blown like a trumpet and idiophones made from turtle shells. These, like the vertical flutes of bamboo cane, clay or bone, have fallen into disuse among the Indian tribes of Colombia. As a rule these flute groups play mainly in the market-place, choosing pieces of music reflecting a mainly European influence. But in the Carnival period they often play purely Indian tunes, with a beat that contrasts with the drum accompaniment. Pan-pipes often reinforce the flute melody at the upper octave. P. C.

Illustration 80

Inga Musicians · San Andres, Putumayo, Colombia

Apart from the transverse flute made of cane and the tubular drum, we also see two young girls with mouth organs and a musician blowing a cow's horn in this illustration. Trumpet-like wind instruments, like the shell trumpet of the cow's horn, are still called *fotutos* in Colombia. Together with flutes they were blown for dancing and ceremonies and also during war expeditions.

The term *chirimía* is used to-day in this region for groups of musicians with the following instruments: a big drum which beats out the basic rhythm, a small drum which serves to subdivide the rhythm and a flute which plays the melody. Every community has its instrumental ensemble. But, in addition, nearly every Indian in the area is able to play the flute. In place of the music of the Catholic church they have introduced various of their own old tunes into the Christian services of worship. P. C.

79

80

Illustration 81

Tucurima with a Vase-Shaped Wind Instrument · Upper Purus, Brazil

Photograph by Harald Schultz

Wind instruments made from fired clay were in widespread use in old Peru even before the Inca period (Nazca). The specimen illustrated here is in the form of a bulging vase that is side-blown through a small hole. Similar aerophones are also to be found among the Jivaro from the Montaña of Ecuador and the Saliva, belonging to the civilisation around the Caribbean. The latter use them for purposes other than ceremonies for the dead. On the upper Rio Negro

and among the Musquilo in Nicaragua it is usual to imitate the roar of the jaguar with this instrument. In Guyana and the Orinoco basin multi-spherical ceramic "trumpets" were also played. The origin of these vase-like wind instruments of fired clay within the Amazon area has not yet been properly established, nor have the limits of their region of distribution.

Among the Tucurima, as among other Indian tribes in South America, for example, the Caraya, Canella, Apinayé, Warrau and among the Carib, we actually find trumpets with a terminal mouthpiece too (text picture). They are made from different kinds of bamboo, also from Cecropia or Lagenaria branches, the pith of which is easy to remove. The bamboo cane is cut right through a knot and one then bores through the middle of the septum, or partition, occurring at that spot. The mouthpiece produced in this way provides a broad support for the blower's lips.

The Tucuriman instrument illustrated here (text picture) is wound round with red and black cotton threads. For the light rings they use golden grass specially cultivated for the purpose. An armadillo tail forms the conically curved bell-mouth. This illustration answers a query put by Izikowitz in 1935 (579, p. 219) regarding an armadillo tail in the Copenhagen collections which had given rise to some confusion. People were not clear whether it was a megaphone or a trumpet. In reality it is, as we can see here, the curved bell-mouth at the lower end of the trumpet tube.

P. C.

Illustration 82

Tucurima with Ducted Whistle · Upper Purus, Brazil

Photograph by Harald Schultz

The ducted whistle occurring in Central and South America only appears sporadically in the Amazon area. It is difficult to decide whether this instrument was imported from Europe or was already known to the Indian tribes

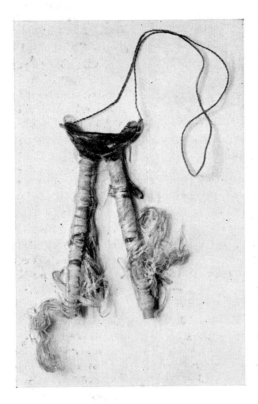

before America was discovered. Various excavation finds and other clues too lead us to conclude that the recorder-type flute occurring in America is possibly of pre-Columbian origin. Such instruments have, for example, been found among the Indian tribes on the Xingu when they were discovered and had had no contact whatsoever with Europeans. The Tucurima manufacture those vertical flutes from a piece of bamboo cane about 60 cm long. The sound opening ends immediately below a knot, the septum of which has been perforated. In Brazil these instruments nearly all have four finger-holes in the lower part of the cane. The labium is situated close to the blow-opening, which is stopped by a wax peg apart from a narrow slit running through the core. Through this slit the current of air is directed against the edge of the sound hole and forms a vibrating air sheet at the labium. In other parts of America we also find recorders made of clay or bone. Among the Cuna they are made from birds' bones and are used by the medicine men. They are played only once and are then strung on a kind of necklace. In the Gothenburg museum we can see a Cuna necklace of this type (region to the east of the Panama Canal) to which thirteen of these flutes are attached. In Yucatan and Colima recorders, or block flutes, made of clay and with four to six finger-holes have been unearthed.

The Uitoto in the north-west of the Amazon area use vertical flutes with two finger-holes and about 110 cm long and pan-pipes made from three bamboo canes, called *toriibakue*, also flutes and whistles whose mouthpiece is formed by the skull of a frog with black resin poured over it and with two small tubes wound round with bast emerging from it (text picture). This instrument, 19 cm long and exhibited in the Ethnological Museum in Munich (59-2-99), is blown by the Uitoto during the frog festival. In the same museum we can see a flute from the Desana (Tucano), who live along the Rio Macu-Parana. It is carved from the upper thigh bone of a deer with a band of fibre wound round it to which shimmering green beetle wings have been attached. The instrument is 19 cm long.   P.C.

146

Illustration 83

Tucuna with Bark Trumpet · Amazon (Upper "Solimões"), Brazil

Photograph by Harald Schultz

The Tucuna live scattered along the upper reaches of the Amazon, here called the Rio Solimões, in the frontier area between Peru, Brazil and Colombia. The puberty rites of the girls, connected with masked dances, are of particular importance in this tribe. During the festivities the Tucuna sing with falsetto voices and so softly that they can hardly be heard. Various kinds of wind instruments predominate here: small whistle- or trumpet-like instruments made from lianas; trumpets four to six metres long made from spirally coiled strips of bark; wooden megaphones six metres long through which they can speak or sing; bamboo trumpets; vertical flutes of bone and pan-pipes. In addition there are shell rattles and cylindrical tube drums with two painted membranes and zigzag cording.

In the illustration opposite a Tucuna is blowing a very long and slightly conical trumpet of coiled bark. This instrument is called a *buburé* in the native language. To prevent the long tube from breaking or sagging, it is attached to a stick, the end of which is rested on a tree stump. Among the Tucuna this instrument is blown at night for the puberty rites of young girls. As in other Amazon areas, women are not allowed to set eyes on the *buburé*. It is stored under water to keep it out of sight of the women and also to preserve the bark more effectively. The bark trumpet is also used among the scattered Tucuna communities as a signalling instrument for calling the members of the tribe to the festivals.

Among the Ipurina on the Rio Purus bark trumpets are blown at the so-called *kamutši* festival, described by Paul Ehrenreich (243, p. 70). The *kamutši* live in a lagoon known only to certain shamans. When it is time for the festival to be celebrated, one of them makes his way to the lake in question and fetches the magic trumpets made from the spirally coiled bark of the jutahy tree or flutes of taboca cane with a peg inserted to form a kind of tongue. The *kamutši* spirits are supposed to be present inside them. In the meantime the men have assembled in the forest some distance away from the village to receive the trumpets, of which there are fifteen to twenty, varying in length according to the tone. They move to and fro several times blowing a variety of tunes, each man laying his right elbow on the shoulder of the man in front. The trumpets are always pointed downwards, to the left. At each blast the whole throng bend their knees. The two leading trumpeters sound the note and blow their instrument briefly every now and then with wild gesticulations as they dance a few times up and down in front of and behind the head of the crowd.

In contrast to the instruments used among the Piaroa (Illust. 86), the Tucuna trumpet is made of rolled bark as far as the blow-hole. Bark trumpets of this type are to be found in various shapes, especially in alpine civilisations, but among other peoples too. In America their distribution area is confined essentially to the region of tropical forest around the Amazon. But it can also be found occasionally among certain Indians of the Algonkin linguistic family in North America and in this case is probably an instrument introduced from Europe. The bark trumpets occurring in America are usually blown in pairs, together with two large clarinets in Guyana and with two flutes on the Orinoco (Illust. 86).   P.C.

83

Illustration 84

Maquiritare Dance · High Parima (Sierra Parima), Venezuela

Photograph by Jean Fichter

The Maquiritare (better known as Yecuana) live along the High Parima and on the Rivers Merivari, Paraba and upper Mazaruni. When this photograph was taken in 1949 they had never seen a white man before. According to Alain Gheerbrandt (821, p. 67), the greatest feast of the Maquiritare is dedicated to the sun, the god and father of all the demi-gods in their mythology. It is at the same time the feast of the wild boar, which they regard as an ancestor. The dancers are attired in palm leaves and are decorated with flowers and chains of wild boar's teeth. They first of all dance in the antechamber of the tribal hut, whose walls are made of bark. The men then move to the village square in front of the hut. . . . The feast goes on for 72 hours. On the evening of the third day a fire is lit in the middle of the village square. The dancers move round along the edge of the shadow, while the Chief stands beside the fire quite motionless and sings the verses of the most sacred song in the Maquiritare tradition. This corresponds to the Book of Genesis in the Bible. The men sing every verse in chorus and then take up their positions in two parallel lines on either side of the flames, coming closer to them as they dance. They throw all their finery, their headdresses, rings and palm-leaf skirts in the fire. Then they trample out the glowing embers with their bare feet. The feast ends when the final spark is extinguished.

There has been some disagreement about the origin of the drum with two membranes which occurs in several areas of South America. Izikowitz refers to the idea supported by Erich Maria von Hornbostel and Curt Sachs, i.e., that this drum is pre-Columbian. Certainly the instrument illustrated here does have a cord running in a zigzag pattern, such as we also find in Europe. But, as we have mentioned before, these Indians never had any contact with Europeans up to the time when this photograph was taken. It is, of course, possible that this model reached them from the Caribbean coast.

The use of large sea shells as wind instruments was widespread in areas where such items were readily obtainable. But they were also blown in countries far away from the sea, e.g., in Tibet, in the heart of Asia. In America the use of shell trumpets extends over an area comprising Mexico, Central America and the Andes regions, extending as far as the Araucanians who live in southern Chile. As a result of trading, they also became introduced to central South America. They occur in the Orinoco basin, but there is no sign of them in the Amazon area (567, p. 228). Although these shells are frequently used for signalling in time of war, they were originally a religious instrument. In the Mochica civilisation of Peru, imitations were made of natural sea shells and so trumpets were produced from fired clay in a stylised shell shape. They are always equipped with a terminal mouthpiece.   P.C.

151

Illustration 85

Jaguar Ceremony of the Piaroa · Orinoco, Venezuela

Photograph by Alain Gheerbrandt and Jean Fichter

Along the Amazon and the upper Orinoco the individual tribes live in isolation in the huge primeval forests. Ethnically different peoples sometimes lived in the same region without unification or even any contact taking place. Some of these tribes were not discovered until a few decades ago and so they often retained their archaic musical traditions without being affected by any strong influence from outside. A remarkable tribe of this kind (probably identical with the ancient Ature) is the Piaroa, visited by Koch-Grünberg. Some of them still live on the unexplored tributaries to the right of the Orinoco.

This illustration reproduces part of the ceremony described in detail by Alain Gheerbrandt (821, p. 29). As he tells us, the festival month is marked, above all, by religious ceremonies. The tribal hut stands on one side of the square in the middle of the village, and on the other side there is a small hut that is strictly guarded — a secret hut which only the men are allowed to enter. It is used for storing the paraphernalia connected with worship, the palm and flower clothing, the conical caps of the priests, the stocks of *niopo* (vessels with a brown doping powder and curare) and the sacred musical instruments which play an important part in the religious and social system of the Piaroa. At certain hours of the morning and evening the "devil" — the fourth person from the right in the illustration — spreads out palm branches, closes the entrance to the sacred hut and enters the village square. After performing a few dance movements in mime and striking the ground with his cleft staff, symbolising a snake, he disappears. Then the real act of worship begins. The five masked figures, the "priests" of the tribe, emerge from the consecrated hut, slowly cross the square and turn to the main entrance of the large hut belonging to the tribe as a whole. Their faces are hidden behind fine palm fibres hanging down from their conical headdresses. Their whole body is concealed, except for one hand, which is stuck through the cloak of palm leaves and is shaking a basket rattle to the rhythm of their steps. The priests enter the tribal hut, which is shrouded in semi-darkness. They dance in a row in the middle and hop from one foot to the other, shaking their *maracas* all the time and chanting monotonous invocations. From time to time they interrupt their chanting to drink some fermented manioc. They turn away as they do so, so that the people cannot recognise their faces. Then they resume their singing. With this performance they hope to win the favour of the good spirits. It takes place twice a day during the festival month, morning and evening, and lasts for over an hour. The second entrance of the masked men is followed by an hour of sacred music, before darkness falls. The women withdraw into the tribal hut, as they are forbidden to see the musicians under pain of death. They do not know that the music they are hearing is being played by the men on instruments made from wood and bark. From childhood upwards they have been taught to regard it as a dialogue between the men and the spirits who have come down to earth during this particular month.

The Piaroa have many musical instruments and, for a primitive people, their range is quite unusual. The collection consists of about twenty instruments — giant bark trumpets, flutes, including a nose flute, a bullroarer and a small instrument in the form of a ceramic vessel (two men, each with a bamboo cane, blow into it — see text picture).

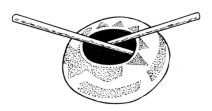 Among the Piaroa the sound of these instruments symbolises the voices of divine beings and certain good and evil spirits. The nose flute, which is blown through the right nostril and produces soft, pleasant sounds, is here called the *guahari* or *u'ufteu*, which means much the same as "soul". It is called after Guahari, the father of the tribe and creator of the Piaroa and other good Indian tribes. They use this flute to imitate his voice. The ceramic vessel that serves as a resonator for the two bamboo trumpets (text picture) is used as a sound symbol for the "wife of the evil spirit". On the extreme right of our illustration two Piaroa are playing this instrument, called a *wola*. One can obtain astonishing sound effects with it by inserting the lower end of the wind instruments into the spherical clay vessel at different depths and blowing in a staccato or legato manner. A piece of rock crystal is always placed inside the pottery vessel, which is decorated with ornaments, as the instrument would not otherwise be able to "get in touch with the spirits" . . . The bullroarer, which is whirled through the air on a cord, produces a kind of whizzing or buzzing sound representing the whirlwind which accompanies the descent of the gods to earth.

85

Illustration 86

Piaroa Musicians with Bark Trumpets and Vertical Flutes · Venezuela

Photograph by Alain Gheerbrandt and Jean Fichter

The trumpets that the two men on the right of the picture are blowing are made from a cylindrical wooden tube and tree bark rolled up together and all secured by strings and long sticks. These instruments may reach a length of two to three metres, but are, in general, 150 cm long. On the left of the picture we can see two men with vertical flutes that have no finger-holes. Among the Piaroa these are always blown in pairs. The shorter, which is a notched flute, is regarded as female, and the longer one, of the recorder type, is considered male. The two instruments always bear a carved or painted symbol in keeping with their sexual significance, but this is often hardly visible. In addition to this ensemble there are also two transverse flutes with finger-holes.

The structure of this music can be described roughly as follows. The flutes play a fairly long melody, with a kind of *bourdon*, or drone produced by the two trumpets in turn, running underneath it. On the rhythmical foundation formed by the trumpets and the deep-toned flutes the high transverse flutes improvise short, charming tunes. In addition the Piaroa use a small trumpet which they call an *aguti*, because the tail of an agouti is used for the bell-mouth. This instrument produces a shrill note. The bark trumpets are stored under water. They are brought out towards five o'clock in the afternoon. In the huts belonging to the settlement the sound of them can be heard as they are blown on the way to the village. The flute music starts up simultaneously at the other end of the township. The two groups then advance towards each other. The women stay in the huts and hear this music and the stamping feet of the men. In addition the bullroarer makes a noise like a storm breaking out. All these acoustic effects create a sensation of fear and foreboding in the womenfolk and a dread of the supernatural. An odd result is produced when they move the trumpets to and fro in front of one another as they blow them. There is interference and so the notes emerging are very deep.

Georg Schünemann tested the sound of a similar trumpet from the Mojo Indians, belonging to the Aruak linguistic family. They also possess rattles made from fruit shells, a wind instrument fashioned from a hollow nut, a big drum and pan-pipes. According to him (739, p. 467) the trumpet consists of a large bamboo cane with a simply attached mouthpiece. The tube is 72.8 cm long and the diameter at the top and bottom is about 11 cm. At the upper end the opening is blocked with natural wax which has been stuck over it, so making it airtight. A blowing pipe is inserted in the mass of wax. This is a perfectly ordinary tube 9.5 cm long and 2.4 cm in diameter ... He managed to play c′, g′ and c″, but the notes depended completely on lip tension. A glissando effect is very easily produced, i. e., the note rose and fell with a howl which was quite intentional and was, in fact, a usual practice.

The vertical flutes illustrated here, which have no finger-holes, have the sound hole partially stopped and are constructed on the ducted principle. Inside the pipe above the sound hole there is a deflector of wax, wood or clay which directs the air current against the edge of the sound hole. Part of the elongated rectangular sound hole is covered with strips of leaf or leather which are wound round the tube of the flute above and below the opening and are secured with a cord. Before blowing it, the player adjusts these two strips and the size and position of the sound hole is corrected thereby. These instruments are to be found in South America only on the Orinoco, the Rio Uaupes, the upper Xingu and the Rio Tiquie, among the Tuyuca Indians.   P.C.

Another common Piaroa instrument is described by Alain Gheerbrandt (821, p. 29). It consists of two thin, flat pieces of wood which are placed between the lips. One blows through them, just like children blowing on a leaf, and a shrill sound is emitted. This instrument is called a *meuotza*, which roughly means "voice of Meuoka". He was the twin brother of Guahari, who caused a great deal of mischief and, amongst other things, created the Makuan tribes who are hated by the Piaroa. While being played, this instrument always acts as a disturbing factor and tends to annoy everyone present.

86

Illustration 87

Craho Master of Ceremonies with Rattle · Brazil

Photograph by Harald Schultz

The Craho are no longer very numerous. There are still about four hundred and fifty of them living in the north-east of Brazil in steppe-land a few hundred miles to the east of the Rio Tocantins. Their rites take the form of cycles extending over periods of from twelve to fifteen years. The pattern of their community songs, which are sometimes performed in three-note parallels, corresponds to that of the Suya who live on the upper Xingu. The use of three-note

parallels is relatively rare, but evidence regarding their distribution would appear to show that the so-called mathematical "simplicity" of the pure fourths and fifths and their "natural" quality are mere illusions on the part of European investigators and theorists with their fondness for rationalising. Among the most primitive peoples the parallels are usually built up, in fact, on irrational intervals, some large and some small. Mathematically rational intervals are only a reality in the more highly advanced civilisations.

The text picture and the following illustration show Craho rites. The master of ceremonies is swinging a calabash rattle in rhythm, and the youths whose manhood is being consecrated on this occasion are marching in time to it. He and the singer sitting beside him are wearing garlands of fresh bast or tree bark. They are sitting on a hollowed-out trunk — we shall have something further to say about this when describing the next illustration — and are closely watching the behaviour of the young initiates and are singing with their lips only just open.   P.C.

Illustration 88

Ritual Song of the Craho · Tocantins, Brazil

Photograph by Harald Schultz

This photograph records another phase of the Craho rite, which, according to their belief, serves to renew the vitality of this Indian tribe from the north-east of Brazil. The master of ceremonies is dancing on the right of the picture. He is wearing rattles made from dry fruit capsules on the calves of his legs as he performs between two hollowed-out tree trunks lying on the ground. He and his assistant take it in turn to summon up the spirits by singing the old songs against the openings in the tree trunks, which represent the souls of departed Craho. Later these trunks, or drums, are rapidly carried into the village in turn. We should remember at this point that the drum is the true representation of fertile, creative power and the embodiment of all things female.

The meaning of the Craho rite is roughly as follows. The song generates the power and, according to the most ancient histories of creation, the first and most elementary force is tonal. This power is directly connected with the drum. The running of the young men and the act of bringing the wooden drums into the villages mean that renewed power has been passed on to the inhabitants.

In the opinion of Harald and Vilma Chiara Schultz (740) the Craho are the most musical Indians in Brazil. The morning song, starting shortly before sunrise, is sung in the village square to the accompaniment of the gourd rattle. It begins slowly and almost ponderously and gradually livens up until it reaches its climax at sunrise. The same ceremony is repeated in the evening after work. When they have all returned to the huts, one or other of the best singers in the tribe raises his voice and his song goes resounding through the night air.

Among the tribes in central Brazil the Craho, the Suya, the Tucuna and others have a special fondness for melodic cadences that include the semi-tone and the third. Among the Craho we find the melodic cadence g sharp—g—e, among the Tucuna e—d sharp—b—g, among the Suya e—e flat—c—b—a flat or d—c sharp—c—a and among the Trumai c—b—b flat—g—f.

"If the Crao Indian does not sing, he is ill," wrote Erich Wustmann (834, p. 98), who stayed with that Indian tribe for a considerable time and brought back a great many photographs of their dances and rites, also tape recordings of their songs. He reported that they had songs to suit a great variety of occasions — festival songs, hunting chants, animal songs, war songs and laments, etc.—and often sang for hours on end without stopping. When he questioned them about the meaning of some of the song texts, the Craho singers had to admit that they no longer knew what the various songs signified.

They dance and sing almost daily, morning and evening, to the rhythm of the calabash rattle of the leading singer and master of ceremonies. The War Dance plays a great part here, as among most of the Indian tribes. In it a group of dancers imitate the conquered enemies in their poses and gestures. The masked dances are connected with demon magic. Giant masks made of palm fronds cover the dancers almost completely as they move about, performing the prescribed figures. The Craho also have women's dances that start up in the morning before sunrise. The women stand side by side in a long line in front of the singing master who shakes his calabash rattle, and they move their slightly bent arms in time to the rhythm of the song.   P.C.

Illustration 89

Camayura Dance Ceremony with Double Clarinets · Xingu, Brazil

Photograph by Erich Wustmann

The main rivers in the northern Matto Grosso are the Rio dos Mortos, the Paramatinga and the Xingu. Tribes of various origins and belonging to a very low cultural level have withdrawn to this area. The natives living on the upper Xingu are members of various linguistic families. The Yaulapiti belong to the Aruak group, the Guicuru and the Apalakiri (Calapalo) are Carib, and the Camayura and Cayabi form part of the Tupian-Guarani group. In spite of their differing languages these tribes show a very considerable degree of cultural unity.

When the Camayura return from fishing or receive a visit from neighbouring tribes, festivities take place and the course of these is regulated and predetermined by certain ritual acts. The centre of all these ceremonies is the village square, which is surrounded by spacious huts with waterproof grass roofs. The sacred wind instruments, the bull-roarers and the masks are stored in the main house. Dancing, fighting contests and initiation rites take place in succession or merge into one another. One of the most remarkable dances is the dance of the wind instrument players, illustrated here. In these long double clarinets, the ergological characteristics of which have been described elsewhere (Illust. 90), the longer tubes are regarded as male and the shorter as female. Simone Dreyfus-Roche (490) has mentioned that the Camayura refer to those wind instruments as *urua*. The instrumentalists run through the settlement in pairs. Their heads are decked with a circlet of yellow feathers and their ankles are bound round with thick layers of bark as a precaution against snake bites. They visit every house, dancing and playing as they go. The women also take part in this dance, laying their hands on the shoulders of the musicians. Finally they dance round the square which has a consecrated enclosure in the centre, marking the grave of a specially revered chieftain. Without interrupting the dancing, the men touch the enclosure with their bows and also swing the calabash rattle (text picture). Their pan-pipes, which are played singly or in pairs, have a varying number of stopped tubes. There is no evidence of drums in the Xingu district. P.C.

89

Illustration 90

Erigpactsa Musicians with Bamboo Clarinets · Juruena, Matto Grosso, Brazil

Photograph by Harald Schultz

This picture was taken inside the tribal hut of the Erigpactsa, the meeting-place of the men. There they eat and lay down their weapons and fishing nets and converse during the day. In the middle of the room there is a receptacle made of fired clay containing a mixture of honey and water. Here they celebrate with their music the beginning of sowing and planting. Their instruments are not flutes or trumpets, as we might be inclined to assume, but clarinets constructed on the reed cap principle. The tubes, about two metres long and without finger-holes, are made of green bamboo. The blow-hole is about 30 to 40 cm above one of the knots. The septum at the first growth knot is pierced through the middle. Into this hole in the septum a thin tube with an idioglottal reed is pushed (cf. drawing on p. 174). The vibrating tongue formed by an oblique incision in this tube causes the air column in the tube of the instrument to pulsate. The pitch is different in each instrument. It is regulated by putting the reed at different depths below the septum. The blowing process is indirect as in reed cap instruments and cannot be influenced by the player's lips. Similar types of instruments also exist among the Umutina (Illust. 94) and the Caingang.

In the centre of the group of Erigpactsa musicians illustrated here a youth with a painted face is sitting quietly, taking no part. We come across him again blowing a set of bamboo pan-pipes outside the hut (text picture). This consists of six tubes arranged according to length and joined together with a cord. The longest pipe is on the left, i.e., the musician's left. As we have already mentioned, pan-pipes reached their most advanced stage of development in the Andean civilisations. There we find instruments of bamboo, plain wood, clay and stone. In the Amazon area they are made exclusively from bamboo cane. It should be pointed out that they are not connected with worship in the south of Brazil.

P.C.

Illustration 91

Worship of the Dead by the Umutina, a Subgroup of the Bororo (living between the upper Paraguay and Sepotuba Rivers)

Photograph by Harald Schultz

The young men from the Umutina village on the upper Paraguay have taken up their position in two lines. Those in the back row have an animal skin hanging down behind and are wearing bunches of foliage in their ears. The ones in front are dressed in palm-leaf skirts. There is a palm strip covering their eyes. The rattles here are made from

calabashes or pottery. In his raised right hand the master of ceremonies is holding an instrument made from a *cujete*, the Crescentia fruit so widely found in Brazil. The fruits are either spherical or oval, according to Izikowitz (579, p. 98). As they have no stalks, a wooden rod is usually driven through the calabash to provide a secure grip. The stem is often attached with wax. The rattle being used by the master of ceremonies illustrated here appears to be of a different type, where only one side of the calabash is perforated and not the whole shell. In this instance four holes are bored at the place where the handle is to be attached and it is tied on with thread or sinews. The rattles, which are meant to exorcise and drive out harmful spirits, are often adorned with feathers. In many tribes the feathers are regarded as the soul of the bird assisting the shaman. The contents of the rattles are very varied—dry seed grains, gravel, pieces of shell, etc. The differences in the material used play no part as a rule—the only decisive factor is the sound effect. But in certain cases the rattling objects inside the capsule are credited with magic powers, especially if they are the gift of a mighty wizard or some other being with supernatural abilities. For example, the Warrau who live on the Orinoco delta as far as the Pomeroon River put small pieces of rock crystal into their *maracas*, as secret powers are attributed to them. We have already referred elsewhere (p. 152) to the use of that mineral in the Piaroa instrument called a *wola*. Rattles of the *maracas* type are to be found nearly all over America. They are used to appease evil spirits and attract good ones and, above all, in shaman healing ceremonies.

The instrument in the text picture consists of a calabash rattle and two basket rattles tied to a pole about 2 m long and decorated with feathers. We come across this type again among the Palikur who live on the Brazilian bank of the Rio Oyapoc. This rattle is intended for men's and women's dances and the ground is struck at regular intervals. It is also used for the male dance known as the *hauyari* on the death of a woman and for the women's dance called a *macquari*, marking the death of a man. This type probably had its origins in Guyana and is very similar to the *chichautzli* of the ancient Maya. In all cases basket rattles display the Guyana weaving design.   P.C.

Illustration 92

Umutina (Bororo) with Transverse Flute · Matto Grosso, Upper Paraguay, Brazil

Photograph by Harald Schultz

This photograph and the following one relate to worshipping of the dead—a ceremony of extreme importance among the Bororo, as shown in Illustrations 91 and 94. A striking feature is the use of the same kind of headgear, equipment and adornments by all the Umutina playing instruments and illustrated here. In one hand they hold an instrument

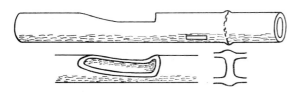

and in the other their bow and arrow. None of their instruments is played with both hands. The transverse flute blown by the Indian is cut out of a bamboo cane (text picture). In the right hand he can be seen holding the instrument near the narrow rectangular blow-hole. With the palm of his hand he covers a second opening cut in the cane. If this is completely closed, the length of the tube determines the height of the note emitted. But the opening can only be partly covered or completely opened. Changes in the position of the hand produce notes of differing pitch, the sequence of which corresponds to a gliding movement from one note to another. Curt Nimuendajú, quoted by Karl Gustav Izikowitz (579, p. 278), described how this instrument was played by the Palikur. The blower always started with a high note, fluctuated for a time around this fundamental note, then went a few tones deeper, wavered again and produced another tremulo, allowing the final note to descend slowly.

An interesting type of transverse flute is used by the Suisi in the north-west of Brazil. It consists of a bamboo rod about 170 cm long, subdivided by the natural partitions occurring at the nodes into five sections. Each part has a rectangular blow-hole. So this instrument is really made up of five different transverse pipes, closed on both sides and without finger-holes. When there is dancing, it is played simultaneously by five men.   P.C.

Illustration 93

Umutina with a Cow's Horn Trumpet · Matto Grosso, Upper Paraguay, Brazil

Photograph by Harald Schultz

Harald Schultz, who took this photograph, wrote that the Indian in the picture was calling to the ghosts of his ancestors to take part in the grand ceremonies commemorating the dead. This wind instrument, also used as a signalling horn, consists of a bamboo cane let into a cow's horn, fastened with wax and wound round with a cord.

Cattle were not introduced into America until after the *Conquista* by the Europeans. But this does not mean that wind instruments of this kind only came into existence in the post-Columbian era. In earlier times the tail of the armadillo was used as a bell-mouth for trumpets. This is a common practice among many Indian tribes even to-day, for example, among the Botocudo. The Maue in central Brazil make a bell-mouth for their trumpet-type instruments from elongated calabashes, the lower part of which has been cut off. To this is attached a blowing tube of bamboo adorned with parrot feathers. The joint is securely bound with cotton cord. The war trumpet of the Mundrucu, who live in the Rio Tapajoz area, consists of two pieces of tubing of different diameter, one being long and narrowish and the other short and wide. The latter serves as the sound opening and runs out into two fork-shaped projections to which the blowing tube is firmly tied. It is a very remarkable fact that the actual tube of the trumpet is closed at the top end by the septum formed by the natural knot, although we would expect to find the mouthpiece there. The blow-hole is cut into the side-wall of the tube. The area of distribution of trumpets that are side-blown and held crosswise extends basically along the Amazon and the country to the south of it.   P.C.

166

92

93

Illustration 94

Umutina (Bororo) with Reed Instruments · Matto Grosso, Upper Paraguay, Brazil

Photograph by Harald Schultz

A number of Umutina Indians have taken up their position in full array outside their huts. They are armed with a spear and a large bow and are carrying a rectangular shield made from animal skin on their back. The curious musical instrument they are holding can be included in the class of idioglottal clarinets. The thin mouthpiece consists of a reed, the upper end of which is stopped by a knot or by the septum. By means of a tangential incision a tongue has been separated from the wall of the tube to such an extent that it is still connected with the mouthpiece at its base, but up towards the top it is free to vibrate. The bottom end of the mouthpiece, which is open, extends into a bamboo cane about 35 cm long and having an appreciably larger diameter. The mouthpiece is stuck through the pierced septum at the head of the instrument and is firmly glued and also tied round with bast fibres. When blowing it, the player takes it right into his mouth, so that the oral cavity serves as the reed cap.

This instrument, which is found in Guyana and along the Amazon, has no finger-holes, so it is only possible to play one note on it. In different tribes several of these clarinets are blown in unison. The individual instruments differ in pitch and complement one another. The "music master" gives each player certain signs when it is his turn to play his instrument. According to Richard Schomburgk (833, p. 152), the young men gather round their music teacher nearly every evening and give concerts under his leadership in the middle of the village. The instrument gives out a high or a deep note according to the size of the bamboo cane and its opening. The whole concert is controlled by a movement of the hand, a nod of the head or a beat of the instrument of the *Hoho-hit* in the direction of the musician whose turn it is to begin or join in. Although each instrument has only one note, the "musical director" has such an accurate knowledge of the notes produced by all the instruments and gives his signs so correctly that there is a basic sense of harmony in the midst of all the noise.

In addition to this idioglottal clarinet, which is occasionally provided with a bell-mouth from a calabash cut open underneath or made from a cow's horn, the Umutina use the deer hoof and the calabash rattle, the bullroarer, a signalling whistle ideal for hunting, compound trumpet-like instruments made from bamboo canes, polyglobular trumpets consisting of three or four calabashes joined together with wax, also vertical flutes without finger-holes. Of the customary dances performed by them, we must certainly mention the War Dance, in which the warriors move with knees bent and utter cries when the chief shakes his calabash rattle. In the Jaguar Dance the hunter of a jaguar that has been killed plays the part of the animal. He wears its skin, claws and teeth and leaps wildly about. The purpose of this dance is to appease the animal's spirit.   P. C.

Illustration 95

Whistling Boy of the Caingang Indians · Rio Ivahy, Parana, Brazil

Photograph by Harald Schultz

Before the advent of musical instruments and even before articulated singing, man was able to make "body music", i.e., he used parts of his body to produce sounds and mark out rhythms. Primitive races throughout the world stamped their feet on the ground and sometimes this formed the only kind of percussion. Some dances from Ruanda and also from the Basque provinces bear witness to this fact. Hand-clapping is also universal, and beating the forearm is a typical activity of the Polynesians. Depending on the position of the teeth or lips, one can produce notes of greatly varying timbre when breathing out, without using the vocal cords at all. Even to-day hissing or whistling form part of magic rites. In Gabon (Equatorial Africa) the magician summons the rain by imitating the sound of drops of water falling on leaves or the whistle of the storm wind or the rushing flight of birds, which is another sound preceding rain. This is a kind of magic by analogy or imitation, or it may involve some challenge or inducement. When Chateaubriand was crossing the English Channel in a sailing-ship during a dead calm, he noticed the cabin boy going to the bows and whistling into the sail in order to encourage the wind. The shamans too use sounds as a kind of exhortation or entreaty. African and Indian hunters imitate the whistling of birds in an attempt to lure them into the path of their arrows.

The young Caingang Indian in our illustration is practising whistling. He is exerting pressure on his lips and cheeks by changing the position of his fingers, so modulating the tone. This forms part of his training as a hunter.   P. C.

Illustration 96

Young Tucurima with a Musical Bow · Upper Purus, Brazil

Photograph by Harald Schultz

The musical bow of the Tucurima is relatively short, measuring about 35 cm, and is broad and thin and very supple. One sets the string vibrating by striking it with a very thin stick, often with the rib from a palm leaf. The player's oral cavity acts as the resonator. The wooden bow, not the string, is held to the open mouth. This musical bow is an "instrument of solitude", as its note is so feeble that it can only be heard by the player himself. It has no special function. The Indian plays it for his own amusement or, as one of them once said, because he is feeling homesick for his own village.

The musical bow is the only pre-Columbian stringed instrument in South America. At the end of the 19th century there were long discussions as to whether the instrument had been invented by the Indians or had been brought in from Africa. No unanimous verdict has been reached on the subject. The most convincing argument in favour of its being a native instrument is the fact that the musical bow was known to the Patagonians who had never up to that time had any contact with Africa or her culture.   P. C.

96

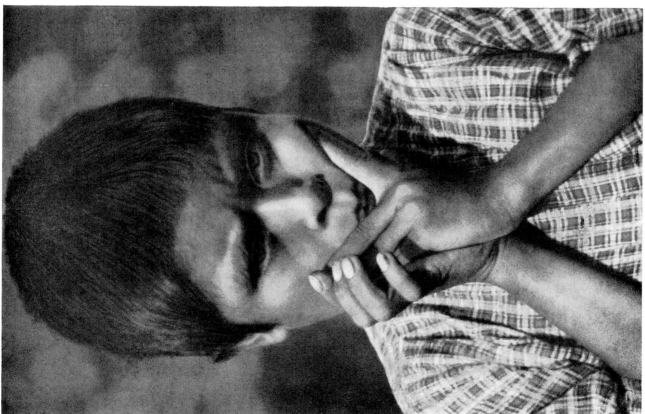

95

171

Illustration 97

A Group of Yahgan Lamenting the Dead · Tierra del Fuego, Navarino Island, Chile

Photograph by Charles Wellington Furlong, November 1907

The Indians of Tierra del Fuego, who, as we know, are divided up into Canoe Indians (Yahgan, Alacaluf) and Land Indians (Ona, Haush), have no properly differentiated musical instruments. But they do certainly have a clearly developed musical awareness. They all sing and Cooper tells how the Alacaluf enjoyed listening to the gramophone and showed a spontaneous liking for American negro spirituals, even managing to hum the tune of these very well after the very first hearing. The Yahgan (who can make a whistle from the wind-pipe of the white kelpgoose) are said to have sung "many songs" of a ritual nature, at mourning and initiation ceremonies, although they also managed to improvise others on more profane occasions. When engaged in ceremonial singing, they beat out the time with staffs. Our photograph of a group of singing Yahgan was taken by Furlong in 1907. He mentions how ceremonial songs were sung typically in a roofed chamber. In the picture a group of men and women have assembled to mourn their dead. The man who had been killed was the husband of the woman with white paint on her face.   E. L.

In contrast to the Yahgan or Yamana, their northern neighbours, the Ona or Selk'nam, knew nothing of musical instruments or of songs suitable for entertainment or merrymaking. Only during performances and ceremonies conducted by the medicine men and the "Klóketen" feast did one hear simple, monotonous songs with a strong emphasis on the rhythmical side.

In the mythical tales of the Ona an ancestor named Kokpómeč was regarded as the chief originator of these songs. With their help he is said to have performed miraculous deeds and he is also supposed to have instructed the medicine men in the art of singing. The shaman song was thought to have a magic effect, always guaranteeing good weather and even causing some large whale to go aground and so meet his death. But the medicine men *(xon)* mainly used their songs to enter into a semi-conscious, dream-like state, supposedly enabling them to heal the sick and prophesy and perform weather magic. In his classic work on the Indians of Tierra del Fuego, Martín Gusinde described his own impressions and observations on such occasions. He said that one most often heard the *xon* starting up their song after midnight or in the very early morning. Its monotonous uniformity always had a very wearying effect on him even after the first ten minutes. As a mere listener he felt that his nerves were being set on edge and his whole brain was in a state of confusion. The usual melody contained only slight modulations around the same fundamental note. There were no differences in the strength of their voices, which were only half audible. The theme remained the same throughout, but the vowels sometimes came out clearly or became rather muffled. The rhythm sounded jerky, because after each fresh intake of breath the same theme was started up again with renewed vigour (260, Vol. I, pp. 753/754).

The "Klóketen" ceremony constituted a climax in the religious and social life of the Ona groups. During it the various youths who had reached manhood were given adult status. There was clear discrimination against the female members of the tribe. What actually happened inside the cult hut was kept a closely guarded secret from the womenfolk and they were all excluded from acts of worship and were temporarily terrorised by the masked men. The men appeared as "spirits" during the "Klóketen" festival, and were unrecognisable because they had painted their bodies and were wearing bark masks. The text picture shows the "spirit" Matan (Photograph by M. Gusinde, St. Gabriel-Mödling, nr. Vienna).   R. K.

The southern mounted tribes of Patagonia, the Tehuelche, possessed a few musical instruments listed by Cooper: a bark rattle which hung from the belt when they were dancing, another rattle made of dried animal bladders or skins, a drum with a skin membrane, a whistle made from the thigh bone of the guanaco and the musical bow.

The Puelche, living to the north of the Tehuelche, were familiar with the use of a kettle-drum. Unfortunately, we have no information regarding their musical life, their songs or their other instruments.   E. L.

172

173

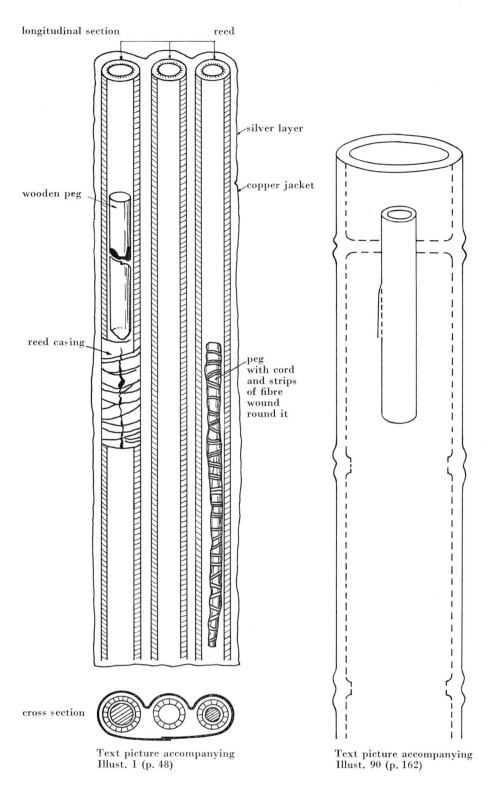

longitudinal section   reed

silver layer

copper jacket

wooden peg

reed casing

peg
with cord
and strips
of fibre
wound
round it

cross section

Text picture accompanying
Illust. 1 (p. 48)

Text picture accompanying
Illust. 90 (p. 162)

APPENDIX

LITERATURE

Important Bibliographies and Reference Works (R.K.)

1 Baldus, H., Bibliografia Critica da Etnologia Brasileira; Comissão do IV Centenario da cidade de São Paulo, Sao Paulo 1954

2 Bernal, I., Bibliografía de Arqueología y Etnografía. Mesoamerica y Norte de México. 1514-1960; Instituto Nacional de Antropología e Historia, Mexico 1962

3 Comas, J., Bibliografía Selectiva de las Culturas Indígenas de América; Publicacion del Instituto Panamericano de Geografía e Historia, Mexico 1953

4 Dockstader, F. J., The American Indian in Graduate Studies. A Bibliography of Theses and Dissertations; Contribution from the Museum of the American Indian, Heye Foundation, Vol. XV, New York 1957

5 Friederici, G., Amerikanistisches Wörterbuch und Hilfswörterbuch für den Amerikanisten; Abhandlungen aus dem Gebiet der Auslandskunde, Vol. 53, Hamburg 1960

6 Gibson, G. D., A Bibliography of Anthropological Bibliographies: the Americas, in: Current Anthropology, Vol. I, pp. 61-75, Chicago 1960

7 Handbook of American Indians North of Mexico, ed. by Frederick Webb Hodge; Bulletin 30 of the Bureau of American Ethnology, 2 Vols., Washington 1907, 1910

8 Handbook of Middle American Indians; General Editor: Robert Wauchope, Vol. 1: Natural Environment and Early Cultures, ed. by Robert C. West, Austin 1964 (10 more volumes in preparation)

9 Handbook of South American Indians, ed. by Julian H. Steward; Bulletin 143 of the Bureau of American Ethnology, 7 Vols., Washington 1946-59

10 Haywood, C., A Bibliography of North American Folklore and Folksongs, 2 Vols., New York 1951

11 Herzog, G., Research in Primitive and Folk Music in the United States. A Survey, in: American Council of Learned Societies, Bulletin 24, pp. 561–657, Washington 1936

12 Kunst, J., Ethno-Musicology, The Hague 1955 (2nd edition)

13 León-Portilla, M., Indians in the Hemisphere Today: Guide to the Indian Population; Indianist Yearbook 22, Mexico 1962

14 Murdock, G. P. Ethnographic Bibliography of North America, New Haven 1960 (3rd edition)

15 O'Leary, J., Ethnographic Bibliography of South America, New Haven 1963

16 Rhodes, W., North American Indian Music: a Bibliographical Survey of Anthropological Theory, in: Notes X, 1952

17 Rosenblat, A., La Población Indígena y el Mestizaje en América, 2 Vols., Buenos Aires 1954

Ethnological Monographs (R.K.)

Most of the standard works listed here present a picture of the native population of America at the time of their ethnographical investigation and cover practically all aspects of their way of life and civilisation. Music, ceremonial life, dancing and musical instruments are described in an expert and painstaking manner, with occasional musical extracts and sketches of movements.

Eskimo

18 Birket-Smith, K., Ethnography of the Egesmind District, in: Meddelelser om Grønland, Vol. LXVI, pp. 1 to 484, Copenhagen 1924

19 – Über die Herkunft der Eskimos und ihre Stellung in der zirkumpolaren Kulturentwicklung, in: Anthropos, Vol. 25, pp. 2–23, Vienna-Mödling 1930

20 – The Eskimos, rev. ed. London 1959; New York 1971; German: Die Eskimos, Zürich 1948

21 – The Chugach Eskimo, Nationalmuseets Skrifter, Etnografisk Raekke, Vol. VI, Copenhagen 1953

22 Boas, F., The Central Eskimo, in: 6th Annual Report of the Bureau of American Ethnology, pp. 390–669, Washington 1888

23 – The Eskimo of Baffin Land and Hudson Bay, in: Bulletin of the American Museum ot Natural History, No. XV, pp. 1–570, New York 1901–07

24 Bogoras, W. G., The Eskimo of Siberia, in: The Jesup North Pacific Expedition, Vol. VIII, Leiden – New York 1913

25 Fried, J. (ed), A Survey of the Aboriginal Populations of Quebec and Labrador, Eastern Canadian Anthropological Series, No. 1, Montreal 1955

26 Hawkes, M. W., The Labrador Eskimo, in: Memoir of the Canada Department of Mines, Geological Survey, Vol. XCI, pp. 1–165, Ottawa 1916

27 Himmelheber, H., Eskimokünstler; Teilergebnisse einer ethnographischen Expedition in Alaska von Juni 1936 bis April 1937, Stuttgart 1938

28 Holm, G., Ethnological Sketch of the Angmagssalik Eskimo, in: Meddelelser om Grønland, Vol. XXXIX, pp. 1–147, Copenhagen 1911

29 Hughes, C. C., An Eskimo Village in the Modern World, Ithaca 1960

30 – Under Four Flags: Recent Culture Change Among the Eskimos, in: Current Anthropology, Vol. VI, No. 1, pp. 3–69, Chicago 1965

31 Ingstad, H., Nunamiut; Unter den Inland-Eskimos von Alaska, Berlin 1952

32 Jochelson, W., History, Ethnology and Anthropology of the Aleut, Carnegie Institution of Washington, Publication No. 432, Washington 1933

33 Kroeber, A. L., The Eskimo of Smith Sound, in: Bulletin of the American Museum of Natural History, No. XII, pp. 265—327, New York 1899

34 Lantis, M., Alaska Eskimo Ceremonialism, Monographs of the American Ethnological Society, Vol. XI, New York 1947

35 Malaurie, J., Les Derniers Rois de Thulé, Paris 1955; German: Die letzten Könige von Thule, Leipzig 1957

36 Mikkelsen, E., The Eskimos of East Greenland, in: Canadian Geographical Journal, Vol. 43, pp. 88—98, Ottawa 1951

37 Mowat, F., People of the Deer, Boston 1952

38 — Moeurs et Coutumes des Esquimaux Caribou, Paris 1953

39 Nelson, E. W., The Eskimo About Bering Strait, in: 18th Annual Report of the Bureau of American Ethnology, pp. 3—518, Washington 1899

40 Petitots, E. F. S., Monographie des Esquimaux Tchiglit du Mackenzie et de l'Anderson, Paris 1876

41 Rasmussen, K., The People of the Polar North, A Record Compiled from the Danish Originals and Edited by G. Herring, London and Detroit 1908

42 — Rasmussens Thulefahrt, Frankfurt (Main) 1934

43 Ray, D. J., Artists of the Tundra and the Sea, Seattle 1962

44 Reports of the Canadian Arctic Expedition 1913—18, Vols. XII—XIV, Ottawa 1922—25

45 Reports of the Fifth Thule Expedition 1921—24, the Danish Expedition to Arctic North America in charge of Knud Rasmussen, Vols. III—X, Copenhagen 1927—52

46 Spencer, R. F., The North Alaska Eskimo, Bulletin 171 of the Bureau of American Ethnology, Washington 1959

47 Steensby, H. P., Contributions to the Ethnology and Anthropogeography of the Polar Eskimos, in: Meddelelser om Grønland, Vol. XXXIV, pp. 253—405, Copenhagen 1910

48 Stefansson, V., The Stefansson-Anderson Arctic Expedition, in: Anthropological Papers of the American Museum of Natural History, Vol. XIV, pp. 1—395, New York 1914

49 Thalbitzer, W., The Ammassalik Eskimo, in: Meddelelser om Grønland, Vol. XL, pp. 113—564, 569—739; Vol. LIII, pp. 435—81, Copenhagen 1917, 1921, 1941

50 — Die kultischen Gottheiten der Eskimos, in: Archiv für Religionswissenschaft, Vol. XXVI, pp. 364—430, Leipzig 1928

51 Turner, L. M., Ethnology of the Ungava District, in: 11th Annual Report of the Bureau of American Ethnology, pp. 159—267, Washington 1894

52 Van Stone. J. W., Point Hope: An Eskimo Village in Transition. Seattle 1962

53 — and W. Oswalt, The Caribou Eskimos of Eskimo Point, Northern Coordination and Research Centre, Department of Northern Affairs and National Resources, Ottawa 1959

54 Victor, P. E., Contributions à l'Ethnographie des Esquimo d'Angmagssalik, in: Meddelelser om Grønland, Vol. CXXV, pp. 1—213, Copenhagen 1940

55 Weyer, E. M., The Eskimos, New Haven 1932

56 Barbeau, M., Medicine Men on the North Pacific Coast, Bulletin 152 of the National Museum of Canada, Ottawa 1958

57 Beals, R. L., Ethnology of Rocky Mountain Park: the Ute and Arapaho, Berkeley 1935

58 — The Aboriginal Culture of the Cahita Indians, Ibero-Americana, Vol. XIX, pp. 1—86, Berkeley 1943

59 Bennett, W. C., and R. M. Zingg, The Tarahumara, Chicago 1935

60 Birket-Smith, K., Contributions to Chipewyan Ethnology, in: Reports of the Fifth Thule Expedition, Vol. V, No. 3, pp. 1—114, Copenhagen 1930

61 — and F. de Laguna, The Eyak Indians of the Copper River Delta, Copenhagen 1938

62 Blair, E. H. (ed.), The Indian Tribes of the Upper Mississippi Valley and Region of the Great Lakes, 2 Vols., Cleveland 1911, 1912

63 Bleeker, S., The Mission Indians of California, New York 1956

64 Boas, F., Tsimshian Mythology, in: 31st Annual Report of the Bureau of American Ethnology, pp. 29—979, Washington 1916

65 — Ethnology of the Kwakiutl, in: 35th Annual Report of the Bureau of American Ethnology, pp. 43—1481, Washington 1921

66 Bourke, J. G., The Medicine Men of the Apache, in: 9th Annual Report of the Bureau of American Ethnology, pp. 451—595, Washington 1892

67 Bowers, A. W., Mandan Social and Ceremonial Organization, Chicago 1950

68 Bunzel, R. L., Introduction to Zuñi Ceremonialism, in: 47th Annual Report of the Bureau of American Ethnology, pp. 467—544, Washington 1932

69 — Zuñi Ritual Poetry, in: 47th Annual Report of the Bureau of American Ethnology, pp. 611—835, Washington 1932

70 — Zuñi Katcinas, in: 47th Annual Report of the Bureau of American Ethnology, pp. 837—1086, Washington 1932

71 Capron, L., The Medicine Bundles of the Florida Seminole and the Green Corn Dance, in: Bulletin 151 of the Bureau of American Ethnology, pp. 155—210, Washington 1953

72 Chafe, W. L., Seneca Thanksgiving Rituals, Bulletin 183 of the Bureau of American Ethnology, Washington 1961

73 Cornplanter, J. J., Legends of the Longhouse, Philadelphia 1938

74 Curtis, E. S., The North American Indian, 20 Vols., Cambridge, Mass. 1907—30

75 Denig, E. T., Indian Tribes of the Upper Missouri, ed. by J. N. B. Hewitt, in: 46th Annual Report of the Bureau of American Ethnology, pp. 375—628, Washington 1930

76 Densmore, F., Chippewa Customs, Bulletin 86 of the Bureau of American Ethnology, Washington 1929

77 Dorsey, G. A., The Cheyenne, in: Anthropological Series of the Field Columbian Museum, Vol. IX, pp. 1—186, Chicago 1905

78 — J. O., A Study of Siouan Cults, in: 11th Annual Report

of the Bureau of American Ethnology, pp. 351–454, Washington 1894

79 Driver, H. E., Wappo Ethnography, in: University of California Publications in American Archaeology and Ethnology, Vol. XXXVI, pp. 179–220, Berkeley 1936

80 Drucker, P., Culture Element Distributions: XXVI, Northwest Coast, in: Anthropological Records, Vol. IX, pp. 157–294, Berkeley 1950

81 – The Northern and Central Nootkan Tribes, Bulletin 144 of the Bureau of American Ethnology, Washington 1951

82 – Indians of the Northwest Coast, New York 1955

83 Du Bois, C., Wintu Ethnography, in: University of California Publications in American Archaeology and Ethnology, Vol. XXXVI, pp. 1–148, Berkeley 1935

84 Dunbar, J., The Pawnee Indians, in: Magazine of American History, Vol. IV, pp. 241–81; Vol. V, pp. 321–42; Vol. VIII, pp. 734–54, New York 1880–82

85 Emmons, G. T., The Tahltan Indians, in: University of Pennsylvania Museum Anthropological Publications, Vol. IV, pp. 1–120, Philadelphia 1911

86 Ewers, J. C., The Blackfeet, Norman 1958

87 Fenton, W. N., Tonawanda Longhouse Ceremonies, in: Bulletin 128 of the Bureau of American Ethnology, pp. 140–66, Washington 1941

88 – The Iroquois Eagle Dance, Bulletin 156 of the Bureau of American Ethnology, Washington 1953

89 – and G. P. Kurath, The Feast of the Dead, or Ghost Dance at Six Nations Reserve, Canada, in: Bulletin 149 of the Bureau of American Ethnology, pp. 139–66, Washington 1951

90 Fewkes, J. W., Hopi Katcinas, in: 21st Annual Report of the Bureau of American Ethnology, pp. 3–126, Washington 1903

91 Flannery, R., An Analysis of Coastal Algonquian Culture, in: Anthropological Series of the Catholic University of America, Vol. VII, pp. 1–219, Washington 1939

92 – The Gros Ventres of Montana, Part I: Social Life; Cooper, J. M., The Gros Ventres of Montana, Part II: Religion and Ritual, in: Anthropological Series of the Catholic University of America, Vol. XV, XVI, Washington 1953, 1956

93 Fletcher, A. C., and F. La Flesche, The Omaha Tribe, in: 27th Annual Report of the Bureau of American Ethnology, pp. 17–654, Washington 1911

94 Forde, C. D., Ethnography of the Yuma Indians, in: University of California Publications in American Archaeology and Ethnology, Vol. XXVIII, pp. 83–278, Berkeley 1931

95 Garfield, V. E., et al., The Tsimshian: Their Arts and Music, Publication of the American Ethnological Society, No. XVIII, New York 1951

96 Gatschet, A. S., The Karankawa Indians, in: Archaeological and Ethnological Papers of the Peabody Museum, Vol. I, No. 2, Cambridge 1891

97 Gifford, E. W., The Kamia of Imperial Valley, Bulletin 97 of the Bureau of American Ethnology, Washington 1931

98 – Central Miwok Ceremonies, in: Anthropological Records, Vol. XIV, pp. 261–318, Berkeley 1955

99 Goddard, P. E., Life and Culture of the Hupa, in: University of California Publications in American Archaeology and Ethnology, Vol. I, pp. 1–88, Berkeley 1903

100 – The Beaver Indians, in: Anthropological Papers of the American Museum of Natural History, Vol. X, pp. 201 to 293, New York 1916

101 – Indians of the Southwest, New York 1931

102 Grinnell, G. B., The Cheyenne Indians, 2 Vols., New Haven 1923

103 Haeberlin, H. K., and E. Gunther, Ethnographische Notizen über die Indianerstämme des Puget-Sundes, in: Zeitschrift für Ethnologie, Vol. LVI, pp. 1–74, Berlin 1924

104 Hassrick, R. B., et al., The Sioux, Norman 1964

105 Hilger, I., Chippewa Child Life and its Cultural Background, Bulletin 146 of the Bureau of American Ethnology, Washington 1951

106 Hoffman, W. J., The Mide'wiwin or "Grand Medicine Society" of the Ojibwa, in: 7th Annual Report of the Bureau of American Ethnology, pp. 143–300, Washington 1891

107 – The Menomini Indians, in: 14th Annual Report of the Bureau of American Ethnology, Part I, pp. 11–328, Washington 1896

108 Honigmann, J. J., The Kaska Indians, in: Yale University Publications in Anthropology, Vol. LI, pp. 1–163, New Haven 1954

109 Howard, J. H., The Plains-Ojibwa or Bungi, Anthropological Paper of the University of South Dakota Museum, No. 1, Vermillion 1965

110 Howley, J. P., The Beothucks or Red Indians, Cambridge 1915

111 Jenness, D., The Sekani Indians of British Columbia, in: Bulletins of the Canada Department of Mines, National Museum of Canada, Vol. LXXXIV, pp. 1–82, Ottawa 1937

112 – The Sarcee Indians of Alberta, in: Bulletins of the Canada Department of Mines, National Museum of Canada, Vol. XC, pp. 1–98, Ottawa 1938

113 – The Indians of Canada, Bulletin 65 of the National Museum of Canada, Ottawa 1955 (3rd ed.)

114 Jones, W., Ethnography of the Fox Indians, Bulletin 125 of the Bureau of American Ethnology, Washington 1939

115 Joseph, A., R. Spicer and J. Chesky, The Desert People, Chicago 1949

116 Kluckhohn, C., and D. C. Leighton, The Navaho, Cambridge, Mass. 1946

117 Krause, A., Die Tlinkit-Indianer, Jena 1885

118 Kroeber, A. L., The Arapaho, in: Bulletin of the American Museum of Natural History, No. XVIII, pp. 1–229, 279–454, New York 1902–7

119 – Handbook of the Indians of California, Bulletin 78 of the Bureau of American Ethnology, Washington 1925

120 La Barre, W., The Peyote Cult, in: Yale University Publications in Anthropology, Vol. XIX, pp. 1–188, New Haven 1938

121 La Flesche, F., The Osage Tribe, in: Annual Report of the Bureau of American Ethnology, Vol. XXXVI, pp. 35–604; Vol. XXXIX, pp. 31–630; Vol. XLIII, pp. 23–164; Vol. XLV, pp. 529–833, Washington 1921 to 1930

122 Lange, C. H., Cochiti, Austin 1959

123 Lewis, A. B., Tribes of the Columbia Valley and the Coast of Washington and Oregon, in: Memoirs of the American Anthropological Association, No. I, pp. 147–209, Lancaster, Pa. 1906

124 Lockwood, F. C., The Apache Indians, New York 1938

125 Lowie, R. H., The Northern Shoshone, in: Anthropological Papers of the American Museum of Natural History, Vol. II, pp. 169–306, New York 1908

126 – The Assiniboine, in: Anthropological Papers of the American Museum of Natural History, Vol. IV, pp. 1–270, New York 1910

127 – The Sun Dance of the Crow Indians, in: Anthropological Papers of the American Museum of Natural History, Vol. XVI, pp. 1–50, New York 1915

128 – Notes on Shoshonean Ethnography, in: Anthropological Papers of the American Museum of Natural History, Vol. XX, pp. 185–314, New York 1924

129 – The Crow Indians, New York 1935

130 – Ethnographic Notes on the Washo, in: University of California Publications in American Archaeology and Ethnology, Vol. XXXVI, pp. 301–52, Berkeley 1939

131 – Indians of the Plains, New York 1954

132 McGee, W. J., The Seri Indians, in: 17th Annual Report of the Bureau of American Ethnology, Part I, pp. 9–298, Washington 1900

133 McIlwraith, T. F., The Bella Coola Indians, 2 Vols., Toronto 1948

134 McKennan, R. A., The Upper Tanana Indians, in: Yale University Publications in Anthropology, Vol. LV, pp. 1–223, New Haven 1959

135 Mandelbaum, D. G., The Plains Cree, in: Anthropological Papers of the American Museum of Natural History, Vol. XXXVII, pp. 155–316, New York 1940

136 Mason, J. A., The Ethnology of the Salinan Indians, in: University of California Publications in American Archaeology and Ethnology, Vol. X, pp. 97–240, Berkeley 1912

137 Matthews, W., Navaho Myths, Prayers, and Songs, ed. by P. E. Goddard, in: University of California Publications in American Archaeology and Ethnology, Vol. V, pp. 21–63, Berkeley 1907

138 Mooney, J., The Ghost-Dance Religion and the Sioux Outbreak of 1890, 14th Annual Report of the Bureau of American Ethnology, Part II, Washington 1897

139 Morgan, L. H., League of the Ho-Dé-No-Sau-Nee or Iroquois, Rochester 1851; reprint New Haven 1954

140 Morice, A. G., The Great Déné Race, in: Anthropos, Vol. I, pp. 229–77, 483–508, 695–730; Vol. II, pp. 1–34, 181–96; Vol. IV, pp. 582–606; Vol. V, pp. 113–42, 419–43, 643–53, 969–90, Vienna and Vienna-Mödling 1906–10

141 Müller, W., Die Religionen der Waldlandindianer Nordamerikas, Berlin 1956

142 Niblack, A. P., The Coast Indians of Southern Alaska and Northern British Columbia, in: Report of the U.S. National Museum for 1888, pp. 225–386, Washington 1890

143 O'Kane, W. C., The Hopis: Portrait of a Desert People, Norman 1953

144 Opler, M. E., An Apache Life-way, Chicago 1941

145 Osgood, C., The Ethnography of the Great Bear Lake Indians, in: Bulletins of the Canada Department of Mines, National Museum of Canada, Vol. LXX, pp. 31–92, Ottawa 1931

146 – Contributions to the Ethnography of the Kutchin, in: Yale University Publications in Anthropology, Vol. XIV, pp. 1–189, New Haven 1936

147 – The Ethnography of the Tanaina, in: Yale University Publications in Anthropology, Vol. XVI, pp. 1–229, New Haven 1937

148 – Ingalik Material Culture, in: Yale University Publications in Anthropology, Vol. XXII, pp. 1–500, New Haven 1940

149 – Ingalik Social Culture, in: Yale University Publications in Anthropology, Vol. LIII, pp. 1–289, New Haven 1958

150 – Ingalik Mental Culture, in: Yale University Publications in Anthropology, Vol. LVI, pp. 1–195, New Haven 1959

151 Park, W. Z., Shamanism in Western North America, Northwestern University Studies in the Social Scineces, Vol. II, pp. 1–166, Evanston, Chicago 1938

152 Parker, A. C., Secret Medicine Societies of the Seneca, in: American Anthropologist, n.s., Vol. XI, No. 2, pp. 161–85, Lancaster, Pa. 1909

153 Parsons, E. C., The Pueblo of Jemez, New Haven 1925

154 – Isleta, in: 47th Annual Report of the Bureau of American Ethnology, pp. 193–466, Washington 1932

155 – Taos Pueblo, in: Landmarks in Anthropology Series, Vol. II, pp. 1–120, New York 1936

156 – Pueblo Indian Religion, 2 Vols., Chicago 1939

157 Radin, P., The Winnebago Tribe, in: 37th Annual Report of the Bureau of American Ethnology, pp. 33–550, Washington 1923

158 Reagan, A. B., Notes on the Indians of the Fort Apache Region, in: Anthropological Papers of the American Museum of Natural History, Vol. XXXI, pp. 281–345, New York 1930

159 Reichard, G. A., Navaho Religion, 2 Vols., New York 1950

160 Riggs, S. R., Dakota Grammar, Texts and Ethnography, in: Contributions to North American Ethnology, Vol. IX, Washington 1893

161 Ritzenthaler, R. E., and F. A. Peterson, The Mexican Kickapoo Indians, in: Publications in Anthropology of the Public Museum of the City of Milwaukee, Vol. II, Milwaukee 1956

162 Roberts, J. M., Zuñi Daily Life, Notebook of the Laboratory of Anthropology of the University of Nebraska, III/2, Lincoln 1956

163 Royce, C. C., The Cherokee Nation of Indians, in: 5th Annual Report of the Bureau of American Ethnology, pp. 121–378, Washington 1887

164 Russell, F., The Pima Indians, in: 26th Annual Report of the Bureau of American Ethnology, pp. 3–390, Washington 1908

165 Schwarzer Hirsch (Black Elk – Hehaka Sapa), Die Heilige Pfeife. Die sieben geheimen Riten der Sioux-Indianer, noted by J. E. Brown, Olten, Freiburg (Breisgau) 1956

166 Shimkin, D. B., Wind River Shoshone Ethnography, in: Anthropological Records, Vol. V, pp. 245—88, Berkeley 1947

167 Skinner, A., Notes on the Eastern Cree and Northern Saulteaux, in: Anthropological Papers of the American Museum of Natural History, Vol. IX, pp. 1—116, New York 1911

168 — Social Life and Ceremonial Bundles of the Menomini Indians, in: Anthropological Papers of the American Museum of Natural History, Vol. XIII, Part. I, New York 1915

169 — Observations on the Ethnology of the Sauk Indians, in: Bulletin of the Public Museum of the City of Milwaukee, Vol. V, pp. 1—180, Milwaukee 1923—25

170 — The Mascoutens or Prairie Potawatomi Indians, in: Bulletin of the Public Museum of the City of Milwaukee, Vol. VI, pp. 1—411, Milwaukee 1924—27

171 — Ethnology of the Ioway Indians, in: Bulletin of the Public Museum of the City of Milwaukee, Vol. V, pp. 181 to 354, Milwaukee 1926

172 Slotkin, J. S., The Peyote Religion, Glencoe 1956

173 — The Menomini Powwow, in: Publications in Anthropology of the Public Museum of the City of Milwaukee, Vol. IV, Milwaukee 1957

174 Speck, F. G., Ethnology of the Yuchi Indians, in: Anthropological Publications of the University of Pennsylvania Museum, Vol. I, Philadelphia 1909

175 — Chapters on the Ethnology of the Powhatan Tribes, in: Indian Notes and Monographs, Vol. I, pp. 227—455, New York 1928

176 — Naskapi, Norman 1935

177 — Oklahoma Delaware Ceremonies, Dances and Feasts, in: Memoirs of the American Philosophical Society, Vol. VII, pp. 1—161, Philadelphia 1937

178 — Catawba Religious Beliefs, Mortuary Customs, and Dances, in: Primitive Man, Vol. XII, pp. 21—57, Washington 1939

179 — Midwinter Rites of the Cayuga Long House, Philadelphia 1949

180 Spicer, E. H., Pascua: A Yaqui Village in Arizona, Chicago 1940

181 — Potam, A Yaqui Village in Sonora, Memoir 77 of the American Anthropological Association, Menasha 1954

182 Spier, L., The Sun Dance of the Plains Indians, in: Anthropological Papers of the American Museum of Natural History, Vol. XVI, Part 7, pp. 451—522, New York 1921

183 — Havasupai Ethnography, in: Anthropological Papers of the American Museum of Natural History, Vol. XXIX, pp. 81—392, New York 1928

184 — Klamath Ethnography, in: University of California Publications in American Archaeology and Ethnology, Vol. XXX, pp. 1—338, Berkeley 1930

185 — Yuman Tribes of the Gila River, Chicago 1933

186 — The Prophet Dance of the Northwest and Its Derivatives, in: General Series in Anthropology, Vol. I, pp. 1 to 74, Menasha 1935

187 Spinden, H. J., The Nez Percé Indians, Memoirs of the American Anthropological Association, No. II, pp. 165 to 174, Lancaster, Pa. 1908

188 Stephen, A. M., Hopi Journal, ed. by E. C. Parsons, Columbia University Contributions to Anthropology, XXXIII, 2 Vols., New York 1936

189 Stevenson, M. C., The Zuñi Indians, in: 23rd Annual Report of the Bureau of American Ethnology, pp. 13 to 608, Washington 1904

190 Swanton, J. R., Social Condition, Beliefs and Linguistic Relationship of the Tlingit Indians, in: 26th Annual Report of the Bureau of American Ethnology, pp. 391 to 486, Washington 1908

191 — Contributions to the Ethnology of the Haida, in: Memoirs of the American Museum of Natural History, Vol. VIII, pp. 1—300, New York 1909

192 — Indian Tribes of the Lower Mississippi Valley and Adjacent Coast of the Gulf of Mexico, Bulletin 43 of the Bureau of American Ethnology, Washington 1911

193 — Social Organization and Social Usages of the Indians of the Creek Confederacy, in: 42nd Annual Report of the Bureau of American Ethnology, pp. 23—472, Washington 1928

194 — Religious Beliefs and Medical Practices of the Creek Indians, in: 42nd Annual Report of the Bureau of American Ethnology, pp. 473—672, Washington 1928

195 — Social and Religious Beliefs and Usages of the Chickasaw Indians, in: 44th Annual Report of the Bureau of American Ethnology, pp. 169—273, Washington 1928

196 — Source Material for the Social and Ceremonial Lite of the Choctaw Indians, Bulletin 103 of the Bureau of American Ethnology, Washington 1931

197 — Indians of the Southeastern United States, Bulletin 137 of the Bureau of American Ethnology, Washington 1946

198 Teit, J. A., The Thompson Indians, in: Memoirs of the American Museum of Natural History, Vol. II, pp. 163 to 392, New York 1900

199 — The Lillooet Indians, in: Memoirs of the American Museum of Natural History, Vol. IV, pp. 193—300, New York 1906

200 — The Shuswap, in: Memoirs of the American Museum of Natural History, Vol. IV, pp. 447—758, New York 1909

201 — The Middle Columbia Salish, in: University ot Washington Publications in Anthropology, Vol. II, pp. 83—128, Seattle 1928

202 — The Salishan Tribes of the Western Plateaus, in: 45th Annual Report of the Bureau of American Ethnology, pp. 37—197, Washington 1930

203 — Field Notes on the Tahltan and Kaska Indians, 1912—1915, in: Anthropologica, Vol. III, pp. 39—171, Ottawa 1956

204 Tooker, E., An Ethnography of the Huron Indians, 1615—1649, Bulletin 190 of the Bureau of American Ethnology, Washington 1964

205 Trowbridge, C. C., Shawnese Traditions, ed. by W. V. Kinietz and E. W. Voegelin, in: Occasional Contributions from the Museum of Anthropology of the University of Michigan, Vol. IX, pp. 1—71, Ann Arbor 1939

206 Turney-High, H. H., The Flathead Indians of Montana, in: Memoirs of the American Anthropological Association, No. XLVIII, pp. 1—161, Menasha 1937

207 — Ethnography of the Kutenai, in: Memoirs of the American Anthropological Association, No. LVI, pp. 1 to 202, Menasha 1941

208 Underhill, R. M., Ceremonial Patterns in the Greater Southwest, American Ethnological Society Monographs, No. XIII, New York 1948

209 Voegelin, E. W., Tübatulabal Ethnography, in: Anthropological Records, Vol. II, pp. 1–84, Berkeley 1938

210 – and J. H. Steward, The Northern Paiute Indians, Washington 1954

211 Walker, J. R., The Sun Dance and Other Ceremonies of the Oglala, in: Anthropological Papers of the American Museum of Natural History, Vol. XVI, pp. 51–221, New York 1917

212 Wallace, E., and E. A. Hoebel, The Comanches, Norman 1952

213 Wallis, W. D., The Canadian Dakota, in: Anthropological Papers of the American Museum of Natural History, Vol. XLI, Part I, pp. 1–225, New York 1947

214 – and R. S. Wallis, The Micmac Indians of Eastern Canada, Minneapolis 1955

215 White, L. A., The Acoma Indians, in: 47th Annual Report of the Bureau of American Ethnology, pp. 17–192, Washington 1932

216 – The Pueblo of San Felipe, in: Memoirs of the American Anthropological Association, Vol. XXXVIII, pp. 1–69, Menasha 1932

217 – The Pueblo of Santo Domingo, in: Memoirs of the American Anthropological Association, Vol. XLIII, pp. 1–210, Menasha 1935

218 – The Pueblo of Santa Ana, in: Memoirs of the American Anthropological Association, Vol. LX, pp. 1–360, Menasha 1942

219 – The Pueblo of Sia, New Mexico, Bulletin 184 of the Bureau of American Ethnology, Washington 1962

220 Wissler, C., North American Indians of the Plains, New York 1912

221 – General Discussion of Shamanistic and Dancing Societies, in: Anthropological Papers of the American Museum of Natural History, Vol. XI, pp. 853–76, New York 1916

222 – Indians of the United States, New York 1940

223 Witthoft, J., Green Corn Ceremonialism in the Eastern Woodlands, in: Occasional Contributions from the Museum of Anthropology of the University of Michigan, Vol. XIII, pp. 11–21, Ann Arbor 1949

Central and South American Indians

224 Ahlbrinck, W., Encyclopaedie der Karaiben, in: Verhandelingen der Koninklijke Akademie van Wetenschapen, Afdeeling Letterkunde, n.s., Part XXVII, No. 1, Amsterdam 1931

225 Albisetti, C., and A. J. Venturelli, Enciclopedia Bororo, Vol. I, Publica çöes do Museu Regional Dom Bosco, I, Campo Grande 1962

226 Arauz, P., El Pipil de la región de los Itzalcos, San Salvador 1960

227 Armellada, C. de, Los Motilones, Caracas 1954

228 Baldus, H., Indianerstudien im nordöstlichen Chaco, Leipzig 1931

229 – Os Tapirape, in: Revista do Arquivo Municipal, Vol. XCVI, pp. 155–66; XCVII, pp. 45–54; XCVIII, pp. 105–26; XCIX, pp. 63–77; C, pp. 191–98, CI, pp. 67 to 75; CII, pp. 123–30; CIII, pp. 183–89; CIV, pp. 93–100; CV, pp. 77–90; CVII, pp. 107–20; CVIII, pp. 121–37; CIX, pp. 75–88; CX, pp. 191–202; CXI, pp. 105–19; CXII, pp. 51–62; CIII, pp. 191–99; CXIV, pp. 185–99; CXV, pp. 255–60; CXVI, pp. 55–61; CXVII, pp. 91–98; CXVIII, pp. 117–25; CXIX, pp 79–87; CXX, pp. 51 to 57; CXXI, pp. 79–82; CXXII, pp. 167–172; CXXIII, pp. 53–56; CXXIV, pp. 139–43; CXXVII, pp. 231–36, São Paulo 1944–49

230 Basauri, C., La Población Indígena de México, 3 Vols., Mexico 1940

231 Beals, R.L., Cherán: a Sierra Tarascan Village, Institute of Social Anthropology Publication, No. 2, Washington 1946

232 Becher, H., Die Surára und Pakidái, Mitteilungen aus dem Museum für Völkerkunde in Hamburg, No. XXVI, Hamburg 1960

233 Biesanz, J., The People of Panama, New York 1955

234 Blom, F., and O. La Farge, Tribes and Temples, 2 Vols., Middle American Research Series, No. 1, New Orleans 1926–27

235 Boggiani, G., I Caduvei (Mbayá o Guaycurú), Rome 1895

236 Bolinder, G., Die Indianer der tropischen Schneegebirge, Stuttgart 1925

237 Carrasco, P., Pagan Rituals and Beliefs Among the Chontal Indians of Oaxaca, Mexico, in: Anthropological Records, Vol. XX, pp. 87–117, Berkeley, Los Angeles 1960

238 Caspar, F., Tupari, Brunswick 1952

239 Conzemius, E., Ethnographical Survey of the Miskito and Sumu Indians of Honduras and Nicaragua, Bulletin 106 of the Bureau of American Ethnology, Washington 1932

240 Cook, S. F., and W. Borah, The Indian Population of Central Mexico, 1531–1610, in: Ibero-Americana. No. 44, Berkeley 1960

241 Covarrubias, M., Mexico South, London, Toronto, Melbourne, Sydney 1948; New York 1964

242 Ehrenreich, P., Über die Botocudos, in: Zeitschrift für Ethnologie, Vol. XIX, pp. 1–46, 46–82, Berlin 1887

243 – Beiträge zur Völkerkunde Brasiliens, in: Veröffentlichungen aus dem Königlichen Museum für Völkerkunde, Vol. II, Berlin 1891

244 Emperaire, J., Les Nomades de la Mer, Paris 1955

245 Farabee, W. C., The Central Arawaks, Publication IX of the University of Pennsylvania Museum, Philadelphia 1918

246 – Indian Tribes of Eastern Peru, in: Archaeological and Ethnological Papers of the Peabody Museum, Harvard University, Vol. X, Cambridge, Mass. 1922

247 – The Central Caribs, Publication X of the University of Pennsylvania Museum, Philadelphia 1924

248 Fejos, P., Ethnography of the Yagua, in: Viking Fund Publications in Anthropology, No. 1, New York 1943

249 Fock, N., Waiwai, Nationalmuseets Skrifter, Etnografisk Raekke VIII, Copenhagen 1963

250 Foster, G. M., Notes on the Popoluca of Vera Cruz, Publicación del Instituto Panamericano de Geografía e Historia, No. 51, Mexico 1940

251 — Empire's Children: the People of Tzintzuntzan, Institute of Social Anthropology Publication, No. 6, Washington 1948

252 Friede, J., Los Indios de Alto Magdalena, Bogotá 1943

253 Gamio, M., La población del valle de Teotihuacán, 2 Vols., Mexico 1922

254 Gann, W.T., The Maya Indians of Southern Yucatan and Northern British Honduras, Bulletin 64 of the Bureau of American Ethnology, Washington 1918

255 Gibson, C., The Aztecs Under Spanish Rule, Stanford 1964

256 Girard, R., Los Chortis ante el problema maya, 5 Vols., Mexico 1949

257 — Indios Selváticos de la Amazonia Peruana, Mexico 1958

258 Goldman, I., The Cubeo, in: Illinois Studies in Anthropology, Vol. II, Urbana 1963

259 Grubb, W. B., An Unknown People in an Unknown Land. An Account of the Life and Customs of the Lengua Indians of the Paraguayan Chaco, London 1911 (2nd edition)

260 Gusinde, M., Die Feuerland-Indianer, Vol. I: Die Selk'-nam; Vol. II: Die Yamana; Vol. III: Anthropologie der Feuerland-Indianer, Vienna-Mödling 1931, 1937, 1939

261 von Hagen, V. W., The Jicaque (Torrupán) Indians of Honduras, in: Indian Notes and Monographs, Vol. LIII, New York 1943

262 Hanke, W., Verlöschende Urzeit im Innern Brasiliens, Kulturgeschichtliche Forschungen, Vol. XI, Brunswick 1964

263 Hissink, K., and A. Hahn, Die Tacana, Vol. I, Stuttgart 1961

264 Holmberg, A. R., Nomads of the Long Bow, Institute of Social Anthropology Publication, No. X, Washington 1950

265 Jahn, A., Los Aborígenes del Occidente de Venezuela, Caracas 1927

266 Johnson, J. B., The Opata: An Inland Tribe of Sonora, in: Publications in Anthropology of the University of New Mexico, Vol. VI, Albuquerque 1950

267 Karsten, R., Blood Revenge, War, and Victory Feasts Among the Jibaro Indians of Eastern Ecuador, Bulletin 79 of the Bureau of American Ethnology, Washington 1923

268 — Indian Tribes of the Argentine and Bolivian Chaco, in: Commentationes Humanarum Litterarum, Societas Scientiarum Fennica, Vol. IV, No. 1, Helsinki 1932

269 — The Head-Hunters of Western Amazonas. The Life and Culture of the Jibaro Indians of Eastern Ecuador and Peru, in: Commentationes Humanarum Litterarum, Societas Scientiarum Fennica, Vol. VII, No. 1, Helsinki 1935

270 Kersten, L., Die Indianerstämme des Gran Chaco bis zum Ausgange des 18. Jahrhunderts, in: Internationales Archiv für Ethnographie, Vol. XVII, Leiden 1905

271 Koch-Grünberg, T., Zwei Jahre unter den Indianern. Reisen in Nordwestbrasilien, 2 Vols., Berlin 1909—10

272 — Vom Roroima zum Orinoco. Ergebnisse einer Reise in Nordbrasilien und Venezuela in den Jahren 1911—13, Vols. I—V, Berlin, Stuttgart 1916—28

273 Krickeberg, W., Die Totonaken, in: Baessler-Archiv, Vols. VII—IX, Berlin 1918—22

274 La Barre, W., The Aymara Indians of the Lake Titicaca Plateau, Bolivia, Memoir LXVIII of the American Anthropological Association, Menasha 1948

275 Latcham, R. E., La organizacion social y las creencias religiosas de los antiguos Araucanos, in: Publicaciones del Museo de Etnología y Antropología, Vol. III, pp. 245—868, Santiago de Chile 1922

276 Lehmann, W., Zentral -America, Part I, Berlin 1920

277 Lenz, R., Estudios Araucanos, in: Anales de la Universidad de Chile, Vol. XC, pp. 359—85, 843—78; XCI, pp. 195—241; XCIII, pp. 427—38, 507—55; XCIV, pp. 95—120, 245—62; 331—52, 491—504, 691—719, 841 to 65; XCVIII, pp. 187—207, 301—38, 495—525, Santiago de Chile 1895—97

278 Lothrop, S. K., The Indians of Tierra del Fuego, in: Contributions from the Museum of the American Indian, Vol. X, New York 1928

279 — Indians of the Parana Delta, in: Annals of the New York Academy of Sciences, Vol. XXXIII, pp. 77—232, New York 1932

280 Lumholtz, C., Unknown Mexico, 2 Vols., London 1902

281 McKim, F., San Blas, An Account of the Cuna Indians of Panama, ed. by H. Wassén, Etnologiska Studier, No. 15, Gothenburg 1947

282 Madsen, W., The Virgin's Children. Life in an Aztec Village Today, Austin 1960

283 Medina, J. T., Los Aborígenes de Chile, Santiago de Chile 1952

284 Mendieta y Nuñez, L. (ed), Etnografía de México, Síntesis Monograficas, Mexico 1957

285 Métraux, A., La Civilisation Matérielle des Tribus Tubi-Guarani, Paris 1928

286 — La Religion des Tupinamba et ses Rapports avec celle des autres Tribus Tupi-Guarani, Paris 1928

287 — Études sur la Civilisation des Indiens Chiriguano, in: Revista del Instituto de Etnología de la Universidad Nacional de Tucumán, Vol. I, pp. 295—493, Tucumán 1930

288 — Les Indiens Uro-Cipaya de Carangas, in: Journal de la Société des Américanistes, n.s., Vol. 27, 28, Paris 1935 to 1936

289 — The Native Tribes of Eastern Bolivia and Western Matto Grosso, Bulletin 134 of the Bureau of American Ethnology, Washington 1942

290 — Le Shamanisme chez les Indiens de l'Amérique du Sud Tropicale, in: Acta Americana, Vol. II, pp. 197 –219, Mexico 1944

291 Mishkin, B., Los Quechuas Contemporáneos, in: Revista del Museo Nacional, Vol. XXIX, pp. 160—221, Lima 1960

292 Müller, F., Beiträge zur Ethnographie der Guarani-Indianer im östlichen Waldgebiet von Paraguay, in: Anthropos, Vol. XXIX, pp. 177—208, 441—60, 695—702; XXX, pp. 151—64, 433—50, 767—83, Vienna-Mödling 1934—35

293 Mujia, R., Bolivia-Paraguay, 8 Vols., La Paz 1914

294 Murphy, R. F., Headhunter's Heritage, Berkeley 1960

295 — and B. Quain, The Trumai Indians of Central Brazil, Monograph of the American Ethnological Society, Vol. XXIV, New York 1955

296 Nimuendajú, C., The Apinayé, in: Anthropological Series of the Catholic University of America, Vol. VIII, Washington 1939

297 — The Šerente, Publication of the Frederick Webb

Hodge Anniversary Publications Fund, Vol. IV, Los Angeles 1942

298 Nimuendajú, C., The Eastern Timbira, in: University of California Publications in American Archaeology and Ethnology, Vol. XLI, Berkeley 1946

299 — Social Organization and Beliefs of the Botocudo of Eastern Brazil, in: Southwestern Journal of Anthropology, Vol. II, pp. 93–115, Albuquerque 1946

300 — The Tukuna, in: University of California Publications in American Archaeology and Ethnology, Vol. XLV, Berkeley 1952

301 Nordenskiöld, E., Indianlif i El Gran Chaco, Stockholm 1910; German: Indianerleben, Leipzig 1912

302 — The Ethnography of South America seen from Mojos in Bolivia, in: Comparative Ethnographical Studies, No. 3, Gothenburg 1924

303 — A Historical and Ethnographical Survey of the Cuna Indians, ed. by H. Wassén, in: Comparative Ethnographical Studies, No. 10, Gothenburg 1938

304 Oberg, K., Indian Tribes of Northern Matto Grosso, Brazil, Institute of Social Anthropology Publication, No. XV, Washington 1953

305 Osborne, H., Indians of the Andes, London 1952

306 Pittier de Fabrega, H., Ethnographic and Linguistic Notes on the Paez Indians of Tierra adentro, Cauca, Colombia, Memoir I of the American Anthropological Association, Lancaster, Pa. 1907

307 Ploetz, H., and A. Métraux, La Civilisation Matérielle et la Vie Sociale et Religieuse des Indiens Zè du Brésil Méridional et Oriental, in: Revista del Instituto de Etnología de la Universidad Nacional de Tucumán, Vol. I, No. 2, Tucumán 1930

308 Preuss, K. T., Die Nayaritexpedition I: Die Religion der Coraindianer in Texten nebst Wörterbuch, Leipzig 1912

309 — Religion und Mythologie der Uitoto, Vol. I–II, Göttingen, Leipzig 1921–23

310 — Forschungsreise zu den Kágaba, Vienna-Mödling 1926

311 Redfield, R., Tepoztlan, a Mexican Village, Chicago 1930

312 — The Folk Culture of Yucatan, Chicago 1941

313 — and R. A. Villa, Chan Kom, a Maya Village, Publication 448 of the Carnegie Institution, Washington 1934

314 Reichel-Dolmatoff, G., Datos Histórico-Culturales sobre las Tribus de la Antigua obernación de Santa Marta, Bogotá 1951

315 Roys, R., The Indian Background of Colonial Yucatan, Publication 548 of the Carnegie Institution, Washington 1943

316 Sapper, K., Quiché und Kekchi, in: Ibero-Amerikanisches Archiv, VIII, No. 3, Berlin 1933

317 Sauer, C. O., Aboriginal Population of Northwestern Mexico, in: Ibero-Americana, No. 10, Berkeley 1935

318 Saville, M. H., Reports on the Maya Indians of Yucatan, in: Indian Notes and Monographs, Vol. IX, No. 3, New York 1921

319 Schaden, E., A Mitologia Heróica de Tribos Indígenas do Brasil, Rio de Janeiro 1959

320 Schmidt, M., Indianerstudien in Zentralbrasilien, Berlin 1905

321 — Die Paressi-Kabiši, in: Baessler-Archiv, Vol. IV, pp. 167–250, Berlin 1914

322 — Die Guato und ihr Gebiet, in: Baessler-Archiv, Vol. IV pp. 251–83, Berlin 1914

323 Scholes, F. V., and R. L. Roys, The Maya Chontal Indians of Acalan-Tixchel, Publication 560 of the Carnegie Institution, Washington 1948

324 Schultze-Jena, L., Indiana I: Leben, Glaube und Sprache der Quiché von Guatemala; II: Mythen in der Muttersprache der Pipil von Izalco in El Salvador; III: Bei den Azteken, Mixteken und Tlapaneken der Sierra Madre del Sur von Mexico, Jena 1933–38

325 Skinner, A., Notes on the Bribri of Costa Rica, in: Indian Notes and Monographs, Vol. VI, No. 3, New York 1920

326 Snethlage, E. H., Atiko y, Berlin 1937

327 Soustelle, J., Notes sur les Lacandon du Lac Peljá et du Rio Jetjá (Chiapas), in: Journal de la Société des Américanistes, n.s., Vol. 25, pp. 153–80, Paris 1933

328 Starr, F., Notes upon Ethnography of Southern Mexico, in: Proceedings of the Davenport Academy of Sciences, Vols. VIII, IX, N.P. 1901, 1902

329 von den Steinen, K., Unter den Naturvölkern Zentralbrasiliens, Berlin 1894

330 Steward, J. H., and L. Faron, Native Peoples of South America, New York 1959

331 Stirling, M. W., Historical and Ethnographical Material on the Jivaro Indians, Bulletin 117 of the Bureau of American Ethnology, Washington 1938

332 Stoll, O., Die Ethnologie der Indianerstämme von Guatemala, in: Supplement to Vol. I, Internationales Archiv für Ethnographie, Leiden 1889

333 Stone, D., The Talamancan Tribes of Costa Rica, in: Papers of the Peabody Museum of American Archaeology and Ethnology, Harvard University, Vol. XLIII, No. 2, Cambridge, Mass. 1962

334 Termer, F., Zur Ethnologie und Ethnographie des nördlichen Mittelamerika, Ibero-Amerikanisches Archiv IV, No. 3, Berlin und Bonn 1930

335 Tessmann, G., Die Indianer Nordost-Perus, Hamburg 1930

336 Thompson, J. E. S., Ethnology of the Mayas of Southern and Central British Honduras, in: Anthropological Series of the Field Museum of Natural History, Vol. XVII, No. 2, Chicago 1930

337 — The Itza of Tayasal, Peten, in: Homenaje al Doctor Alfonso Caso, pp. 384–400, Mexico 1951

338 Thurn, E. F. im, Among the Indians of Guiana, London 1883; New York 1967

339 Toor, F., Treasury of Mexican Folkways, New York 1947

340 Tozzer, A. M., A Comparative Study of the Mayas and the Lacandones, New York 1907

341 Trimborn, H., Tres Estudios para la Etnografía y Arqueología de Colombia, in: Revista de Indias, Vol. IV, pp. 43 to 91, 331–47, 441–56, 629–81; V, pp. 27–39, 199–226, Madrid 1943–44

342 Tschopik, H. Jr., The Aymara of Chucuito, Peru, in: Anthropological Papers of the American Museum of Natural History, Vol. XLIV, pp. 133–308, New York 1951

343 Vellard, J., Les Indiens Guayaki, in: Journal de la Société des Américanistes, n.s., Vol. XXVI, pp. 223–92; XXVII, pp. 175–244, Paris 1934–35

444 Verneau, R., and P. Rivet, Ethnographie Ancienne de l'Équateur, 2 Vols., Paris 1912, 1922

345 Villa, R. A., The Maya of East Central Quintana Roo, Publication 559 of the Carnegie Institution, Washington 1945

346 Wagley, C., and E. Galvão, The Tenetehara Indians of Brazil, in: Columbia University Contributions to Anthropology, Vol. XXXV, New York 1949

347 Wassén, H., Contributions to Cuna Ethnography, Etnologiska Studier, No. 16, Gothenburg 1949

348 – Estudios Chocoes, Etnologiska Studier, No. 26, Gothenburg 1963

349 Wilbert, J., Zur Kenntnis der Yabarana, Supplement to Antropologica, Vol. I, Cologne 1959

350 – Indios de la región Orinoco-Ventuari, Caracas 1964

351 Wisdom, C., The Chorti Indians of Guatemala, Chicago 1940

352 Zerries, O., Wild- und Buschgeister in Südamerika, Wiesbaden 1954

353 – Waika. Die kulturgeschichtliche Stellung der Waika-Indianer im Rahmen der Völkerkunde Südamerikas, Munich 1964

Music and Musical Instruments of the Indians and Eskimo (P.C./R.K.)

354 Abraham, O., and E. M. von Hornbostel, Phonographierte Indianermelodien aus British Columbia, in: Boas Anniversary Volume, pp. 447–74, New York 1906; also in the series Sammelbände für Vergleichende Musikwissenschaft, Vol. I, Berlin, Munich 1922

355 Acosta-Saignes, M., El Maremare. Baile del Jaguar y la Luna, in: Archivos Venezolanos de Folklore, Vol. I, No. 2, Caracas 1952

356 Alba, G. H. de, De la Música indígena en Colombia, in: Boletín Latinoamericano de Música, Vol. IV, Bogotá 1938

357 Alcina Franch, J., Sonajas rituales en la cerámica mejicana, in: Revista de Indias, Vol. XIII, 54, pp. 257–38, Madrid 1953

358 Allende, U., Chilean Folk Music, in: Bulletin of the Pan-American Union, Vol. LXV, No. 9, Washington 1941

359 – Los Orígenes de la Música Popular Chilena, in: Antarctica, No. 2, October 1944

360 Alvina, L., La Musica Incaica, in: Revisty Universitaria de la Universidad Nacional de Cuzco, Vol. XVIII, Cuzco 1929

361 Amezquita Borja, F., Música y danza de la sierra norte de Puebla, Puebla 1943

362 Anderson, A. J. O., Aztec Music, in: The Western Humanities Review, No. VIII, pp. 131 ff., Salt Lake City 1954

363 Andree, R., Alte Trommeln indianischer Medizinmänner, in: Globus, Vol. LXXV, pp. 14–16, Brunswick 1899

364 Angulo, J. de, and M. Béclard d'Harcourt, La Musique des Indiens de la Californie du Nord, in: Journal de la Société des Américanistes, n.s., Vol. XXIII, Paris 1931

365 Aretz-Thielle, I., Música tradicional argentina, in: Tucumán, Historia y Folklore, Buenos Aires 1946

366 – Músicas Pentatónicas en Sudamérica, in: Archivos Venezolanos de Folklore, Vol. I, No. 2, Caracas 1952

367 Arguedas, J. M., Cuentos Mágico-Religiosos y Canciones de Fiestas tradicionales, in: Folklore Americano, Vol. I, Lima 1953

368 Arguedas, J. M., Songs of the Quechuas, in: The Americas, Vol. IX, No. 8, pp. 30–34, Washington 1957

369 – Cuentos mágico-realistas Quechuas de Lucanamarca, in: Folklore Americano, Vol. VIII/IX, pp. 142–216, Lima 1960/61

370 – and Ruth Stephan, The Singing Mountaineers: Songs and Tales of the Quechua People, Austin 1957; Edinburgh, London 1958

371 – and F. Izquierdo Río, Mitos, Leyendas y Cuentos Peruanos, Lima 1947

372 Arnao, A., Cuentos Peruanos, Lima 1939

373 Augusta, F. J. de, Zehn Araukanerlieder, in: Anthropos, Vol. VI, pp. 684–98, Vienna-Mödling 1911

374 Ayestarán, L., La Música Indígena en el Uruguay, Montevideo 1949–53

375 Azevedo, L. H. C. de, Escala, ritmo e melodia na música dos Indios brasileiros, Rio de Janeiro 1938

376 – Tupinamba Melodies in Jean de Léry's Histoire d'un Voyage fait en la Terre du Brésil, in: Papers of the American Musicological Society, Annual Meeting 1941

377 Baker, T., Über die Musik der Nordamerikanischen Wilden, Leipzig and New York 1882

378 Bakkegard, P. M., and E. A. Morris, Seventh Century Flutes from Arizona, in: Ethnomusicology, Vol. V, No. 3, Middletown 1961

379 Barbeau, M., Asiatic Survivals in Indian Songs, in: The Musical Quarterly, Vol. XX, pp. 107 ff., New York 1934

380 – The Dragon Myths and Ritual Songs of the Iroquoians, in: Journal of the International Folk Music Council, Vol. III, pp. 81 ff., Cambridge 1951

381 Barlow, R., and H. Lehmann, Statuettes-Grelots Aztèques de la Vallée de Mexico, in: Tribus, Vol. IV, Stuttgart 1956

382 Barrera Vázques, A., Canción de la danza del arquero flechador, in: Tlalocan, Vol. I, pp. 273–77, Mexico 1943

383 Barton, F. R., American Primitive Music, New York 1909

384 Béclard d'Harcourt, M., La Musique Indienne chez les Anciens Civilisés d'Amerique. Le Folklore Musical de la Région Andine Equateur, Pérou, Bolivie, in: Lavignac, Histoire de la Musique, Paris 1922

385 Beyer, H., Mexican Bone Rattles, in: Middle American Research Series Publication, No. V/7, New Orleans 1934

386 Boas, F., On Certain Songs and Dances of the Kwakiutl, in: Journal of American Folklore, Vol. I, pp. 49–64, New York 1888

387 – Chinook Songs, in: Journal of American Folklore, Vol. I, pp. 220–26, New York 1888

388 – Dance and Music in the Life of the Northwest Coast Indians of North America, in: The Function of Dance in Human Society, pp. 7–18, New York 1944

389 Bogert, C. M., and R. Martha, Tarascan and Other Music of Mexico, in: Ethnic Folkways Album FW 8867, New York 1958

390 Boglár, L., and I. Halmos, La Flûte Nasale chez les Indiens Nambicuara, in: Acta Ethnographica, Vol. XI, pp. 437–446, Budapest 1962

391 Bose, F., Die Musik der Uitoto, in: Zeitschrift für Vergleichende Musikwissenschaft, Vol. II, pp. 1–14, 25–50, 1934

392 — Musikalische Völkerkunde, Freiburg (Breisgau) 1953

393 — Südamerikanische Musikforschung, in: Acta Musicologica, Vol. XXIX, Cassel 1953

394 Bose, F., Die Musik der Chibcha, in: Internationales Archiv für Ethnographie, Vol. XLVIII, pp. 149–99, Leiden 1958

395 Boulton, L., Indian Music, in: Ethnic Folkways Album FW 8850, New York 1957

396 Bowra, C. M., Primitive Song, London 1962

397 Brasseur de Bourbourg, C. E., Grammaire de la Langue Quiché . . . servant d'Introduction au Rabinal Achi, Drame Indigène, avec la Musique Originale, Paris 1862

398 Brinton, D. G., Native American Stringed Musical Instruments, in: American Antiquarian, Vol. XIX, pp. 19 to 20, Chicago 1897

399 Burlin, N., American Indian Cradle Songs, in: The Musical Quarterly, Vol. VII, New York 1921

400 Burton, F. W., American Primitive Music, with especial attention to the Songs of the Ojibways, New York 1909

401 Bushnell, G., Some Post-Columbian Whistling Jars from Peru, in: Proceedings of the 33rd International Congress of Americanists, pp. 416–20, San José 1959

402 Buttree-Seton, J. M., The Rhythm of the Red Man, New York 1930

403 Cabral, J., La Música Incaica, Buenos Aires 1915

404 Cáceres de Pastor, C., Instantáneas Musicales Andinas del Departamento de Junín, Lima 1944

405 Campobello, N., and G. Campobello, Ritmos indígenas de México, Mexico 1940

406 Capron, L., Notes on the Hunting Dance of the Cow Creek Seminole, October 1946, in: Florida Anthropologist, Vol. IX, Nos. 3–4, pp. 67–78, Tallahassee 1957

407 Castañeda, D., Las Flautas en las Civilizaciones azteca y tarasca, in: Música, Revista Mexicana, Vol. II, No. 2–4, Mexico 1930–31

408 — and V. T. Mendoza, Los Percutores precortesianos, in: Anales del Museo Nacional de Arqueología, Vol. VIII, Mexico 1933

409 — Los Teponaztlis en las Civilizaciones precortesianas, in: Anales del Museo Nacional de Arqueología, Vol. VIII, Mexico 1933

410 — Los pequeños Percutores en las Civilizaciones precortesianas, in: Anales del Museo Nacional de Arqueología, Vol. XXV, pp. 449–576, Mexico 1933

411 Chafe, W. C., Seneca Thanksgiving Rituals, Bulletin 183 of the Bureau of American Ethnology, Washington 1961

412 Chase, G., America's Music, New York, Toronto, London 1955; Chapter XX: Indian tribal music

413 Chavez, C., La Música, Parte I: La Música en las Culturas Indias, in: México y la Cultura, pp. 475 ff., Mexico 1946

414 Coimbra, G., La Música y la Danza del Pueblo Aymara, in: Revista Geográfica Americana, Vol. XVI, pp. 331 to 338, Buenos Aires 1941

415 — Danzarines y Músicos Aymaras, in: Revista Geográfica Americana, Vol. XVII, pp. 89–96, Buenos Aires 1942

416 Colby, L. W., The Ghost Song of the Dakota, in: Proceedings and Collections of the Nebraska State Historical Society, Series 2, Vol. I, pp. 131–50. Lincoln 1895

417 Collaer, P., Musique Caraïbe et Maya, in: Studia memoriae Bela Bartok, Budapest 1957

418 Conklin, H. C., and W. C. Sturtevant, Seneca Indian Singing Tools at Coldspring Longhouse: Musical Instruments of the Modern Iroquois, in: Proceedings of the American Philosophical Society, Vol. 97, pp. 262–90, New York 1953

419 Correa, G., Texto de un baile de diablos, in: Native Drama in Guatemala and Mexico, pp. 97–104, New Orleans 1958

420 Cosio, J. G., La Música Incaica, in: Revista Universitaria de la Universidad Nacional de Cuzco, Vol. IV, No. 12, pp. 31–35, Cuzco 1915

421 Cresson, H. T., Aztec Music, in: Proceedings of the Academy of Natural Sciences of Philadelphia, Vol. XXXV, Philadelphia 1883

422 Cringan, A. T., Pagan Dance Songs of the Iroquois, in: Annual Archaeological Report, being Part of Appendix to the Minister of Education, Ontario, pp. 168–89, Toronto 1899

423 — Iroquois Folk Songs, in: Annual Archaeological Report, being Part of Appendix to the Report of the Minister of Education, Ontario, pp. 137–52, Toronto 1902

424 Cronyn, G. W. (ed.), The Path On the Rainbow: An Anthology of Songs and Chants from the Indians of North America, New York 1934 (2nd edition)

425 Densmore, F., An Onondaga Thanksgiving Song, in: Indian School Journal, Vol. VII, pp. 23–24, 1907

426 — Chippewa Music I, II, Bulletins 45 and 53 of the Bureau of American Ethnology, Washington 1910, 1913

427 — Preservation of Indian Music, in: Smithsonian Miscellaneous Collections, Vol. LXV, No. 6, pp. 81–85, Washington 1915

428 — The Study of Indian Music, in: The Musical Quarterly, Vol. I and II, New York 1915, 1917

429 — Music in Its Relation to the Religious Thought of the Teton Sioux, in: Holmes Anniversary Volume, pp. 67 to 79, Washington 1916

430 — Poems from Sioux and Chippewa Songs, Washington 1917

431 — Study of Indian Music, in: Smithsonian Miscellaneous Collections, Vol. LXVI, No. 17, pp. 108–11, Washington 1917

432 — Teton Sioux Music, Bulletin 61 of the Bureau of American Ethnology, Washington 1918

433 — The Rhythm of Sioux and Chippewa Music, in: Art and Archaeology, Vol. IX, pp. 59–67, Washington 1920

434 — Indian Action Songs, Boston 1921

435 — The Music of the Papago and Pawnee, in: Exploration and Fieldwork of the Smithsonian Institution in 1920, Washington 1921

436 — Northern Ute Music, Bulletin 75 of the Bureau of American Ethnology, Washington 1922

437 — Mandan and Hidatsa Music, Bulletin 80 of the Bureau of American Ethnology, Washington 1923

438 — Music in the Treatment of the Sick by American Indians, in: Hygieia, pp. 29 ff., April 1923

439 — Rhythm in the Music of the American Indian, in: Proceedings of the International Congress of Americanists, Vol. XX, 1, pp. 85–89, Rio de Janeiro 1924

440 — How the Indian Seeks Power Through Dream Music, in: Musical America, Jan. 11th, 1926

441 — Music of the Tule Indians of Panama, in: Smithsonian

Miscellaneous Collections, Vol. LXXVII, No. 11, Washington 1926

442 — Studies of Indian Music Among the Menominee of Wisconsin, in: Exploration and Fieldwork of the Smithsonian Institution in 1925, Washington 1926

443 Densmore, F., Studies of Indian Music Among the Menomini, in: Smithsonian Miscellaneous Collections, Vol. LXXVIII, 1, pp. 119—25, Washington 1926

444 — The American Indians and Their Music, New York 1926

445 — The Songs of the Indians, in: American Mercury, Vol. VII, pp. 65—68, 1926

446 — Handbook of the Collection of Musical Instruments in the United States National Museum, Bulletin 136 of the U.S. National Museum, Washington 1927

447 — Music of the Winnebago Indians, in: Exploration and Fieldwork of the Smithsonian Institution 1927, pp. 189 to 198, Washington 1928

448 — The Melodic Formation of Indian Songs, in: Journal of the Washington Academy of Sciences, Vol. XVIII, pp. 16 ff., 1928

449 — Papago Music, Bulletin 90 of the Bureau of American Ethnology, Washington 1929

450 — Music ot the Winnebago and Menominee Indians of Wisconsin, in: Exploration and Fieldwork of the Smithsonian Institution 1928, pp. 189—98, Washington 1929

451 — Pawnee Music, Bulletin 93 of the Bureau of American Ethnology, Washington 1929

452 — What Intervals the Indians Sing, in: American Anthropologist, n.s., Vol. XXXI, Menasha 1929

453 — Peculiarities in the Singing of the American Indians, in: American Anthropologist, n.s., Vol. XXXII, pp. 651 to 660, Menasha 1930

454 — Music of the Winnebago, Chippewa, and Pueblo Indians, in: Exploration and Fieldwork of the Smithsonian Institution in 1930, pp. 217—24, Washington 1931

455 — Menominee Music, in: Bulletin 102 of the Bureau of American Ethnology, pp. 1—230, Washington 1932

456 — Seminole Music Related to Cocopa, in: El Palacio, Vol. XXXII, pp. 172—3, Santa Fé 1932

457 — Yuman and Yaqui Music, Bulletin 110 of the Bureau of American Ethnology, Washington 1932

458 — A Resemblance Between Yuman and Pueblo Songs, in: American Anthropologist, n.s., Vol. XXXIV, pp. 694—700, Menasha 1932

459 — Recording Seminole Songs in Florida, in: Exploration and Fieldwork of the Smithsonian Institution in 1932, pp. 93—96, Washington 1933

460 — A Survey of Indian Music in the Gulf States, in: American Anthropologist, n.s., Vol. XXXVI, Menasha 1934

461 — Cheyenne and Arapaho Music, Southwest Museum Paper, No. 10, Los Angeles 1936

462 — The Alabama Indians and Their Music, in: Straight Texas, Publication of the Texas Folk-Lore Society, No. 13, pp. 270—93, Austin 1937

463 — The Influence of Hymns on the Form of Indian Songs, in: American Anthropologist, n.s., Vol. XL, pp. 175—77, Menasha 1938

464 — Music of Santo Domingo Pueblo, New Mexico, Southwest Museum Paper, No. 12, Los Angeles 1938

465 — Musical Instruments of the Maidu Indians, in: American Anthropologist, n.s., Vol. XLI, pp. 113—18, Menasha 1939

466 — Nootka and Quileute Music, Bulletin 124 of the Bureau of American Ethnology, Washington 1939

467 — The Poetry of Indian Songs, in: So Live the Works of Men, ed. by D. D. Brand and F. E. Harvey, pp. 121—30, Albuquerque 1939

468 Densmore, F., Native Songs of Two Hybrid Ceremonies Among the American Indians, in: American Anthropologist, n.s., Vol. XLIII, pp. 77—82, Menasha 1941

469 — The Use of Meaningless Syllables in Indian Songs, in: American Anthropologist, n.s., Vol. XLV, pp. 160—62, Menasha 1942

470 — The Study of Indian Music, in: Annual Report of the Board of Regents of the Smithsonian Institution for 1491, pp. 527—550, Washington 1942

471 — A Search for Songs Among the Chitimacha Indians in Louisiana, in: Bulletin 133 of the Bureau of American Ethnology, pp. 1—15, Washington 1944

472 — Music of the Indians of British Columbia, in: Bulletin 136 of the Bureau of American Ethnology, pp. 1—99, Washington 1943

473 — Choctaw Music, in: Bulletin 136 of the Bureau of American Ethnology, pp. 101—188, Washington 1943

474 — The Survival of Omaha Songs, in: American Anthropologist, n.s., Vol. XLVI, Menasha 1944

475 — Traces of Foreign Influence in the Music of the American Indians, in: American Anthropologist, n.s., Vol. XLVI, pp. 106—12, Menasha 1944

476 — The Importance of Recordings of Indian Song: in American Anthropologist, n.s., Vol. XLVII, pp. 637—39, Menasha 1945

477 — Folk-Songs of the American Indians, in: The Masterkey, Vol. XXIV, pp. 14—18, Los Angeles 1950

478 — Technique in the Music of American Indians, in: Bulletin 151 of the Bureau of American Ethnology, pp. 211—16, Washington 1953

479 — The Belief of the Indian in a Connection Between Song and Supernatural, in: Bulletin 151 of the Bureau of American Ethnology, pp. 217—23, Washington 1953

480 — The Use of Music in the Treatment of the Sick by American Indians, in: Annual Report of the Board of Regents of the Smithsonian Institution for 1952, pp. 439—54, Washington 1953

481 — Seminole Music, Bulletin 161 of the Bureau of American Ethnology, Washington 1956

482 — Music of Acoma, Isleta, Cochiti and Zuñi Pueblos, Bulletin 165 of the Bureau of American Ethnology, Washington 1957

483 — Music of the Indians in Our Western States, in: Journal of American Folk-Lore, Vol. LXX, pp. 176—78, Bloomington 1957

484 — Music of the Maidu Indians of California, in Publications of the F. W. Hodge Anniversary Publication Fund, Southwest Museum, Vol. VII, Los Angeles 1958

485 Deuber, A., Musikinstrumente und Musik der Arapai, in: Speiser, F., Im Düster des brasilianischen Urwaldes, pp. 320—22, Stuttgart 1926

486 Domínguez, F., Yaqui Music, in: Mexican Folk-Ways, Yaqui Number, July, Mexico 1937

487 Dorsey, J. O., Omaha Songs, in: Journal of American Folk-Lore, Vol. I, pp. 209—13, Boston 1888

488 — Songs of the Hecucka Society, in: Journal of American Folk-Lore, Vol. I, pp. 65—68, Boston 1888

489 — Ponka and Omaha Songs, in: Journal of American Folk-Lore, Vol. II, pp. 271—76, Boston 1889

490 Dreyfus-Roche, S., Musique Indienne du Brésil (Collection du Musée de l'Homme; Disque MC 20.137), Paris

491 — Chants Indiens du Vénézuela. Séance de Chamanisme Collection du Musée de l'Homme; Disque LD1), Paris

492 Driver, H. E., The Spatial and Temporal Distribution of the Musical Rasp in the New World, in: Anthropos, Vol. XLVIII, pp. 578—92, Freiburg (Switzerland) 1953

493 — and S. H. Riesenberg, Hoof Rattles and Girls' Puberty Rites in North and South America, Memoir IV of the Indiana University Publications in Anthropology and Linguistics, pp. 1—31, Bloomington 1950

494 Eberhardt, C. C., Sound-Signalling by Indians of Tropical South America, in: Smithsonian Miscellaneous Collection, Vol. V, pp. 269—71, Washington 1909

495 Ekholm, G. F., and H. Yurchenko, Indian Music of Mexico (Ethnic Folkways Album P 413), New York

496 Estreicher, Z., The Music of the Caribou-Eskimo, in: Encyclopedia Arctica II: Anthropology, New York 1931

497 — Zur Polyrhythmik in der Musik der Eskimos, in: Schweizerische Musikzeitung, Vol. LXXXVII, pp. 411 to 15, Zürich 1947

498 — La Musique des Esquimaux-Caribous, in: Bulletin LIV de la Société Neuchâteloise de Géographie, pp. 1—53, 1948

499 — La Polyphonie chez les Esquimaux, in: Journal de la Société des Américanistes, Vol. XXXVII, pp. 259ff., Paris 1948

500 — Die Musik der Eskimos, in: Anthropos, Vol. XLV, pp. 659—720, Freiburg (Switzerland) 1950

501 — Eskimo-Musik, in: Musik in Geschichte und Gegenwart, Vol. III, Cassel and Basle 1954

502 — Cinq Chants des Esquimaux Ahearmiut, in: van den Steenhoven, Research-Report on Caribou-Eskimo Law, The Hague 1956

503 Farwell, A., American Indian Melodies, New York 1901

504 Fenton, W. N., Songs From the Iroquois Longhouse, Smithsonian Publication 3691, Washington 1942

505 — Seneca Songs from Coldspring Longhouse, Program Notes to Album 17, Folk Music of the United States, Library of Congress Collection, Archives of American Folk Song, Washington 1947

506 — and G. P. Kurath, The Feast of the Dead, or Ghost Dance at Six Nations Reserve, Canada, in: Bulletin 149 of the Bureau of American Ethnology, pp. 139—65, Washington 1951

507 Fewkes, J. W., Tusayan Flute and Snake Ceremonies, in: 19th Annual Report of the Bureau of American Ethnology, pp. 957—1011, Washington 1900

508 — A Few Summer Ceremonials at Zuñi Pueblo, in: Journal of American Ethnology and Archaeology, Vol. I, pp. 1—61, Boston 1891

509 Fillmore, J. C., The Harmonic Structure of Indian Music, in: American Anthropologist, n.s., Vol. I, pp. 297—318, New York 1899

510 Fischer, E., Patagonische Musik, in: Anthropos, Vol. III, pp. 941—51, Vienna 1908

511 Fletcher, A. C., Indian Story and Song from North America, Boston 1900

512 — Indian Games and Dances with Native Songs, Boston 1915

513 — and F. La Flesche, A Study of Omaha Indian Music; With a Report on the Structural Peculiarities of Music, by J. C. Fillmore, in: Archaeological and Ethnological Papers of the Peabody Museum, Vol. I, No. 5, pp. 1—152, Cambridge, Mass. 1893

514 Fortún, J. E., La Danza de los Diablos, La Paz 1961

515 Fourdrignier, E., Musique Bolivienne, in: Bulletin de la Société des Américanistes de Belgique, Series 5, Vol. VII, pp. 450—60, Brussels 1906

516 Gallice, P., Notes sur un Instrument Musical Andin, in: Travaux de l'Institut Français d'Études Andines, Vol. VI, pp. 47—49, Paris, Lima 1957/58

517 Gallop, R., The Music of Indian Mexico, in: The Musical Quarterly, Vol. XXXV, pp. 210ff., New York 1939

518 — Otomi Indian Music from Mexico, in: The Musical Quarterly, Vol. XXVI, pp. 87ff., New York 1940

519 Galpin, F. W., Aztec Influence on American Indian Instruments, in: Sammelbände der Internationalen Musikgesellschaft, No. IV, pp. 661ff., Leipzig 1902/03

520 — The Whistles and Reed Instruments of the American Indians of the Northwest Coast, in: Proceedings of the Musical Association, Vol. XXIX, pp. 115—38, London 1903

521 Garay, N., Tradiciones y Cantares de Panamá, Brussels 1930

522 Garces, B., and M. Garces, La Música Incaica No Es Pentafónica, in: Revista Universitaria de la Universidad Nacional de Cuzco, Vol. XXV, No. 72, pp. 54—60, Cuzco 1936

523 — Evolución Técnica de la Música Peruana, Gama Eptafónica, in: Proceedings of the International Congress of Americanists, Vol. XXVII, pp. 25—32, 1943

524 Geiringer, K., Musical Instruments, Oxford 1945

525 Gilman, B. I., Zuñi Melodies, in: Journal of the American Archaeological and Ethnological Society, Vol. I, pp. 63 to 91, Boston 1891

526 — Hopi Songs, in: Journal of the American Archaeological and Ethnological Society, Vol. V, pp. 1—226, Boston 1908

527 Gonzáles, B. A., Clasificación de los Sicus Aymaras, in: Revista de Estudios Musicales, Vol. I, No. 1, Mendoza 1949

528 Grinnell, G. B., Notes on Some Cheyenne Songs, in: American Anthropologist, n.s., Vol. V, pp. 312—22, New York 1903

529 Groven, A., Eskimolieder fra Alaska. Studier over Tone-Systemer og Rytmer (Stencilled), Oslo n.d.

530 Guerrero, R. G., La Música Zapoteca, in: Neza, Vol. IV, No. 1, Mexico 1939

531 — Consideraciones sobre la Música Tarasca, in: Boletín Latinoamericano, Vol. 4, Montevideo 1941

532 — Música de Chiapas, in: Revista de Estudios Musicales, Vol. I, No. 2, Mendoza 1949

533 Gustaver, B., On a Peculiar Type of Whistle Found in Ancient American Indian Graves, in: American Anthropologist, n.s., Vol. XXV, pp. 307—17, Menasha 1923

534 Hague, E., Latin American Music: Past and Present, Santa Ana, Calif. 1934

535 Haile, B., Navaho Chantways and Ceremonials, in: American Anthropologist, n.s., Vol. XL, pp. 639–52, Menasha 1938

536 Halmos, I., Das Verhältnis von Instrument, Stimmung und Tonart in Längsflöten-Melodien der Nambikuara-Indianer, in: Abhandlungen und Berichte des Staatlichen Museums für Völkerkunde Dresden, Vol. XXIV, pp. 49–59, Berlin 1965

537 Harcourt, M. d', Mélodies Populaires Indiennes, Milan 1923 (cf. also 384)

538 – R. d', and M. d'Harcourt, La Musique dans la Sierra Andine de la Paz à Quito, in: Journal de la Sociéte des Américanistes, n.s., Vol. XII, pp. 21–53, Paris 1920

539 – La Musique des Incas et ses Survivances, Paris 1925

540 – L'Ocarina à Cinq Sons dans l'Amérique préhispanique, in: Journal de la Société des Américanistes, Vol. XXIII, pp. 189 ff., Paris 1931

541 – Sifflets et Ocarinas du Nicaragua et du Mexique, in: Journal de la Société des Américanistes, Vol. XXXI, Paris 1941

542 – La Musique chez les Mayas, in: Bulletin de la Société Suisse des Américanistes, Vol. III, Geneva 1951

543 – Les Formes du Tambour à Membrane dans l'Ancien Pérou, in: Journal de la Société des Américanistes, Vol. XLIII, Paris 1954

544 – La Musique des Aymara, in: Journal de la Société des Américanistes, n.s., Vol. XLVIII, pp. 5–133, Paris 1959

545 Hatch, J., Tachi Yokuts Music, in: Publications of the Kroeber Anthropological Society, Vol. XIX, pp. 47–66, Berkeley 1958

546 Hauser, M., Grønlandske trommesange, Gronland, Charlottensund 1960

547 Hawkes, D. W., The Dance Festivals of the Alaska Eskimos, Anthropological Publication of the University of Pennsylvania, Vol. VI, Philadelphia 1914

548 Hawley, E. H., Distribution of the Notched Rattle, in: American Anthropologist, o.s., Vol. XI, pp. 344–46, Washington 1898

549 Haywood, C., A Bibliography of North American Folklore and Folksongs, II, pp. 749–1159, New York 1951

550 Heinitz, W., Strukturprobleme in primitiver Musik, Hamburg 1931

551 Helfritz, H., Musik und Tänze der Aimaras und Quechuas, in: El México Antiguo, Vol, VII, pp. 283–93, Mexico 1955

552 Hernándes de Alba, G., De la Música Indígena en Colombia, in: Boletín Latino-Americano de Música, Vol. IV, pp. 721–31, Bogotá 1938

553 Herzog, G., Musical Styles in North America, in: Proceedings of the 23rd International Congress of Americanists, pp. 455–58, New York 1928

554 – The Yuman Musical Style, in: Journal of American Folklore, Vol. XLI, pp. 183–231, 1928

555 – Special Song Types in North American Indian Music, in: Zeitschrift für Vergleichende Musikwissenschaft, Vol. III, pp. 23–33, 1935

556 – Plains Ghost Dance and Great Basin Music, in: American Anthropologist, n.s., Vol. XXXVII, pp. 403–19, Menasha 1935

557 – A Comparison of Pueblo and Pima Musical Styles, in: Journal of American Folklore, Vol. XLIX, pp. 283–417, 1936

558 – Music in the Thinking of the American Indian, in: Peabody Bulletin, May 1938

559 Hissink, K., Die Medizinmann-Trommel der Tacana, in: Mitteilungen aus dem Museum für Völkerkunde zu Hamburg, Vol. XXV, pp. 177–81, Hamburg 1959

560 Hoffmann, C., American Indian Songs and Dances (Disc Ethnic Album 161), Washington

561 Holmer, N. M., Dos Cantos Shamanísticos de los Indios Cuna (Etnologiska Studier 27), Gothenburg 1963

562 – and S. H. Wassén, The Complete Mu-igala in Picture Writing. A Native Record of a Cuna Indian Medicine Song (Etnologiska Studier 21), Gothenburg 1953

563 – and S. H. Wassén, Nia-ikala, Canto Mágico para Curar la Locura (Etnologiska Studier 23), Gothenburg 1958

564 Hornbostel, E. M. von, Über einige Panpfeifen aus Nordwest-Brasilien, in: Koch-Grünberg, T., Zwei Jahre unter den Indianern Nordwest-Brasiliens, Vol. II, pp. 378–91, Berlin 1910

565 – Zwei Gesänge der Cora-Indianer, Melodien und Formanalysen, in: Preuss, K.T., Die Nayarit-Expedition, Vol. I, pp. 367–76, Leipzig 1912

566 – Musik der Makuschí, Taulipáng und Yekuaná, in: Koch-Grünberg, T., Vom Roroima zum Orinoco. Vol. III, pp. 397–442, Berlin 1923; Spanish in: Archivos Venezolanos de Folklore, Vol. III, 4, pp. 137–58, Caracas 1955/56

567 – Fuegian Songs, in: American Anthropologist, n.s., Vol. XXXVIII, pp. 357–67, Menasha 1936

568 – The Music of the Fuegians, in: Ethnos, Vol. XIII, pp. 61–97, Lund 1948; Spanish in: Archivos Venezolanos de Folklore, Vol. IV, Caracas 1955/56

569 Hough, W., Music of the Hopi Flute Ceremony, in: American Anthropologist, o.s., Vol. X, pp. 162–63, Washington 1897

570 – The Hopi Indian Collection in the United States National Museum, Washington 1918

571 Howard, J., and G. P. Kurath, Ponca Dances, Ceremonies and Music, in: Ethnomusicology, Vol. III, No. 1, Middletown 1959

572 Igualada, F. de, Musicología Indígena de la Amazonia Colombiana, in: Bolétín de la Sociedad Geográfica de Colombia, ser. 2, Vol. V, pp. 281–91, Bogotá 1938

573 Iribarren, C. J., La Flauta de Pan y otros Instrumentos Indígenas, in: Boletín del Museo y d e la Sociedad Arqueológica de la Serena, Chile, No. IX, 1957

574 Isamitt, C., Un Instrumento Araucano – la Trutruka, in: Boletín Latino-Americano de Música, Vol. I, pp. 43–46, Bogotá 1935

575 – Cuatro Instrumentos Musicales Araucanos, in: Boletín Latino-Americano de Música, Vol. III, pp. 55–56, Bogotá 1937

576 – Los Instrumentos Araucanos, in: Boletín Latino-Americano de Música, Vol. IV, pp. 310 ff., Bogotá 1938

577 – La Danza entre los Araucanos, in: Boletín Latino-Americano de Música, Vol. V, pp. 601–05, Bogotá 1941

578 Israel, H., Ein grönländischer Singstreit, in: Abhandlungen und Berichte des Staatlichen Museums für Völkerkunde Dresden, Vol. XXII, pp. 1–13, Berlin 1963

579 Izikowitz, K. G., Musical and Other Sound-Instruments of the South American Indians, Gothenburg 1927; Elmsford, N.Y. 1934

580 — Le Tambour à Membrane au Pérou, in: Journal de la Société des Américanistes, n.s., Vol. XXIII, pp. 163—75, Paris 1931

581 — Les Instruments de Musique des Indiens Uro-Chipaya, in: Revista del Instituto de Etnología de la Universidad Nacional de Tucumán, Vol. II, pp. 263—91, Tucumán 1922

582 Jeançon, J. A., Indian Song Book, Denver 1924

583 — Indian Musical and Noise-Making Instruments, in: Denver Art Museum, Indian Leaflet Series, Vol. XXIX, pp. 1—4, Denver 1931

584 Jenness, D., Eskimo Music in Northern Alaska, in: The Musical Quarterly, Vol. VIII, pp. 377—83, New York 1922

585 Jiménez Borja, A., Instrumentos Musicales Peruanos, in Revista del Museo Nacional, Vol. XIX/XX, pp. 37 to 190, Lima 1950/51

586 Johnson, C. I., Navaho Corn Grinding Songs, in: Ethnomusicology, Vol. VIII, No. 2, Middletown 1964

587 Keiler, B., Instruments and Music of Bolivia (Ethnic Folkways Album FM 4012), New York 1962

588 Kelm, H., Der Morgengesang der Sirionó, in: Kulturhistorische Studien (Festschrift H. Trimborn), pp. 42—64, Brunswick 1961

589 Key, M., Music of the Siriono (Guaranian), in: Ethnomusicology, Vol. VII, No. I, pp. 17—21, Middletown 1963

590 Kluckhohn, C., The Great Chants of the Navajo, in: Theatre Arts Monthly, Vol. XVII, pp. 639—45, 1933

591 — Navaho Women's Knowledge of Their Song Ceremonials, in: El Palacio, Vol. XLV, pp. 87—92, Santa Fé 1938

592 — and L. Wyman, An Introduction to Navaho Chant Practice, in: Memoir LIII of the American Anthropological Association, pp. 1—204, Menasha 1940

593 Kollmann, P., Flöten und Pfeifen aus Alt-Mexiko, in: Bastian-Festschrift, pp. 559—74, Berlin 1896

594 Krause, F., Der Trommelbaum im Schinguquellgebiet Zentral-Brasiliens, in: Mitteilungsblatt der Deutschen Gesellschaft für Völkerkunde, Vol. XI, pp. 20—55, Leipzig 1942

595 Kunike, H., Musikinstrumente aus dem alten Michoacan, in: Baessler-Archiv, Vol. II, pp. 282 ff., Berlin 1911

596 Kurath, G. P., Los Concheros, in: Journal of American Folklore, Vol. LIX, pp. 387—99, Philadelphia 1946

597 — Iroquois Midwinter Medicine Rites, in: Journal of the International Folk Music Council, Vol. III, pp. 96—100, Cambridge 1951

598 — Local Diversity in Iroquois Dance and Music, in: Symposium on Local Diversity in Iroquois Culture, ed. by W. N. Fenton, Bulletin 149 of the Bureau of American Ethnology, pp. 109—37, Washington 1951

599 — Matriarchal Dances of the Iroquois, in: Proceedings of 29th International Congress of Americanists, Vol. III, pp. 123—30, Chicago 1952

600 — An Analysis of the Iroquois Eagle Dance and Songs, in: Bulletin 156 of the Bureau of American Ethnology, pp. 223—306, Washington 1953

601 — Native Choreographic Areas of North America, in: American Anthropologist, n.s., Vol. 55, pp. 153—62, Menasha 1953

602 — Chippewa Sacred Songs in Religious Metamorphosis, in: Scientific Monthly, Vol. LXXIX, pp. 311—17, New York 1954

603 — The Tutelo Fourth Night Spirit Release Singing, in: Midwest Folklore, Vol. IV, pp. 87—105, Bloomington 1954

604 Kurath, G. P., The Tutelo Harvest Rite, in: Scientific Monthly, Vol. LXXVI, No. 3, pp. 87—105, New York 1954

605 — Ceremonies, Songs and Dances of Michigan Indians, in: Michigan History, Vol. XXXIX, pp. 466—68, Lansing 1955

606 — Songs of the Wigwam, Delaware 1955

607 — Antiphonal Songs of Eastern Woodland Indians, in: The Musical Quarterly, Vol. 42, pp. 520—26, New York 1956

608 — Pan-Indian Dances and Songs of Midwest, in: Journal of Health, Physical Education and Recreation, Vol. XXVII, No. 9, pp. 44—45, 51—52, Washington 1956

609 — Songs and Dances of Great Lakes Indians (Ethnic Folkways Album P 1003), New York 1956

610 — Catholic Hymns of Michigan Indians, in: Anthropological Quarterly, Vol. XXX, pp. 31—44, Washington 1957

611 — Game Animal Dances of the Rio Grande, in: Southwestern Journal of Anthropology, Vol. XIV, pp. 438—48, Albuquerque 1958

612 — Plaza Circuits of Tewa Indian Dancers, in: El Palacio, Vol. 65, pp. 11—26, Santa Fé 1958

613 — Menomini Indian Dance Songs in a Changing Culture, in: Midwest Folklore, Vol. IX, No. 1, pp. 31—38, Bloomington 1959

614 — Cochiti Choreographies and Songs, in: The Pueblo of Cochiti, ed. by C. H. Lange, pp. 539—56, Austin 1960

615 — Panorama of Dance Ethnology, in: Current Anthropology, Vol. I, No. 3, pp. 233—54, Chicago, 1960

616 — The Sen'ason Rattle of the Yaqui Indian Pascolas, in: Ethnomusicology, Vol. IV, No. 2, pp. 60—63, Middletown 1960

617 — Effects of Environment on Cherokee-Iroquois Ceremonialism, Music, and Dance, in: Symposium on Cherokee and Iroquois Culture, Bulletin 180 of the Bureau of American Ethnology, pp. 173—95, Washington 1961

618 — Iroquois Music and Dance: Ceremonial Art of Two Seneca Longhouses, Bulletin 187 of the Bureau of American Ethnology, Washington 1964

619 — and S. Martí, Dances of Anáhuac, The Choreography and Music of Precortesian Dances, Viking Fund Publication in Anthropology, No. 38, Chicago 1964

620 Lach, R., Die Musik der Inkas, in: Der Auftakt, Vol. VI, pp. 124 ff., Prague 1926

621 Lavin, C., La Musique des Araucans, in: Revue Musicale, Vol. VI, No. 5, Paris 1925

622 — Un País con Cuatro Nacionalidades Musicales, in: Folklore Americano, Vol. I, pp. 21—27, Lima 1953

623 — La Música de los Araucanos, in: Anuario Musical, Vol. XVI, pp. 201—16, Barcelona 1961

624 Leden, C., Musik und Tänze der grönländischen Eskimos und die Verwandtschaft der Musik der Polareskimos mit der der Indianer, in: Zeitschrift für Ethnologie, Vol. XLIII, pp. 260—70, Berlin 1911

625 — Die Musik der Naturvölker (Eskimo und Indianer), in: Leden, C., Über Kiwatins Eisfelder. Drei Jahre unter kanadischen Eskimos, pp. 264—78, Leipzig 1927

626 — Über die Musik der Smith Sund Eskimos, in: Meddelelser om Grønland, Vol. CLII, No. 3, Copenhagen 1952

627 — Über die Musik der Ostgrönländer, Meddelelser om Grønland, Vol. CLII, No. 4, Copenhagen 1954

628 Lehmann, W., Ein Tolteken-Klagegesang, in: Seler-Festschrift, pp. 281–319, Stuttgart 1922

629 Lehmann-Nitsche, R., Patagonische Gesänge und Musikbogen, Phonogrammaufnahmen und Einleitung, in: Anthropos, Vol. III, pp. 916–40, Vienna 1908

630 Lima, E. de, Las Flautas Indígenas Colombianas, in: Estudios Latino-Americanos, Vol. III, pp. 67ff., Mendoza 1937

631 List, G., Music in the Culture of the Jibaro Indians of the Ecuadorian Montaña, Inter-American Music Bulletin, Nos. 40–41, Washington 1964

632 Lizardi, R. E., La Música Precortesiana, in: Cuadernos Americanos, Vol. XV, No. 1, Mexico 1956

633 McAllester, D. P., Peyote Music, Viking Fund Publication in Anthropology, Vol. XIII, New York 1949

634 — Menomini Peyote Music, in: Menomini Peyotism, by J. S. Slotkin, Transactions of the American Philosophical Society, Vol. 43, Part 4, pp. 681–700, Philadelphia 1952

635 — Notes on the Music of the Navajo Creation Chants, in: Navajo Creation Chants, issued by the Peabody Museum, Harvard University, pp. 33ff., Cambridge, Mass. 1952

636 — Enemy Way Music, Peabody Museum Papers, Vol. XLI, No. 3, Cambridge, Mass. 1954

637 — An Apache Fiddle, Ethnomusicology Newsletter, No. 8, Middletown 1956

638 — The Role of Music in Western Apache Culture, in: Acts of the International Congress of the Anthropological and Ethnological Sciences, Vol. V, pp. 468–72, Philadelphia 1960

639 — (ed.), The Myth and Prayers of the Great Star Chant and the Myth of the Coyote Chant, Navajo Religion Series, Vol. IV, Santa Fé 1956

640 MacLeish, K., A Few Hopi Songs from Moenkopi, in: The Masterkey, Vol. XV, pp. 178–84, Los Angeles 1941

641 Manicer, G. G., Muzyka i Muzykal'nye Instrumenty Nekotorich Plemen Brazilii, in: Sbornik Muzej Antropologii i Etnografie, Vol. V, No. 1, pp. 319–50, Petrograd 1918

642 Marsh, D. B., Padlermiut Drum Dance, in: The Beaver, Vol. CCLXXVI, pp. 20–21, Winnipeg 1945

643 Martens, F., Music in the Life of the Aztecs, in: The Musical Quarterly, Vol. XVI, pp. 413ff., New York 1928

644 Martí, S., Música de las Américas, in: Cuadernos Americanos, Vol. LII, pp. 153–68, Mexico 1950

645 — Flautilla de la Penitencia, in: Cuadernos Americanos, Vol. LXXII, pp. 145–57, Mexico 1953

646 — Música Primitiva, in: Revista YAN, México I, pp. 10 to 17, Vol. 1953

647 — Guía de la Sala de Música Prehispánica (Museo Nacional de Antroplogía), Mexico 1954

648 — Precortesian Music, in: Ethnos, Vol. XIX, pp. 69–79, Stockholm 1954

649 — Instrumentos Musicales Precortesianos, Mexico 1955

650 — Música Mixteco-Zapoteca, in: Boletín Bibliográfico de la Sección de Hacienda y Crédito Público No. 128, Mexico 1958

651 — Danza Precortesiana, in: Cuadernos Americanos, Vol. CVI, Mexico 1959

652 — Canto, Danza y Música Precortesianos, Mexico 1961

653 Matthews, W., The Mountain Chant, in: 5th Annual Report of the Bureau of American Ethnology, pp. 379 to 467, Washington 1887

654 — Navajo Gambling Songs, in: American Anthropologist, Vol. II, os., pp. 1–19, New York 1889

655 — The Basket Drum, in: American Anthropologist, Vol. VII, pp. 202–08, Washington 1894

656 — Songs of Sequence of the Navajos, in: Journal of American Folklore, Vol. VII, pp. 185–94, Boston 1894

657 — Songs of the Navajos, in: Land of Sunshine, Vol. V, pp. 197–201, Los Angeles 1896

658 — Navaho Night Chant, in: Journal of American Folklore, Vol. XIV, pp. 12–19, 1901

659 — The Night Chant, Memoir VI of the American Museum of Natural History, New York 1902

660 Mead, C. W., The Musical Instruments of the Incas, Anthropological Papers of the American Museum of Natural History, Vol. XV, Part 3, New York 1924

661 Mendoza, V. T., Música Indígena de México, in: México en el Arte IX, Mexico 1950

662 — Supravivencias de la Cultura Azteca. La Canción de Baile de la Música Indígena de México, in: México en el Arte IX, Mexico 1950

663 — Música Indígena Otomi, in: Revista de Estudios Musicales, Vol. V/VI, pp. 351ff., Mendoza 1951

664 — Panorama de la música tradicional de México, Mexico 1956

665 — El ritmo de los Cantares Mexicanos recolectados por Sahagún, in: Miscellanea Paul Rivet octogenario dictada 1958, Vol. II, pp. 777–85, Mexico 1958

666 Merriam, A. P., Notes on Cheyenne Songs, in: Journal of the American Musicological Society, Vol. III, pp. 289ff., Richmond 1950

667 — Flathead Indian Instruments and Their Music, in: The Musical Quarterly, Vol. XXXVII, pp. 368–75, New York 1951

668 — Music of the Flathead Indians, in: Tomorrow, Vol. IV, No. 3, pp. 103–07, New York 1956

669 — and W. L. d'Azevedo, Washo Peyote Songs, in: American Anthropologist, n.s., Vol. LIX, pp. 615–41, Menasha 1957

670 — and B. W. Merriam, Songs and Dances of the Flathead Indians (Ethnic Folkways Album P445), New York 1953

671 — and F. G. Spier, Chukchana Yokuts Songs, in: Actas del XXXIII Congreso Internacional de Americanistas, San José 1958, San José 1959

672 Miller, D. C., Flutes of the American Indian, in: Flutist, Vol. II, pp. 509–12, 1921

673 Montell, G., Yaqui Dances, in: Ethnos, Vol. III, No. 6, pp. 145–66, Stockholm 1938

674 Mooney, J., A Kiowa Mescal Rattle, in: American Anthropologist, o.s., Vol. V, pp. 64–65, New York 1892

675 Moreno, S. L., Música y Danzas Autóctonas del Ecuador, Quito 1949

676 — La Música de los Incas, Quito 1957

677 Murillo, E., Indigenous Music in Columbia, in: Bulletin of the Pan American Union, Vol. LVII, pp. 34–36, Washington 1923

678 Nettl, B., The Shawnee Musical Style, in: Southwestern Journal of Anthropology, Vol. IX, pp. 277–85, Albuquerque 1953

679 Nettl, B., Observations on Meaningless Peyote Song Texts, in: Journal of American Folklore, Vol. LXVI, pp. 161–64, Bloomington 1953

680 — Stylistic Variety in North American Indian Music, in: Journal of the American Musicological Society, Vol. VI, pp. 160–68, Richmond 1953

681 — North American Indian Musical Styles, in: Journal of American Folklore, Vol. LXVII, pp. 45–56, 297–308, 351–68, Bloomington 1954

682 — North American Indian Musical Styles, Memoir 45 of the American Folk-Lore Society, Boston 1954

683 — Text-Music Relationships in Arapaho Songs, in: Southwestern Journal of Anthropology, Vol. X, pp. 192 to 99, Albuquerque 1954

684 — Musical Culture of the Araphao, in: The Musical Quarterly, Vol. XLI, pp. 235–31, New York 1955

685 — Michigan American Music, in: Michigan History, Vol. XXXIX, Lansing 1955

686 — Music in Primitive Culture, Cambridge 1956

687 — Indianermusik, in: Musik in Geschichte und Gegenwart, Vol. VI, Cassel and Basle 1957

688 Newcomb, F. J., and G. A. Reichard, Sandpaintings of the Navajo Shooting Chant, New York 1937

689 Nowotny, K. A., Die Notation des "Tono" in den aztekischen Cantares, in Baessler-Archiv, n.s., Vol. IV, pp. 185–89, Berlin 1956

690 Osburn, M. H., Some Prehistoric Musical Instruments of North America, in: Hinrichsen's Musical Yearbook, Vol. VII, pp. 243 ff., London 1952

691 Paredes, R., Música Indígena en la Altiplanicie, in Revista de la Biblioteca Muncipal "Mariscal Andrés de Santa Cruz", Vol. I, No. 2, pp. 15–17, La Paz 1949

692 Parsons, E. C., Note on the Night Chant at Tuwelchedu, in: American Anthropologist, n.s., Vol. XXIII, pp. 240–43, 1921

693 Payer, Ein am Amazoenstrom gebräuchlicher Trommelapparat, in: Zeitschrift für Ethnologie Vol. XXXV, pp. 481–83, Berlin 1903

694 Peabody, C., A Prehistoric Wind-Instrument from Pecos, New Mexico, in: American Anthropologist, n.s., Vol. XIX, pp. 30–33, Lancaster, Pa. 1917

695 Peacock, K., Indian Music of the Canadian Plains, in: Ethnic Folkways Album P 464, New York 1955

696 Perdomo Escobar, J. I., Esbozo histórico sobre la Música Colombiana, in: Boletín Latino-Americano de Música, Vol. IV, pp. 387 ff., Bogotá 1938

697 Pike, K. L., The Flea: Melody Types and Perturbations; in an Mixtec Song, in: Tlalocan, Vol. II, pp. 128 ff., Mexico 1946

698 Pozo, M. J., La Música Vernacular Ayacuchana, in: Huamanga, Vol. X, Nos. 57–58, pp. 1–7, Ayacucho 1944

699 Rasmussen, K., Schneehüttenlieder, Essen and Freiburg (Breisgau) 1947

700 Reichard, G. A., The Story of the Navajo Hail Chant, New York 1944

701 Reinhard, K., Die Musik des mexikanischen Fliegerspiels, in: Zeitschrift für Ethnologie, Vol. LXXIX, pp. 59–74, Brunswick 1954

702 Rhodes, W., Acculturation in North American Indian Music, in: Proceedings of the International Congress of Americanists, Vol. XXIX, 2, pp. 127–32, Chicago 1952

703 Rhodes, W., American Indian Music, in: Tomorrow, Vol. IV, 3, pp. 97–102, New York 1956

704 — A Study of Musical Diffusion Based on the Wandering of the Opening Peyote Song, in: Journal of the International Folk Music Council, Vol. X, pp. 42–49, Cambridge 1958

705 — The Christian Hymnology of the North American Indians, in: Acts of the International Congress of the Anthropological and Ethnological Sciences, Vol. V, pp. 324–31, Philadelphia 1960

706 Rivet, P., La Musique des Incas, in: Journal de la Société des Américanistes, n.s., Vol. XVIII, pp. 349–50, Paris 1926

707 — La Musique Indienne en Amérique, in: La Natur, Vol. XLIX, pp. 244–47, Paris 1927

708 Robb, J. D., Rhythmic Patterns of the Santo Domingo Corn Dance, in: Ethnomusicology, Vol. VIII, No. 2, Middletown 1964

709 Roberts, H. H., Chakwena Songs of Zuni and Laguna, in: Journal of American Folklore, Vol. XXXVI, pp. 177 to 84, 1923

710 — Form in Primitive Music, Ancient Southern Californian Indian Songs, New York 1933

711 — Musical Areas in Aboriginal North America, in: Yale University Publications in Anthropology, Vol. XII, pp. 1–41, New Haven 1936

712 — and H. K. Haeberlin, Some Songs of the Puget Sound Salish, in: Journal of American Folklore, Vol. XXXI, pp. 496–520, 1918

713 — and D. Jenness, Songs of the Copper Eskimos, in: Report of the Canadian Arctic Expedition, Vol. XIV, pp. 1–506, Ottawa 1925

714 — and M. Swadesh, Songs of the Nootka Indians of Western Vancouver Island, in: Transactions of the American Philosophical Society, Vol. 45, Part 2, Philadelphia 1955

715 Robins, R. H., and N. MacLeod, A Yurok Song Without Words, in: Bulletin of the School of Oriental and African Studies of the University of London, Vol. XX, pp. 501 to 506, London 1957

716 Rodrigues, J. B., O Canto e la Dança selvicola, in: Revista Brasileira, ser. III, Vol. IX, Rio de Janeiro 1881

717 Román Ramírez, M., Una ocarina antropomorfa de El Salvador en el Museo Etnológico de Barcelona, in: Boletín Americanista, Vol. I, 1, pp. 67–68, Barcelona 1959

718 Romero, J., Música precortesiana, in: Anales del Instituto Nacional de Antropología e Historia, Vol. II, Mexico 1947

719 Rovsing Olsen, P., Rapport fra en Reise til Øst-Grønland, in: Dansk Musiktidskrift, No. III, Copenhagen 1962

720 — Dessins Mélodiques dans les Chants Esquimaux du Groenland de l'Est, in: Dansk Aarbog for Musikforskning, Copenhagen 1963

721 Sachs, C., Eine Weltgeschichte des Tanzes, Berlin 1933; Histoire de la Danse, Paris 1938; World History of the Dance, New York 1963

722 — The History of Musical Instruments, New York 1940

723 Safford, W. E., The Pan-Pipes of Ancient Peru, in: American Anthropologist, n.s., Vol. XVIII, pp. 124–26, Lancaster, Pa. 1916

724 Saldivar, G., Historia de la Música en México, Mexico 1934

725 Samper, B./F. Domínguez/L. Sandi/R. Tellez Girón, Investigación folklorística en México. Materiales, Vol. I, Mexico 1962

726 Sánchez Malga, C., Peruvian Music, in: Bulletin of the Pan American Union, Vol. LXV, pp. 606–11, Washington 1931

727 Sapir, E., Song Recitative in Paiute Mythology, in: Journal of American Folklore, Vol. XXIII, pp. 455–72, 1910

728 – Songs for a Comox Dancing Mask, in: Ethnos, Vol. IV, pp. 49–55, Stockholm 1939

729 Sargent, W., Types of Quechua Melody, in: The Musical Quarterly, Vol. XX, pp. 230–45, New York 1934

730 – Folk and Primitive Music in Canada, in: Journal of the International Folk Music Council, Vol. IV, Cambridge 1952

731 Sas, A., Aperçu sur la Musique Inca, in: Acta Musicologica, Vol. VI, pp. 1 ff., Basle 1934

732 – La Música de los Incas, in: Pro-Arte Musical, Vol. VII, 2, pp. 48–51, Havana 1955

733 Schaden, E., Ethnographische Notizen zu einem Chicha-Tanzlied der Kayová, in: Beiträge zur Völkerkunde Südamerikas (Festschrift H. Baldus), pp. 283–91, Hanover 1964

734 – F. S. G., Música e Dança entre os Indios do Brasil, in: Paulistânia, Vol. XXVI, pp. 13–15, São Paulo 1948

735 Schinhan, J. P., The Music of the Papago and Yurok, in: Bulletin of the American Musicological Society, Vol. I, pp. 13 ff., 1936

736 Schneider, M., Geschichte der Mehrstimmigkeit, I, Berlin 1934

737 – Bemerkungen über südamerikanische Panpfeifen, in: Archiv für Musikforschung, Vol. II, pp. 496–97, 1937

738 – Contribución a la Música Indígena del Mato Grosso (Brasil), in: Anuario Musical, Vol. VII, pp. 159–76, Barcelona 1952

739 Schünemann, G., Musikinstrumente der Indianer. Aus der Sammlung der Frankfurter Südamerika-Expedition (1927–1929), Archiv für Musikforschung, Vol. I, 1936

740 Schultz, H., and V. C. Schultz, Brazilian Indian Music (Ethnic Folkways Album 4311), New York 1962

741 Seler, E., Altmexikanische Knochenrasseln, in: Globus, Vol. LXXIV, pp. 85–93, Brunswick 1898

742 – Mittelamerikanische Musikinstrumente, in: Globus, Vol. LXXVI, pp. 109–12, Brunswick, 1899

743 – Die religiösen Gesänge der alten Mexikaner, in: Gesammelte Abhandlungen zur Amerikanischen Sprach- und Altertumskunde, Vol. II, pp. 959–1107, Berlin 1904

744 – Die holzgeschnitzte Pauke von Malinalco und das Zeichen atltlachinolli, in: Gesammelte Abhandlungen zur Amerikanischen Sprach- und Altertumskunde, Vol. III, pp. 221–304, Berlin 1908

745 Selvas, E. J., Música y Danzas Indígenas de Chiapas, in: Ateneo, Vol. V, Mexico 1954

746 Simmons, M. L., Pre-Conquest Narrative Songs in Spanish America, in: Journal of American Folklore, Vol. LXXIII, pp. 103–11, Bloomington 1960

747 Skinner, A., Songs of the Menomini Medicine Ceremony, in: American Anthropologist, n.s., Vol. XXVII, pp. 290 to 314, Menasha 1925

748 Snethlage, E. H., Musikinstrumente der Indianer des Guaporégebietes, Baessler-Archiv, Suppl. X, Berlin 1938

749 Speck, F. G., Ceremonial Songs of the Creek and Yuchi Indians (Musical Transcriptions by Jacob Sapir), University of Pennsylvania Museum Anthropological Publications, Vol. I, pp. 157–245, Philadelphia 1911

750 – and L. Broom (in collaboration with Will West Long), Cherokee Dance and Drama, Berkeley, Los Angeles 1951

751 – and G. Herzog, The Tutelo Spirit Adoption Ceremony, Harrisburg 1942

752 Spence, L., Myth and Ritual in Dance, Game, and Rhyme, London 1947

753 Spicer, E. H., La Danza Yaqui del Venado en la Cultura Mexicana, in: Américan Indígena, Vol. XXV, No. 1 pp. 117–39, Mexico 1965

754 Spinden, H. J., Home Songs of the Tewa Indians, in: American Museum Journal, Vol. XV, pp. 73–78, New York 1915

755 – Songs of the Tewa, New York 1933

756 Starr, F., Notched Bones from Mexico, in: Proceedings of the Davenport Academy of Natural Sciences, Vol. VII, pp. 101–07, 1900

757 – Notes on Mexican Musical Instruments – Past and Present, in: American Antiquarian, Vol. XXV, pp. 303–10, Chicago 1903

758 Stevenson, R., The Music of Peru, Lima 1959

759 – Early Peruvian Folk Music, in: Journal of American Folklore, Vol. LXXIII, pp. 112–32, Bloomington 1960

760 Strelnikov, I. D., La Música y la Danza de las Tribus Indias Kaa-ihwua (Guarani) y Botocudo, in: Proceedings of the 23rd International Congress of Americanists, pp. 796–802, New York 1930

761 Stricklen, E. G., Notes on Eight Papago Songs, in: University of California Publications in American Archaeology and Ethnology, Vol. XX, pp. 361–66, Berkeley 1923

762 Stumpf, C., Lieder der Bellakula-Indianer, in: Sammelbände für Vergleichende Musikwissenschaft, Vol. I, Berlin, Munich 1922

763 – Phonographierte Indianermelodien, in: Vierteljahrsschrift für Musikwissenschaft, Vol. VIII, 1892, and in: Sammelbände für Vergleichende Musikwissenschaft, Vol. I, Berlin, Munich 1922

764 Svensson, S. E., Studier i Eskimo-Musikens Intervallförräd och Tonalitet, Svensk Tidskrift för Musikforskning, Vol. XXXVIII, Stockholm 1957

765 Termer, F., Los Bailes du Culebra entre los Indios Quichés en Guatemala, in: Proceedings of the 23rd International Congress of Americanists, pp. 661–67, New York 1930

766 – El palo de Volador in Guatemala, in: El México Antiguo, Vol. III, pp. 13–23, Mexico 1931–36

767 Thalbitzer, W., Eskimomusik und Dichtkunst in Grönland, in: Anthropos, Vol. VI, pp. 485–96, Vienna-Mödling 1911

768 – Cultic Games and Festivals in Greenland, in: Proceedings of the 20th International Congress of Americanists, Gothenburg 1925

769 – Légendes et Chants Esquimaux du Groenland, Paris 1929

770 – Inuit sange og danse fra Grønland, Copenhagen 1939

771 Thalbitzer, W., and H. Thuren, Musik aus Ost-Grönland. Eskimoische Phonogramme, in: Zeitschrift der Internationalen Musikgesellschaft, Vol. XII, pp. 33 ff., 1910/11

772 — and H. Thuren, La Musique chez les Esquimaux, in: Mercure Musical, Paris 1911

773 Thuren, H., On the Eskimo Music of Greenland, in: Meddelelser om Grønland, Vol. XL, pp. 1–45, Copenhagen 1911

774 — an W. Thalbitzer, Melodies from East Greenland, in: Meddelelser om Grønland, Vol. XL, No. 2, pp. 97–112, Copenhagen 1923

775 Tinoco, M. F. de, and G. Aguilar Machado, Una Ocarina Huetar de 18 Notas del Museo Nacional de Costa Rica, San José 1937

776 Titiev, M., Social Singing Among the Mapuche, Anthropological Paper of the University of Michigan, Vol. II, Ann Arbor 1949

777 Titus, M. E., A Treatise on American Indian Music, Indianapolis 1920

778 Toor, F., A Treasury of Mexican Folkways, Part. III: Music — Verse — Dance, New York 1947

779 Troyer, C., Indian Music Lecture: The Zuñi Indians and their Music, Philadelphia 1913

780 Tschopik, H. J., Music of Peru (Ethnic Folkways Album P 415), New York 1949

781 — Indian Music of the Upper Amazon (Ethnic Folkways Album P 458), New York 1954

782 — Music from Mato Grosso (Ethnic Folkways Album P 446), New York 1955

783 Underhill, R. M., Singing for Power. The Song Magic of the Papago Indians of Southern Arizona, Berkeley 1938

784 Vásquez Santa Ana, H., Fiestas y Costumbres Méxicanas, Mexico 1940

785 Vedova, G. Dalla, Alcune Canzoni degl' Indiani Abitanit sull' Alto Ucayali, in: Bollettino della Società Geografica Italiana, Vol. XXI, pp. 717–18, Rome 1884

786 Vega, C., La Flauta de Pan Andina, in: Proceedings of the 25th International Congress of Americanists, Part I, pp. 333–48, Buenos Aires 1934

787 — Tonleitern mit Halbtönen in der Musik der alten Peruaner, in: Acta Musicologica, Vol. IX, pp. 41 ff., Basle 1939

788 — Panorama de la Música Popular Argentina, Buenos Aires 1944

789 — Los instrumentos musicales aborígenes y criollos de la Argentina, Buenos Aires 1949

790 Viaggiano, E. J., La Musicalidad de los Tupi-Guarani, Publicación del Instituto de Arqueología, Lingüística y Folklore "Dr. Pablo Cabrera", No. XXV, Cordoba 1944

791 — Instrumentología Musical Popular Argentina, Publicación del Instituto de Arqueología, Lingüística y Folklore "Dr. Pablo Cabrera", Vol. XX, Cordoba 1948

792 Vizcarra Rojas, A., Folklore Musical Peruano, in: Revista Universitaria de la Universidad Nacional de Cuzco, Vol. XXIX, No. 78, pp. 163–98, Cuzco 1940

793 Voegelin, E. W., Shawnee Musical Instruments, in: American Anthropologist, n.s., Vol. XLIV, pp. 463–75, Menasha 1942

794 — C. F., and R. C. Euler, Introduction to Hopi Chants, in: Journal of American Folklore, Vol. LXX, pp. 115–36, Bloomington 1957

795 Vogeler, E., Lieder der Eskimos, Copenhagen 1930

796 Walton, E. L., Dawn Boy. Blackfoot and Navaho Songs, New York 1926

797 — Navajo Song Patterning, in: Journal of American Folklore, Vol. XLIII, pp. 105–18, 1930

798 Wasson, V., and R. G. Pand, Mushroom Ceremony of the Mazatec Indians of Mexico (Ethnic Folkways Album FR 8975), New York 1957

799 Waterman, T. T., Native Musical Instruments of California, in: Out West, Vol. XXVIII, pp. 276–86, Los Angeles 1908

800 Weinstock, H., Mexican Music, New York 1940

801 Wheelwright, M. C., The Hail and Water Chants, Museum of Navajo Ceremonial Art, Navajo Religions Series, Vol. II, Santa Fé 1946

802 — The Myth and Prayers of the Great Star Chant, Santa Fé 1956

803 Wilbert, J., Los Instrumentos Musicales de los Warrau, in: Antropológica, Vol. I, pp. 2–22, Caracas 1956

804 Wilder, C. S., The Yaqui Deer Dance: A Study in Cultural Change, in: Bulletin 186 of the Bureau of American Ethnology, pp. 145–210, Washington 1963

805 Wiora, W., Älter als Pentatonik, in: Studia memoriae Bela Bartok, pp. 158 ff., Budapest 1956

806 — Die vier Weltalter der Musik, Stuttgart 1961

807 Wren, C., Turtle Shell Rattles and Other Implements From Indian Graves, in: Proceedings and Collections of the Wyoming Historical and Geological Society, Vol. X, pp. 195–210, Wilkes Barre 1909

808 Wyman, L. C., The Female Shooting Life Chant, in: American Anthropologist, n.s., Vol. XXXVIII, pp. 634 to 53, Menasha 1936

809 — and C. Kluckhohn, Navaho Classification of Their Song Ceremonials, in: Memoirs of the American Anthropological Association, Vol. L, pp. 1–38, Menasha 1938

810 Yeomans, W. H., The Inca Scale of Music, in: New World Antiquity, Vol. VII, pp. 10–12, 1954

811 Yurchenko, H., Investigaciones sobre Música Indígena, in: Boletín Indigenista, Vol. VI, Mexico 1946

812 — Indian Music of Mexico and Guatemala, in: Bulletin of the American Musicological Society, Vol. XI–XIII, pp. 58 ff., 1948

813 Zerries, O., Das Schwirrholz, Stuttgart 1942

814 — Kürbisrassel und Kopfgeister in Südamerika, in: Paideuma, Vol. V, pp. 323–39, Bamberg 1953

815 — The Bullroarer Among South American Indians, in: Revista do Museu Paulista, n.s., Vol. VII, pp. 275–309, São Paulo 1953

816 — La maraca y los espíritus cefaliformes en Suramérica, in: Estudios Americanos, Vol. XXI, 107, pp. 119–40, Seville 7961

Other Literature Quoted

817 Acosta, P. J. de, Historia Natural y Moral de las Indias, Seville 1590; Edición de Edmundo O'Gorman, Mexico 1940

818 Canals-Frau, S., Prehistoria de América, Buenos Aires 1950; French edition, Paris 1953

819 Dorsinfang-Smets, A., La Recherche du Salut chez les Indiens d'Amérique, in: Religions de Salut, Brussels 1962

820 Eliade, M., Le Chamanisme et les Techniques Archaïques de l'Extase, Paris 1951

821 Gheerbrandt, A., Des Hommes Qu'On Appelle Sauvages (Orénoque-Amazonie), Paris 1952

822 Giddings, J. L., The Archaeology of Bering Strait, in: Current Anthropology, Vol. I, No. 2, Chicago 1960

823 Jelinek, A., An Index of Radiocarbon Dates Associated with Cultural Materials, in: Current Anthropology, Vol. III, No. 5, Chicago 1962

824 Jenness, D., The Ojibwa Indians of Parry Island, Their Social and Religious Life, in: National Museum of Canada Bulletin 78, Ottawa 1935

825 Krickeberg, W./H. Trimborn/W. Müller/O. Zerries, Die Religionen des Alten Amerika, Stuttgart 1961

826 Lesser, A., The Pawnee Ghost Dance Hand Game, New York 1933

827 Mason, R. J., The Paleo-Indian Tradition in Eastern North America, in: Current Anthropology, Vol. III, No. 3, Chicago 1962

828 Merriam, A. P., The Ethnography of Flathead Indians, in: Western Anthropology, No. 2, 1955

829 Motolinía, T. de Benavente, Memoriales, Publicado de Luís García Pimental, Mexico 1941

830 Palacios, E. J., En los Confines de la Selva Lacandonia. Exploraciones en al Estado de Chiapas, Mexico 1928

831 Rhodes, W., Music of the American Indian: Northwest, Puget Sound; Music of the American Indian: Kiowa, Washington, Library of Congress, N.D.

832 Schmieder, O., Die Neue Welt, Vol. II: Nordamerika, Munich 1963

833 Schomburgk, R., Reisen in British Guiana, Vol. I, Leipzig 1841

834 Wustmann, E., Crao. Indianer der Roten Berge, Radebeul 1958

ADDENDA

Music and Musical Instruments of the Indians and Eskimo

835 Aretz-Thielle, I., El Folklore Musical Argentino, Buenos Aires 1952

836 Barbeau, M., Songs of the Northwest, in: The Musical Quarterly, Vol. XIX, pp. 101–11; Vol. XX, pp. 107–16, New York 1933, 1934

837 Baratta, M. de, Ensayo sobre Música Indígena de El Salvador, in: Revista de Estudios Musicales, Vol. I, pp. 61 ff., Mendoza 1950

838 Boulton, L., and H. Cowell, Music of the Eskimo of Hudson Bay and Alaska (Ethnic Folkways Album P 444). Record by L. Boulton; Notes by L. Boulton and H. Cowell, New York

839 Campos, R. M., La Música Popular de México, in: Revista de Estudios Musicales, Vol. I, pp. 81 ff., Mendoza 1950

840 Capitan, L'omichicahuaztli mexicain et son ancêtre de l'Époque du Renne en Gaule, in: Proceedings of the International Congress of Americanists, Vol. XVI, Vienna 1908

841 Curtis, N., Two Pueblo Indian Grinding Songs, in: Craftsman, Vol. VII, pp. 35—41, 1904

842 Delgadillo, L. A., La Música Indígena y Colonial en Nicaragua, in: Revista de Estudios Musicales, Vol. I, pp. 43 ff., Mendoza 1950

843 Densmore, F., Recent Developments in the Study of Indian Music, in: Proceedings of the International Congress of Americanists, Vol. XIX, Washington 1918

844 — Field Studies of Indian Music, in: Exploration and Fieldwork of the Smithsonian Institution in 1923, pp. 119 ff., Washington 1924

845 — Study of Tule Music, in: Exploration and Fieldwork of the Smithsonian Institution in 1924, pp. 115 ff., Washington 1925

846 — The Study of Indian Music in the 19th Century, in: American Anthropologists, Vol. XXIX, pp. 77 ff., Menasha 1927

847 — The Use of Music in the Treatment of the Sick by American Indians, in: The Musical Quarterly, Vol. XIII, pp. 555 ff., New York 1927

848 — Some Results of the Study of American Indian Music, in: Journal of the Washington Academy of Science, Vol. XVIII, 1928

849 — Music of the American Indians at Public Gatherings, in: The Musical Quarterly, Vol. XVII, pp. 464 ff., New York 1931

850 — The Music of the North American Indians, in: Proceedings of the International Congress of Americanists, Vol. XXV, pp. 119 ff., 1932

851 — The Songs of Indian Soldiers During the World War, in: The Musical Quarterly, Vol. XX, pp. 419 ff., New York 1934

852 — On "Expression" in Indian Singing, in: American Anthropologist, Vol. XXXVI, pp. 487 ff., Menasha 1934

853 — La Música de los Indios Norte-Americanos, in: Boletín Latino-Americano de Música, Vol. V, pp. 863 ff., Bogotá 1941

854 — Importance of Rhythm in Songs for the Treatment of the Sick by American Indians, in: Scientific Monthly, Vol. LXXIX, pp. 109 ff., New York 1954

855 Dixon, R. B., The Musical Bow in California, in: Science, n.s., Vol. XIII, pp. 274 ff., 1901

856 Duran, S. M., La Musique Aborigène et Populaire de l'Equateur, in: Art Populaire, Vol. II, pp. 117 ff., Paris 1931

857 Ebner, C. B., Beiträge zur Musikgeschichte am Amazonas, in: Anais missionarios de preciosissimo sangue, Belem 1950

858 Ehrenreich, P., Flötentanz der Moki, in: Zeitschrift für Ethnologie, Vol. XXXII, pp. (494)/(495), Berlin 1900

859 Genin, A., Notes on the Dances, Music, and Songs of the Ancient and Modern Mexicans, Publication of the Smithsonian Institution, Washington 1920

860 — The Musical Instruments of the Ancient Mexicans, in: Mexican Magazine, Vol. III, pp. 355 ff., 1927

861 Harcourt, R. d', La Musique Indienne chez les Anciens Civilisés d'Amerique I. Les Instruments de Musique des Mexicains et des Péruviens, in: Lavignac, Histoire de la Musique, Vol. V, pp. 3337 ff., Paris 1920

862 Heinitz, W., Chirimia- und Tembór-Phonogramme aus Nordwest-Guatemala, in: Vox, Vol. XIX, pp. 4 ff., 1933

863 Herzog, G., The Collections of Phonograph Records in: North America and Hawaii, in: Zeitschrift für Vergleichende Musikwissenschaft, Vol. I, pp. 58–62, 1933

864 – Maricopa Music, in: Spier, L., Yuman Tribes of the Gila River, Chicago 1933

865 – Speechmelody and Primitive Music, in: The Musical Quarterly, Vol. XX, pp. 452 ff., New York 1934

866 – Songs (of the Coast Salish), in: Adamson, T., Folk Tales of the Coast Salish, in: Memoirs of the American Folklore Society, Vol. XXVI, pp. 422 ff., New York 1934

867 – Transcription and Analysis of Tutelo Music, in: Speck, F., The Tutelo Spirit Adoption Ceremony, Harrisburg 1942

868 – Investigación sobre música primitiva y folklórica en los Estados Unidos, in: Boletín Latino-Americano de Música, Vol. V, pp. 393 ff., Bogotá 1941

869 – African Influences in North American Indian Music, in: Papers Read at the International Congress of Musicology Held at New York 1939, pp. 130–43, New York 1944

870 – Salish Music, in: Indians of the Urban Northwest, ed. by M. W. Smith, pp. 93 ff., New York 1949

871 Huot, M. C., Peyote Songs, in: Transition, Vol. XXIV, pp. 117–9, 1936

872 Jackson, W., Shell-Trumpets and their Distribution in the Old and New World, in: Memoirs of the Manchester Literary Society, Vol. LX, Fasc. 8, 1916

873 Knosp, G., La Musique des Indiens de l'Amérique du Nord, in: Lavignac, Histoire de la Musique, Vol. V, pp. 3333 ff., 1920

874 Lach, R., Das musikalische Konstruktionsprinzip der altmexikanischen Tempelgesänge, in: Johannes-Wolf-Festschrift, pp. 88 ff., 1929

875 – Die Musik der Inkas, in: Der Zuschauer, 1925/26, Fasc. 8

876 Lachmann, R., Musik der ausereuropäischen Natur- und Kulturvölker, in: Bücken's Handbuch der Musikwissenschaft, Vol. I, Wildpark-Potsdam 1929

877 Lara, M. de, and M. L. Escobar, Ritmo y melodía nativos de Venezuela, in: Estudios Latino-Americanos, Vol. III, pp. 121 ff., 1937

878 Leden, C., Musikethnologische Grönlandexpedition, in: Zeitschrift der Internationalen Musikgesellschaft, Vol. XII, pp. 370 ff., 1910

879 Marschall, W., Die Panpfeife im circumpazifischen Raum, in: Abhandlungen und Berichte des Staatlichen Museums für Völkerkunde Dresden, Vol. XXV, pp. 127–51, Berlin 1965

880 Martí, S., Música Precortesiana, in: Cuadernos Americanos, Vol. LXXVII, Mexico 1954

881 – La Música de Mesoamérica, Boletín Bibliográfico de la Secretaria de Hacienda y Crédito Publico, No. 113, Mexico 1954

882 Martí, S., Notable Instrumental Prehispánico, in: Cuadernos Americanos, Vol. CXLIV, Mexico 1966

883 Mason, B., Drums, Tom-toms and Rattles, New York 1938

884 Merriam, A. P., and B. W. Merriam, Flathead Indian Music, Report on Field Research, Evanston 1950

885 Michel, C., Cantos Indígenas de México, Mexico 1951

886 Miles, C., Aboriginal Musical Instruments in North America, in: Hobbies, Vol. LVII, pp. 134 ff., 1953

887 Nettl, B., Historical Perspective Music: the Shawnee Musical Style, in: Journal of the American Musicological Society, Vol. V, No. 2, 1952

888 – Historical Aspects of Ethnomusicology, in: American Anthropologist, n.s., Vol. LX, pp. 518–32, Menasha 1958

889 Nicholson, H. S., Four Songs From a Yuma Version of Los Pastores, in: University of Arizona General Bulletin, Vol. IX, pp. 25–28, 1945

890 Rhodes, W., Music of the Sioux and the Navajo (Ethnic Folkways Album P 104), New York

891 – Music of the American Indians of the Southwest (Ethnic Folkways Album P 420), New York

892 Saville, M. H., A Primitive Maya Musical Instrument, in: American Anthropologist, o.s., Vol. X, pp. 272–73, Washington 1897

893 – The Musical Bow in Ancient Mexico, in: American Anthropologist, o.s., Vol. XI, Washington 1898

894 Schultze-Jena, L., Alt-Aztekische Gesänge, published by G. Kutscher, Quellenwerke zur Alten Geschichte Amerikas, Vol. VI, Berlin 1957

895 Stevenson, R., Music in Mexico, New York 1952

896 Stone, D., Music of the Black Caribs of Honduras; Records by P. Kite Smith; Notes by D. Stone (Ethnic Folkways Album P 435), New York

897 Thalbitzer, W., Eskimo-Liederen van Oost Groenland, Santpoort 1933

898 Thuren, H., The Eskimo Music, Copenhagen 1912

899 Wolf, S., Zum Problem der Nasenflöte, Abhandlungen und Berichte aus dem Staatlichen Museum für Tier- und Völkerkunde Dresden, New Series, B, Völkerkunde, No. 1, Leipzig 1941

Other Literature Quoted

900 Dräger, L., Einige indianische Darstellungen des Sonnentanzes aus dem Museum für Völkerkunde in Leipzig, in: Jahrbuch des Museums für Völkerkunde zu Leipzig, Vol. XVIII, pp. 59–86, Berlin 1961

901 Torquemada, J. de, Los veintiún libros rituales y Monarquía Indiana, con el origen y guerras de los indios occidentales . . ., Seville 1615

LIST OF ILLUSTRATIONS

Illustration 1
Pan-Pipes from the Hopewell Civilisation · Ca. 100 A.D. ·
Found at Helena Crossing, Arkansas. · American Museum of
Natural History, New York, Neg. No. 126,285. p. 49.

Illustration 2
Painted Pottery Plate from the Hohokam Civilisation · Ca.
800 A.D. · Snaketown, Arizona · Diameter 26.7 cm · Arizona
State Museum, University of Arizona, Tucson, Neg. No.
GP-820. p. 49

Illustration 3
Human Bone Whistle · Hopewell Civilisation · Ca. 200 A.D. ·
Bourneville, Ohio · Length 21 cm · Ohio State Museum,
Columbus, Ohio. p. 51

Illustration 4
Stone Flute · San Nicolas Island, California · Length 18.4 cm ·
Museum of the American Indian, Heye Foundation, New York,
Cat. No. 20/3836, Neg. No. 22,835. p. 51

Illustration 5
Bullroarer of the Nascapi · Davis Inlet · Length 39.4 cm,
Breadth 6.4 cm · National Museum of Canada, Ottawa,
Inv. No. III-B-349, Neg. No. T 9138. p. 53

Illustration 6
Bullroarers of the Central and Copper Eskimo · Length 26 cm,
21.6 cm and 22.2 cm. · National Museum of Canada, Ottawa,
Inv. No. IV-C-1402, IV-C-994, IV-D-162, Neg. No. T 9372.
p. 53

Illustration 7
Singing Nuwungmiut Eskimo with Rim Drums · Cape Bar-
row, Alaska · Laura Boulton Collection of Traditional and
Liturgical Music, Columbia University, New York. p. 55

Illustration 8
Eskimo Drumming Contest · Angmagssalik, East Greenland ·
Photograph by William Thalbitzer (1906) · Photographic
Collection of the Arktisk Institut Charlottenlund, Denmark,
No. 7656. p. 57

Illustration 9
Dance of the Copper Eskimo · Photograph by Leo Hansen ·
Photographic Collection of the Nationalmuseum, Copenhagen,
No. 2274. p. 59

Illustration 10
Singing Eskimo with his Two Wives and Daughter · Angmagssalik, East Greenland · Photograph by William Thalbitzer
(1906) · Photographic Collection of the Arktisk Institut
Charlottenlund, Denmark, No. 7678. p. 59

Illustration 11
Wooden Box Drum of the Yakutat · Alaska · Height 94 cm,
Breadth 83.5 cm, Depth 35.5 cm · Museum of the American
Indian, Heye Foundation, New York, Cat. No. 19/9099. p. 61

Illustration 12
Chief's Rattle from the Haida · Skidegate, Queen Charlotte
Islands, British Columbia · Length 33 cm. · Museum of the
American Indian, Heye Foundation, New York, Cat. No.
I/8082, Neg. No. 14,564. p. 63

Illustration 13
Tsimshian Clapper · British Columbia · Length 26.7 cm ·
National Museum of Canada, Ottawa, Cat. No. VII-C-485,
Neg. No. T 6165. p. 63

Illustration 14
Wooden Kitksan Rattle · Skeena River, British Columbia ·
Length 30 cm · Museum of the American Indian, Heye
Foundation, New York, Cat. No. 9/7998, Neg. 29,426. p. 65

Illustration 15
Salish Rattle · Vancouver Island, British Columbia · Length
37 cm · Museum of the American Indian, Heye Foundation,
Cat. No. 20/347, Neg. No. 29,427 . p. 65

Illustration 16
Haida and Makah Reed Instruments · British Columbia and
the State of Washington · Length 32-45.7 cm · Museum of
the American Indian, Heye Foundation, New York, Cat. No.
19/3535, 10/649, 6/38. p. 67

Illustration 17
Vertical Haida Flute, Front and Side View · Queen Charlotte
Islands · Length 42 cm · Übersee-Museum, Bremen, Cat. No.
C 198 · Photograph by Helmut Jäger. p. 67

Illustration 18
Haida Wind Instrument · Queen Charlotte Islands · Length
18 cm · National Museum of Canada, Ottawa, Neg. No. 78,657.
p. 67

Illustration 19
Four-toned Kitksan Whistle · British Columbia · Length
44.5 cm · Museum of the American Indian, Heye Foundation,
New York, Cat. No. 6/6279, Neg. No. 29,246. p. 69

Illustration 20
Musical Bow of the Tlingit (Alaska) and the Maidu (California) · Length 152 and 200 cm · Museum of the American
Indian, Heye Foundation, New York, Cat. No. 21/456 and
21/1645. p. 71

Illustration 21
Musical Bow of the Yokuts from Fresno · California · Robert
H. Lowie Museum of Anthropology, University of California,
Berkeley, Cat. No. 1–10,789. p. 71

Illustration 22
Musical Bow of the Yokuts from Madera · California · Length
90 cm · Robert H. Lowie Museum of Anthropology, University
of California, Berkeley, Cat. No. 1–10,427.   p. 71

Illustration 23
Papago with Scraping Stick · Smithsonian Institution, Bureau
of American Ethnology, Washington, D.C., Neg. No. 2775.
p. 73

Illustration 24
Hopi Scraping Stick · Arizona · Length 39.4 cm · Museum of
the American Indian, Heye Foundation, New York, Cat. No.
6/2057, Neg. No. 21,007.   p. 73

Illustration 25
Medicine Rites of the Sia-Pueblo · Jemez River, New Mexico ·
Smithsonian Institution, Bureau of American Ethnology,
Washington, D.C., Neg. No. 2189 · Photograph by M. C. Ste-
venson, 1888/89.   p. 75

Illustrations 26 and 27
Indian Water-Colour Paintings from the Pueblo of Isleta,
New Mexico · Ritual in a Worship Chamber in the Pueblo of
Isleta (Illust. 26) · "Hot Cornhusk Dance", One of the Dances
Performed in Isleta on the Four Days after Christmas (Illust.
27). For the originals see the Archives of the American Philo-
sophical Society, Philadelphia.   p. 77

Illustration 28
Green Corn Ceremony of the Pueblo Indians · Gouache Paint-
ing by Awa Tsireh (Alfonso Roybal) · Size: 49×70.5 cm. ·
Museum of Modern Art, New York, Abby Aldrich Rockefeller
Fund · Photograph by Soichi Sunami.   p. 79

Illustration 29
Zuñi Clay Drum · New Mexico · Height 47 cm · Museum of
the American Indian, Heye Foundation, New York, Cat. No.
10/8790, Neg. No. 21,008.   p. 81

Illustration 30
Peyote Drum · Museum of the American Indian, Heye Foundation, New York, Cat. No. 22/4435, Neg. No. 29,121.   p. 81

Illustration 31
Niman-Katčina Dance of the Hopi · Arizona · Smithsonian
Institution, Bureau of American Ethnology, Washington, Neg.
No. 42, 189-F · Photograph by A. C. Vroman, 1901   p. 83

Illustration 32
Papago Flute-Player · Smithsonian Institution, Bureau of
American Ethnology, Washington, D.C., Neg. No. 2774.   p. 85

Illustrations 33 and 34
Dance of the Deer · Dancer and Yaqui Musician with Flute
and Drum · Photograph by Luís Márquez.   p. 87

Illustration 35
Pascola Dance in Pascua · Arizona · Photograph from "Arizona Highways", January 1949.   p. 89

Illustration 36
Apache with Stringed Instrument · Smithsonian Institution,
Bureau of American Ethnology, Washington, D.C., Neg. No.
2580-b-4.   p. 91

Illustration 37
Apache Fiddle with Bow · Arizona · Length 54 cm · Museum
of the American Indian, Heye Foundation, New York, Cat.
No. 8/4561, Neg. No. 21,009.   p. 91

Illustration 38
Apache War Dance · Part of a Picture by George Catlin, 1855 ·
American Museum of Natural History, New York, Neg. No.
324,939.   p. 93

Illustration 39
Hidatsa Warrior with Deer-Hoof Rattle in the Dog Dance ·
Copper Engraving by René Rollet from a Painting by Carl
Bodmer, 1834 · From "Reise in das innere Nord-America in
den Jahren 1832–1834" (Coblenz 1839/41), a Travel Book by
Prince Maximilian zu Wied.   p. 95

Illustration 40
Exponents of the Arapaho Sun Dance with Bone Whistles in
their Mouths · Cheyenne, Arapaho Reservation, Oklahoma
1901 · Photograph by George A. Dorsey, from G. A. Dorsey,
The Arapaho Sun Dance; The Ceremony of the Offerings
Lodge, in: Anthropological Series of the Field Columbian Museum, Vol. IV, Chicago 1903, Pl. 86, Fig. 1.   p. 97

Illustration 41
Picture of an Episode from the Sun Dance · Indian Leather
Painting (probably Dakota work) · Museum für Völkerkunde,
Leipzig, Cat. No. N Am 3445.   p. 97

Illustration 42
Arapaho Ghost Dance · Oklahoma · Pictorial Archives of the
Smithsonian Institution, Washington, Neg. No. 35(R) · Pho-
tograph by James Mooney, 1893.   p. 99

Illustration 43
Vertical Dakota Flute · Museum of the American Indian,
Heye Foundation, New York, Cat. No. 8/3237, Neg. No.
21,007.   p. 101

Illustration 44
Mandan Warrior Decked in Wooing Finery · Upper Missouri ·
From "Reise in das innere Nord-America in den Jahren
1832–1834" (Coblenz 1839/41), a Travel Book by Prince
Maximilian zu Wied, Illust. XXIV.   p. 101

Illustration 45
Whistle Language in Courtship (demonstrated by a man from
the Mexican Kickapoo group) · Milwaukee Public Museum,
Milwaukee, Wis. ·   Photograph by Ritzenthaler/Peterson.
p. 101

Illustration 46
Osage Song Record Stick · Box Cover with Pictographic Song
Records of the Chippewa (Ojibwa) · Museum of the American
Indian, Heye Foundation, New York, Cat. No. 2/891 and
10/6938, Neg. No. 21,033.   p. 103

Illustration 47
Delaware Deerskin Drum with Beaters · Length about 100 cm ·
Museum of the American Indian, Heye Foundation, New York,
Cat. No. 2/1087, Neg. No. 21,006.   p. 105

INDEX

202